303

CD-ROMs

TO USE IN YOUR LIBRARY

Descriptions, Evaluations,
and Practical Advice

Patrick R. Dewey

AMERICAN LIBRARY ASSOCIATION
Chicago and London 1996

Series Note

101 Software Packages to Use in Your Library
101 Microcomputer Projects to Do in Your Library
202+ Software Packages to Use in Your Library
101 Desktop Publishing and Graphics Programs

Project editor: Joan A. Grygel
Cover designed by Charles Bozett
Composed by Digital Book Works, Inc., in Linotype Times and Helvetica, using T_EX.
Printed on 50-pound Glatfelter, a pH-neutral stock, and bound in 10-point C1S by McNaughton & Gunn, Inc.

The paper used in this publication meets the minimum requirements of American National Standard for Information Sciences—Permanence of Paper for Printed Library Materials, ANSI Z39.48-1992 ⊗

Library of Congress Cataloging-in-Publication Data
Dewey, Patrick R., 1949–
    303 CD-ROMs to use in your library : descriptions, evaluations,
  and practical advice / Patrick R. Dewey.
    p. cm. — (101 micro series)
  Includes bibliographical references (p.) and index.
  ISBN 0-8389-0666-4
    1. CD-ROMS—United States—Catalogs. 2. Libraries—United States—
  Special collections—CD-ROMs. I. Title. II. Series.
Z1040.D49 1995
028.1'3—dc20
                                95-23607

00 99 98 97 96   5 4 3 2 1

For my dog Software,
who went to the "big doghouse in the sky"
at the wonderful age of 14

Contents

Children's Literature   *32*

Introduction

The growth of the CD-ROM (*C*ompact *D*isc—*R*ead-*O*nly *M*emory) market is quite astonishing. Just a few years ago there were only a few titles. At this writing, however, there are more than 10,000 consumer titles from which to choose, of which some 2,000 are multimedia. The installed base of CD-ROM drives, the devices that permit a computer to access the data on a CD-ROM, doubled worldwide from 1985 to 1995.

CD-ROMs contain the same type of information that the traditional computer media of diskettes and hard-disk drives contain, but on a scale orders of magnitude larger. The physical arrangement of a CD is quite simple. The shiny side, which contains the data, consists of a single line of *1*s and *0*s approximately three and one-half miles long and is the same size as the standard 5.25-inch floppy disk. The resemblance stops there, however. A single CD may contain the equivalent of 345 floppy disks, or 350,000 pages of text. The scale of such storage space has had profound implications for software.

Thousands of books or even hundreds of thousands of periodical or newspaper articles can be squeezed onto a single CD, all easily searchable. Prior to this, just lifting the paper equivalent was impossible for a human without the aid of a forklift. No longer do you have to look for a particular volume or struggle with the tonnage of the *Oxford English Dictionary*. The advent of CD-ROM makes large, well-organized databases available to even the smallest library.

This vast storage capacity has made possible the development of multimedia, which includes sound, pictures, text, and even video in the same program. Graphics and sound, the core components of multimedia, use a lot of memory, so multimedia programs prior to the development of CD-ROM were limited and primitive. The CD-ROM's capability opened the door to innovative products to enhance information. For example, a pioneering product, NautilusCD, is a magazine on disc that contains stories, pictures, video, sound, and software demos and shareware. However, multimedia is not just entertainment; it has legitimate reference and research advantages. Interactive encyclopedias are a good example. Paper encyclopedias may become as extinct as dinosaurs within just a few years. An innovative entry into this market is Microsoft's Encarta, which is ablaze with multimedia elements. Users of this resource can see animated demos of concepts and videos of important historical events in addition to being able to read the full text of countless articles. Another example, The American Indian: A Multimedia Encyclopedia, presents research information in the form of hundreds of source documents, pictures, authentic recordings of tribal songs, maps, and much more.

CD-ROM technology makes it much easier for libraries to circulate software. Older floppy disk technology, for example, was very difficult to circulate, for two reasons. First it was very susceptible to damage. Even if this could be avoided, diskettes were easily duplicated, which is prohibited by simple copyright, not to mention any license agreements. In contrast, CD-ROMs generally hold so much data that it is not practical to copy the great majority of them. Also, CD-ROMs are fairly indestructible, at least when compared with floppy disks. Only grave physical abuse can compromise the data they hold.

Libraries may choose to loan to patrons a wide range of educational and entertainment software on CD. A good example is World Library's Stories of Murder, Mystery, Magic, Terror & More and others in this series. Patrons have access to a sizable library that can be searched and read right at their fingertips. Prices have fallen to the point where making CDs available to the public is also economically sound. Of course, not every person in the community owns a personal computer or one with a CD and multimedia peripherals, but the number is growing each day.

Software Requirements

For those librarians who know little about computers, a good entry-level manual or book will be useful. The software component, or set of instructions that tells the computer what to do, is multilayered and almost as complicated as the people who operate it. All software is ultimately composed of 1s and 0s. By adding up this binary code made up of the two logical states of electricity, the computer can count and keep track of vast amounts of data. The part of the software package that humans use to interact with the computer is called an *interface*. In the past this was the Disk Operating System (DOS). DOS is a text-based system, allowing one program at a time to be used. A more-advanced Graphical User Interface (GUI), such as Windows, uses images and a pointing device called a *mouse* to input commands to the computer. In Windows many programs may be operated simultaneously, provided the computer has enough hardware resources such as memory and clock speed (explained in the following section). Windows is very similar to the GUI used by the Macintosh. Programs such as WordPerfect are applications programs and may be run from within Windows. Some of the CDs listed in this book run under DOS; others require a Windows environment or operate under the Macintosh system.

Hardware Requirements

The most popular microcomputer is the IBM and its clones. (Actually, the clones outsell the IBM by a wide margin.) Generations of IBMs and their clones are identified by their central processing unit (CPU) number: the 286, 386, or 486. A break in this tradition has been the Pentium (which was to have been the 586). The greater the number, the more powerful the computer, generally speaking.

The size of any attached hard-disk drives is also important. Computer memory, whether long-term mass storage or transient Random Access Memory, is measured in kilobytes (1 kilobyte equals 1,008 bytes). One thousand kilobytes (one million bytes) is known as a *megabyte*. A thousand megabytes is known as a *gigabyte*. A hard drive should not be less than approximately 500 megabytes, although one gigabyte is not unwise. No matter how large the hard drive, however, on machines that are used for more than a solitary purpose, it will not be too long before the drive space has filled up. You must then clean out no longer needed information to free up space. The larger the hard drive, the more software that can be installed and maintained at one time. At least 100 megabytes of space should be kept free and available as a work space for the computer.

An important consideration is whether to purchase an IBM or clone or a Macintosh computer. Overall, Macs are easier to get up and running. Their hardware/software makeup is more straightforward, and problems are fewer. Furthermore, multimedia is more built-in with a Mac. Apple Computer, the producer of Macintosh, has only 10 percent of the market, however. The rest of the market is IBM and its clones. This makes IBM more appealing in terms of competitive pricing and variety of add-on products. The differences between the Macintosh and the Windows operating environments narrowed considerably on August 24, 1995, when Microsoft released the much-anticipated Windows 95. This program makes it much easier to configure hardware and software, especially multimedia components.

However, selection of the microprocessor is not the only component of quality and speed when selecting a microcomputer system. Another way to gauge computer power is to look at its processing, or clock, speed, which is measured in megahertz (MHz). This will provide a baseline with which to compare machines. In addition to CPU speed, you need to consider the speed of the peripheral components. For example, the speed of the printer and the speed of hard drives vary. Another component that can significantly impair the processing speed of a computer is the amount of random access memory (RAM) that the computer uses to hold and process programs and data. In short, it is possible to purchase a very fast Pentium but with very slow and weak peripherals.

The main downside to CD-ROM technology and multimedia is that they require additional hardware. CD-ROMs won't work on just any drive, they require a special CD-ROM drive. These drives come in different speeds and sizes. Speed starts with single speed, and goes to double, triple, or quadruple. Just reaching the market is a new six-speed drive. The advantage of the higher speeds is not having to wait as long for a program to load or to find the needed information. The disadvantage is that the faster a drive, the greater the price tag. Double speed is now the bottom line for acceptability.

Another problem occurs when more than one CD-ROM is needed. For example, to have six years of the *Chicago Tribune* available on CD-ROM requires the use of six discs. There are several solutions. Popular CD-ROM changers, sometimes called jukeboxes, will handle six, eighteen, and even one hundred CD-ROMs. This makes it convenient to have many CDs at one work station without having to change them. CD changers typically have just one or several CD drives, making it impossible to use more than a few discs. For six years of the *Chicago Tribune*, a six-disc CD changer is a good solution for some libraries. The other, more costly, solution is to put each CD into its own drive in a tower arrangement.

Multimedia also requires a sound card and improved graphics. A sound card provides the computer with sound playback and record capabilities and provides a connection for external stereo speakers, a microphone, or an amplifier. Three major standards for sound are SoundBlaster, Ad Lib, and Windows. Sampling size is important in selecting a card. An 8-bit sound card samples analog signals 256 times per second; a 16-bit card samples analog signals 65,536 times per second. The larger the number, the higher the quality of the output.

The quality of graphic output depends on the graphics card and the monitor. A video card that supports 256 colors (not just the 16 colors of nonmultimedia) is required for multimedia. The common IBM video-display standard is called video graphics display (VGA). An enhanced form of this is called super VGA (SVGA). If the display card that came with a computer does not support SVGA, an SVGA card may be added.

Monitors come in different sizes, including 12-, 17-, and 21-inch screens. For desktop publishing, it is often useful to own a large screen. One other way to judge the quality of a monitor is by its dot pitch, measured from .28 to .51mm, the distance between dots on the screen. The closer the dots (i.e., the smaller the number), the sharper the screen image.

Many computers now come fully equipped and "multimedia-ready" with a CD player, a 256-color graphics adapter, and a sound card. Computers not equipped for multimedia may be made so with a multimedia upgrade kit that includes both a CD-ROM drive and a sound card. There are two standards of Windows-based multimedia: MPC and MPC2. To meet MPC2 requirements and to run the latest software, a computer should have at least:

a clock speed of at least 25 MHz

a 4MB RAM, 160MB hard-disk drive

a CD-ROM drive

SVGA graphics

a 16-bit sound card

CD-ROM drives may also be mounted on local area networks (LANs) to accommodate CD-ROM sharing between work stations. A LAN is a communications network in which computers share programs and data. In such an arrangement, each CD is usually put in its own separate drive, and all CDs are available at all work stations. Using a LAN also safeguards all CDs since they are kept out of harm's way by being stored in a central area, remote from the work stations without any need to change or handle them physically. This arrangement also eliminates the need to change discs whenever a patron wants to use a different one.

When purchasing a work station, consider the following:

CPU speed of 50 to 66 MHz

disk drive capacity and speed (on a CD, both seek and transfer rates)

8 to 12MB RAM minimum with the capacity for expansion

Printer quality and speed (a 12-page-per-minute laser printer at 600 dots per inch is acceptable for most library jobs)

Modem speed (14,400-baud is now the minimum standard)

Video display card (256 colors for multimedia)

Sound card (for multimedia)

Monitor (especially size and color)

LAN

Evaluation Criteria for CDs: Facts and Opinions

To properly select CD-ROMs for library use, several types of information are important: facts, opinions, and review copies. To the extent that you can obtain this information, your selection will be better.

Selecting CD-ROM software for a library falls into two broad categories: in-house library use (reference) and circulation. Generally speaking, it is fair to evaluate CDs on the basis of quality, compatibility, appropriateness, and cost. Databases on CD should be evaluated in terms of their coverage of the areas needed.

It is important to understand the distinctions between different products from the same company covering the same general areas. Some may cover full text, some have only bibliographic citations. Some cover many magazines, some fewer. Obviously, the more information that is in a database, the more expensive it will be to purchase. A good example is a set of products by Infotrac. Seven different, yet similar, products cover magazines and periodicals. These are aimed at different markets and different budgets. Magazine ASAP contains the full text of 250 magazines, whereas Magazine ASAP Select I has the full text of 50 magazines. Magazine ASAP Select II provides the full text of 100 titles. Some CD-ROM products are available as full-year or school-year editions.

For more-expensive CDs it is important to see and use them prior to purchase. Generally, very expensive CDs, such as those offered by Infotrac and other companies, are purchased only for use in the library. Their licensing agreements usually prohibit any other use. Important considerations for selecting reference databases include

cost

scope of information

quality of product, including graphic elements

ease of use

interface (Windows, DOS, etc.)

hardware requirements

Many potential buyers ask where they can find the information necessary to make an intelligent decision. Just as with other computer software, many sources exist, including magazines, books, and even CD-ROMs themselves. Many computer magazines contain countless reviews, though this does entail looking through a lot of information. A few CD-ROM sources contain warehouses of information, though of differing degrees of quality and in differing amounts. You will find some of these described in this book in the section "Computers and Software," which lists products such as CD-ROMs in Print on CD-ROM and CD-ROM of CD-ROMs. Many of the larger companies will send them for a period to preview.

This book itself is a good source of information. It provides the most-complete information possible in a variety of categories of interest to libraries. Within each category are entries in more than one cost range as well, making it possible for both large and small libraries to find appropriate products.

Nonreference CD-ROMs, those intended to be circulated to patrons' homes, require some additional scrutiny. A checklist includes

cost

hardware requirements

its fit within the library's media selection policy

publisher's prohibitions against circulation

quality

All librarians can review and select circulating CDs. The children's librarian can easily select educational CDs for kids. Reference staff will need to select CDs for periodical and magazine indexes.

One favorable attribute becoming increasingly commonplace is the multiplat-form CD. Such CDs can be used on both an IBM clone and a Macintosh. This is ideal for the library with limited funds trying to decide which computer platform to establish. Another suggestion is to purchase the popular and inexpensive packages of CDs seen in many stores that sell computer software and offered by software vendors through the mail. Such packages contain CDs bundled together at an excellent price. They are sometimes products that are beyond their prime, though still popular with patrons and worth owning.

In evaluating CD-ROMs for circulating to patrons' homes, it is important to check the copyright or license provisions. Some permit circulation, some do not. A good example is Shareware Bonanza, which has 25,000 shareware and public-domain programs on a four-disc set. For explorers, this set of discs can be a wonderland. Shareware is a good arrangement for libraries because copyright responsibilities fall to the end user.

The results from a literature survey helped to determine which CD-ROMs should be included and recommended in this book. I used this information to help determine the areas in which CD-ROMs are used by librarians, such as history, genealogy, etc. Then I tried to include a range of products and prices in each category. After consulting numerous sources of software information (electronic and print catalogs, software magazine reviews, etc.), I decided on the selections for inclusion. Next, I requested review copies or purchased products. The effort to acquire CD-ROMs for hands-on review was largely successful, and I obtained several hundred. The actual number of product entries with detailed information in this volume is more than 300. There are many more that are listed and suggested. For example, the Jane's Information Group listing includes more than a dozen products. I installed and used all available products and examined manuals. With each product I considered the following questions:

How could this be used in a library?

Does it have any advantages over any similar print products that are perhaps already used in libraries?

Which type of library (special, academic, school, public) and size (small, medium, large) library would best use this product?

How to Use This Book

Ideally, every library will have a technology plan in place that includes CD-ROM technology in its many aspects, including LAN, circulating, multimedia, reference, etc. Even if no plan is yet written, the need for CD-ROM technology will have to be addressed. A good way to start is to have a complete survey of all hardware, including CD-ROMs, that the library owns. Another excellent tool is a patron survey. This can be used to justify the need for circulating CD-ROMs. If few people in the community own computers with CD-ROM drives, then a circulating collection may be a bit premature. Otherwise, resources appropriate to the perceived demand may be allocated.

In any case, nothing can be done without sufficient information, including knowledge about CD-ROMs. Staff should become familiar with computers and

CD-ROM technology. Even a casual browsing of this book will reveal many areas in which reference may be assisted. Not everything included in this book is useful to every library, especially when considering budgets and interests.

Once the library staff has identified areas in which the library will benefit, additional information, including the CDs themselves, may be obtained from many vendors. Information that is included in this book includes price; vendor, including name, address, and phone and fax where possible; hardware requirements; comments on what the product does; and bibliographic citations, such as reviews, when available.

I hope that the librarians reading this book will have as much fun making their selections as I did gathering and reviewing the CDs contained herein. I made very effort to ensure the accuracy of information contained in this book and made changes even as the manuscript was going through its last editorial stages. Unfortunately, some few products will have new editions, price changes, or even have been discontinued. Therefore, the wise consumer should check with the vendor (numbers supplied in the appendix) to ascertain the most-current data.

Almanacs

While there are some advantages and improvements available in an electronic almanac, most librarians will not want to give up their paper almanacs to rely solely on an electronic one. A paper almanac is extremely handy to keep on a desktop for quick reference; an electronic CD almanac is an excellent tool, however, for use with young people or when speed is not a critical factor. Most electronic almanacs contain multimedia elements, such as speeches and videos of famous events, and are well organized to provide an overall learning package. In addition, the ability to search an electronic almanac instead of just leafing through an index can yield a great deal of additional useful information that might otherwise be lost.

Name:	**Guinness Multimedia Disc of World Records**
Vendor:	Grolier Electronic Publishing
Cost:	$29.95
Hardware requirements:	IBM PC and compatibles, 4MB RAM, 4MB free hard-disk space, Windows 3.1 or later, DOS 5.0 or later, 256-color adapter, sound card, 150K or later CD-ROM transfer rate; Macintosh LC II or later, 68020 CPU 16 MHz or later, System 7.1 or later, 2MB free RAM, 256-color capability, sound card, 125K/second or higher CD-ROM transfer rate
Comments:	This disc makes it easy to look up the longest, biggest, heaviest, smallest, most number of something—there are 89 superlatives in all to choose from—and thousands of other world record entries. Information is accessible in several ways, including an automated slide show that will fascinate kids. Search features include the ability to search for specific items or to browse the database entry-by-entry. A button bar on the bottom of the screen indicates when an entry has a picture or movie available. Multimedia makes the program especially fun, since short video clips will show trains in motion, the *Hindenburg* exploding, etc. Video clips can also be selected as a group without the need to find corresponding

entries in the text. A picture index allows for quick navigating through the many pictures contained within the database. There are 800 color photos that are informative and fun. Search strategies can involve some Boolean terms: AND, NOT, and OR. The "Topic Index" is a quick way to explore certain areas (technology, science, buildings and structures, etc.). Another feature, particularly useful for kids, is the 89-superlative index that makes it easy to locate categories of records.

Name: **Multimedia World Factbook**

Vendor: Bureau of Electronic Publishing

Cost: $99

Hardware requirements: Multimedia IBM PC and compatibles, Windows, 2MB RAM; Macintosh

Comments: This multimedia disc is excellent for school libraries. It contains 248 country profiles with information about geography, population, language, literacy, laborforce, government, national holidays, current leaders, suffrage, voting strength, political pressure groups, gross national product, inflation rate, agriculture, currency, communications, highways, railroads, defense forces, and much more. Multimedia elements include color flags, national anthem performances, and color Hammond maps.

Name: **Wayzata World Fact Book**

Vendor: Wayzata Technology

Cost: $24.95

Hardware requirements: IBM PC and compatibles; Macintosh

Comments: Users will easily find their way around this atlas and gazetteer. This world fact book can be used for browsing or for more-serious study by world travel enthusiasts—children or adults. It covers all of the countries of the world. If desired, the basic facts about each country may be superimposed upon its map. Facts include all of the usual areas children ask questions about when researching school papers: religion, topology, industry, agriculture, and much more. More than 200 photos show street and market scenes, important buildings, and other cultural aspects of countries plus a collection of flags, in color, from around the world. The entire disc (all of the fact sheets of the individual countries plus all other documents) may be searched at one time. Particularly useful in this mountain of data are the many "Special Topics." These include adoption, child abduction, crime, HIV testing, medical tips, immigration numbers, safe tips for trips, residing abroad, terrorist group information, citizenship, and a list of documents that are available from the U.S. State Department. Many excellent tables and charts are in the "Compare All Countries" section. Statistics for birth and death, literacy, life expectancy, etc. are ranked from highest to lowest and lowest to highest (side by side).

Art and Music

CD-ROMs present art and music in new and exciting ways, giving greater context to the music for young and old alike. Music CD-ROMs from Microsoft feature music of famous classical composers. A student of music can explore Beethoven's symphonies for purely educational or recreational purposes. These programs offer complete control over the music, giving the user the freedom to explore and revisit any section. Explanatory text, photographs, and artwork from the age in which the composer lived provide a fuller background and history. Similarly, compilations of artwork give students the opportunity to compare and enjoy hundreds of works of art from various periods.

For the American Bandstand generation, All Music Guide provides an excellent way to find just about any song or popular tune, band, or performer. Apple Pie Music is a multimedia look at American music since its beginnings.

Additional products available:

An Introduction to Classical Music (Attica Cybernetics)

The Orchestra (Time Warner Interactive Group)

World Beat (Medio Multimedia)

Name:	**All Music Guide**
Vendor:	Compton's NewMedia
Cost:	$59.95
Hardware requirements:	IBM PC and compatibles, 1MB RAM, 4MB hard-disk space, DOS 3.1 or later, Windows 3.0 or later
Comments:	All Music Guide is a vast database of music information. It contains listings of some 200,000 albums; 30,000 artists and groups; 190,000 sidemen and instrumentalists; 70,000 in-print classical albums; 120,000 separate classical compositions; 7,000 music books and magazines; and 600 essays, instrument maps, articles, resources, mail order numbers, etc. It also contains an 800-entry glossary of musical terms.

One of the selling claims of this CD is that it has "ratings and reviews by 150 of the country's best music reviewers and reviews from more than 60 music magazines." This is true, but don't expect too much here since the reviews, while interesting, are often no more than one or two sentences at best. Needless to say, the utility of this database is the access to basic album information.

The search interface uses hotkeys, making finding a name easy. A search can be by artist/group, album/title, or record company. The search menu is completely push-button. A search for the name of an individual track is performed by pressing the "track" button under album search, then pressing hotkeys until you find what you want. Other album search fields are titles and sidemen. Artists can be located by musical style, by instrument played, and by name. (When looking up *bagpipes*, only two artists play them in the rock/popular database.) A search for *Anka* results in the names of Anka's albums and includes the date of each along with its label and number. It even allows a place for two separate notes by users. Albums can also be tagged with "have" or "want." The classical music database albums may be looked up by performance, performer, conductor, orchestra, instrument, composition, or composer. Brief biographies, available for some selected artists, include the person's musical history and influence. Any search may be sorted by any field.

The final part of the database is "Music Library and Resources." Information about books and magazines includes the author, title, publisher, date of publication, name of any artist who is the subject of a book, musical category, and notes and a rating. The system also lists record companies. Other resources include the addresses for record labels, jazz radio stations, online computer access to music resources, women's music, children's music, and much more.

Name:	**Apple Pie Music**
Vendor:	Lintronics Publishing Group
Cost:	$95
Hardware requirements:	MPC with 4MB RAM; Macintosh System 7.1, 8MB RAM, 25 MHz (both Macintosh and IBM versions on one disc)
Comments:	Many people will enjoy this database of more than 400 complete folk, religious, and popular compositions of American music from the past 350 years. Approximately half of the recordings come from archival records of the original artists (Native Americans, sailors, coal miners, etc.).

Approximately 200 MIDI files are "reproduced note for note from 17th–20th century sheet music." These files can be played with the computer with different selections of instruments. Also contained on the disc are more than 300 photographs and paintings representative of the periods. Other information on the disc includes song histories and notes about performances, instruments, lyrics, and composers. It's filled with hypertext links to related information. This makes it easy and fun to examine lyrics while listening to a song or while reading its history.

Material may be accessed in numerous ways: by lyrics, song cards (songs that are performed), composers, instruments, the pages of the informative text, or all of these. An alternate way to browse is to select a category from the main menu: resources, history of music, music of history, or music-alley (song performances) or to use the manual. Each category is subdivided into other sections, making it easy to locate and enjoy melodies from an era or of a particular type.

Clearly, a multimedia computer is required for this program. Moreover, if a library were to make this available to the general public, it would have to locate listening facilities in a secluded or soundproofed area or provide users with earphones.

Name:	**Beethoven's Fifth: The Multimedia Symphony for Windows; Beethoven's Fifth: The Multimedia Symphony for Macintosh**
Vendor:	InterActive Publishing
Cost:	$59.95
Hardware requirements:	IBM PC and compatibles, Windows 3.x, 2MB RAM; Macintosh, 2MB RAM, 3.5MB hard-disk space
Comments:	The program plays Beethoven's famous symphony accompanied by explanatory text. It is a highly educational disc sure to improve one's cultural standing and an excellent way to effortlessly learn more about classical music. Also included is a biography of Beethoven and a glossary of musical terms.

Other programs in this series offer music from Beethoven, Mozart, Schubert, and Stravinsky. Each CD features a "Pocket Guide" that allows the user to move from section to section throughout the music at will. "The Composer's World" gives the social and personal context within which the music was written. "Instruments" explains the significance of each instrument in the orchestra and how the composer puts them to work in music. "A Close Reading" gives a running commentary as the music plays. "Art of Listening" illustrates and discusses the composer's underlying techniques. There is even a game that can be played based on the content of the CD.

Name: **Electronic Library of Art: Impressionism and Its Sources; Renaissance Masters I & II; Survey of Western Art**

Vendor: Ebook

Cost: $49.95 each

Hardware requirements: IBM PC 386 or better and compatibles, SVGA (256 colors), 2MB RAM (4MB recommended), Windows 3.1 or later, DOS 3.1 or later, sound card

Comments: Impressionism and Its Sources contains examples of Monet, van Gogh, and other French impressionist artists. A search may be made by title, medium, artist, date, schools, or object. This and the Renaissance Masters CDs contain more than 1,300 images using multimedia elements. Each package acts as a slide collection of artworks. The Impressionism CD is recommended for ages 12 to adult.

Renaissance Masters I & II includes examples of painting, sculpture, and architecture of the Renaissance. Volume I covers the early Renaissance; Volume II covers the High Renaissance. Searches may made be by title, medium, date, schools, or object. Volume I is recommended for ages 12 to adult. Volume II is recommended for ages 8 to adult.

The Survey of Western Art contains more than 1,000 images of sculpture, painting, and architecture from ancient Egypt to contemporary America. Also included are audio explanations, artist biographies, and other text discussing the artworks. Searches may be made by title, artist's name, biographical information, dimensions of a painting, and even its location. Recommended for ages 8 to adult.

Name: **Microsoft Musical Instruments**

Vendor: Microsoft

Cost: $79.95

Hardware requirements: IBM PC and compatibles, DOS 3.1 or later, Windows 3.1 or later

Comments: This is the easy way to become acquainted with more than 200 musical instruments. Included are more than 500 photographs and 1,500 sound samples. In a section called "Musical Ensembles," students may hear music played with the different instruments. Text accompanies the music and photographs, making it a multimedia educational experience.

Name: **MUSE**
Vendor: National Information Services
Cost: $1,395 annual subscription, annual updates
Hardware requirements: IBM PC and compatibles, 512K RAM
Comments: The database contains bibliographic records, music abstracts, and a catalog of sound recordings. Of the RILM abstracts, 158,000 are from the *Répertoire International de Littérature Musicale* (*RILM Abstracts*) and 161,000 records are from the Library of Congress (*The Music Catalog*). The Library of Congress database corresponds to the print editions of *Music*, *Books on Music*, and *Sound Recordings*. Both databases may be searched separately or simultaneously. Areas of music covered include music theory and composition, composers and performers, sound recordings with song listings, performance reviews and analyses, ethnomusicology, music history, musical instruments (ancient and modern), voice and liturgy, and acoustics and technology.

Name: **MUZE**
Vendor: EBSCO Publishing
Cost: $299 annual; $499 quarterly
Hardware requirements: IBM PC and compatibles, 640K RAM (2MB recommended), DOS 5.0 or later, 5MB hard-disk space required; Macintosh, 1.5MB RAM, System 6.0.5 or later, 1MB hard-disk space
Comments: MUZE provides bibliographic access to more than 120,000 musical recordings that represent more than 665,000 songs and musical works. It is used by several national stores. CD, cassette, MiniDisc, Digital Compact Cassette, and music video formats that are for sale in the United States are included. Each record includes biographies of the composer and performer. You can search using the menu-driven system with 25 different categories, including album title, performer, composer, genre, song title/musical work, etc. A glossary of musical terms is also online. When using the database, many hypertext links lead users to additional related information. Each quarterly update adds approximately 5,000 new entries to the database.

Name: **The Viking Opera Guide**
Vendor: Attica Cybernetics
Cost: $59.95
Hardware requirements: IBM PC and compatibles, Windows 3.x, 2MB RAM
Comments: This fact-filled database contains three hours of music and information on more than 1,500 operas, including early

monodies and masques and comic, grand, tragic, etc. operas. Suitable for ages 12 and up, this guide gives the title, composer, premiere information, orchestration, and librettist. It includes 800 composer profiles that give the full name of each composer and his or her birth date and place, date of death, bibliography, and more.

Name: | **Wilson Art Abstracts; Wilson Art Index**
Vendor: | H. W. Wilson
Cost: | $2,495, abstracts; $1,495, index
Hardware requirements: | IBM PC and compatibles, 640K RAM, 3MB free hard-disk space, DOS 3.1 or later, Hayes compatible modem optional
Comments: | These databases provide abstracting and indexing of more than 260 international art publications: English-language periodicals and museum bulletins. Also included are publications in French, Japanese, Italian, German, Spanish, Dutch, and Swedish. Wilson Art Abstracts contains 50- to 150-word abstracts of each article from spring 1994 and indexing from September 1984. Art Index contains indexing only. Both products are updated twice weekly online. Three search levels make it easy for beginners, but more-advanced researchers can search effectively as well. A single-subject search mode (browse) will locate authors of articles or reviews or artists by searching on author's or artist's name or title of a work. Multiple-subject search using Wilsearch mode can be used to search by field: genre, nationality, language, gender, century/period, birthday, and keyword. A command-language search can also be implemented. This system, the same one used by Wilsonline, supports nested Boolean logic, proximity searching, free-text and controlled-vocabulary searching, truncation, ranging, multifile searching, saving of data and of search, and more. In addition, subscribers to any of Wilson's CD-ROM services also have unlimited online access time to provide the latest information when needed.

Astronomy and Space

With the aid of computer software, the amateur astronomer can chart the heavens and watch the changes in the night sky unfold. For example, Astronomer CD can be used to provide a virtual planetarium on the computer screen. Many computer programs and utilities yield information such as asteroid data and databases that calculate the position of stars and planets. Some of the discs contain thousands of photographs of heavenly bodies, including some photographed from the Hubble space observatory. Some programs, such as Amazing Universe, let users experiment with filters and colors to enhance and alter images of star clusters and planets. For the hardcore space junkie, anyone with an avid interest in space technology and space travel, programs such as Space Shuttle are ideal for learning about the manned missions into space. Students can see video clips of actual launches, learn about how missions are planned and operated, how spacesuits work, and how astronauts live during an actual mission.

Additional products available:

Distant Suns (Virtual Reality Laboratories)

Murmurs of Earth (Time Warner Interactive)

Space: A Visual History of Manned Spaceflight (Sumeria)

Voyage to the Planets (Astronomical Research Network)

Name:	**Amazing Universe III**
Vendor:	Hopkins Technology
Cost:	$49.95
Hardware requirements:	IBM PC and compatibles, 640K minimum RAM required; Macintosh, 2MB RAM required, sound card
Comments:	This multimedia program contains more than 550 color photographs of stellar bodies, such as moons, planets, star clusters, etc., taken by NASA space probes, Hubble photos, and the National Optical Astronomy Observatory. These can be viewed and manipulated in a variety of ways. Some of the

images include the "face" on Mars, active volcano on Io, a geyser on Triton, Saturn's rings, Great Red Spot on Jupiter, nebulae, Supernova 1987A, several black-hole candidates, and quasars. Images may be magnified and filtered and colors changed. For instance, there are eighteen special filters, eight color palettes, background and foreground color control, contrast control, image enhancement, 8/16/32-bit images, histograms, and browse functions. This new version, III, contains a built-in planetarium, a great deal of text explaining the pictures, and original music. It also includes a range of pictures showing some of the tiniest objects in the universe: diatoms, algae, bacteria, pollen, and the piercing end of a mosquito.

Further information: Charles Seiter, "Amazing Universe," *MacWorld*, Aug. 1993, 163.

Name: **Expert CD-ROM Astronomer for Windows**
Vendor: Expert Software
Cost: $49.95
Hardware requirements: IBM PC and compatibles
Comments: Expert CD-ROM Astronomer for Windows is two software programs in one: Expert Astronomer Multimedia and Expert Astronomer. The two are linked so information can be drawn from one when in the other. Amateur astronomers will go wild over this package. It is extensive in its coverage of astronomy and easy to use.

Expert Astronomer Multimedia provides coverage of the solar system; deep-sky astronomy; observation of the sky; space exploration; photo gallery; video gallery; and a guide to the universe, the solar system, and the sky. It contains many photos of space objects, including planets, stars, and galaxies, some from the Hubble space telescope. Any specific object is described and can be plotted by the program onto a star chart, if desired. Essays on black holes, radio astronomy, Mars exploration, and many other topics are found throughout the program. In addition to a general table of contents and a table of contents for each section, there is also an index. Hundreds of photographs and dozens of videos with sound provide a rich environment for learning about space by seeing actual footage of space and shuttle liftoffs.

The second program, Expert Astronomer, turns the computer into a planetarium. Users may select from different sky views and manipulate by changing the date, enlarging the view, or selecting a specific object from among the many thousands of celestial objects. The computer will then identify the object and give basic details. Users may insert grids and various reference lines as well as planet names, etc., on the screen.

Name:	**Our Solar System**
Vendor:	Chestnut Software
Cost:	$12.95
Hardware requirements:	IBM PC and compatibles
Comments:	This shareware disk provides several areas of interest, including programs, pictures, and text files. There are literally hundreds of photos, including the sun, planets, asteroids, the moon, astronauts, and many more. They can be viewed in several ways, including directly from the CD. Several viewers are supplied on the disc, including CSHOW, BrowseMaster, and others. Files may also be loaded directly onto a hard drive for use with other programs. The material is shareware, so it may be traded and swapped freely. The disc is truly a treasure trove of software treats, since the young astronomer will find a great number of interesting files beyond the visuals. These include quite a few programs: demos, almanacs of various astronomical occurrences (including phases of the moon in a particular location), a database for the Herschel catalog of deep space, NSS Space Catalog, star and planet positions, moonrise, sunrise, and much, much more. A variety of utilities for performing operations on DOS files are also available. These include archive programs, graphic utilities, and others. The disc is easy to operate, and the DOS interface is menu driven. Many young people and adults alike will enjoy taking this disc home to assume the role of amateur astronomer.

Name:	**Space and Astronomy**
Vendor:	Walnut Creek CDROM
Cost:	$39.95
Hardware requirements:	IBM PC and compatibles; Macintosh
Comments:	A collection of 1,080 image files, 5,000 text files, and astronomy- and space-related shareware make this an extraordinary document of space technology and research for the amateur astronomer or space buff. The collection was put together by Space Station Freedom bulletin board system. The images include space-related artistic renderings of moons, spacecraft, and astronauts in space. It includes a variety of lunar and astronaut photos that may be used for

Windows wallpaper or screen saver slide shows. In addition, there are many images of celestial objects such as galaxies. Clip art includes images of spacecraft, NASA logos, planets, and space camp. Five sound files are of astronauts or ground control calling each other. Text files contain many things, including *Space Digest* (17 volumes), *Space Power Digest*, *NASA Daily News*, Jet Propulsion Laboratory Press Releases, space station and Hubble telescope information files, and a press kit for the Space Transportation System. Fourteen files contain information about the astronauts, including which ones are deceased, which were in the Boy Scouts, which have more than 500 hours of space time, etc. There is even a list of the requirements for becoming an astronaut. For dedicated amateur astronomers, the Dressler and ESO astronomical catalogs are included. For anyone with a real bent toward the esoteric, the disc contains a book entitled *Asteroids II*, assembled at the Jet Propulsion Laboratory, with much information about the asteroids. Also included is a series of "fact sheets" giving details about many space projects (Magellan, Mars Observer, etc.). These fact sheets are relatively brief, but they provide clear and concise data about what each mission was to accomplish. The disc's interface makes it possible to view all images and read all files directly from disc without moving to hard drive. The disc is also "BBS ready," meaning it can be mounted on any of a number of electronic bulletin board systems, including RBBS, Opus, PCBoard, Spitfire, Maximum, and Wildcat BBS. Also on the disc are Usenet sci.space archives from the Internet. Shareware computer programs of interest to future or amateur astronomers, space scientists, or astronauts are also included.

Name:	**Space Shuttle; Space Shuttle MPC**
Vendor:	Software Toolworks (MindScape)
Cost:	$49.95
Hardware requirements:	IBM PC and compatibles; Macintosh (multimedia PC version also requires Windows 3.x)
Comments:	This program is an outstanding multimedia educational tool about the U.S. space shuttle program. The first fifty-three shuttle flights are highlighted, including mission objectives, crew (with pictures), and flight details. The central feature of the program, however, is its many video clips. These clips contain actual footage of each blastoff. The program is divided into orientation, training, and mission launch; a

liftoff game; and a glossary. Users will learn what it takes to become an astronaut and a shuttle pilot. They also learn about equipment such as the space suit, how a zero gravity toilet works, and much more. The training section shows how and what astronauts must learn about mission objectives and work. The liftoff game, intended for young children, is a simple quiz in which players race against the clock to reach the shuttle prior to its departure for space.

Business and Industry

Libraries have long been a good source of business information, whether about making investments or going into business. Such information comes in the form of databases. Several CDs provide basic business information, such as the names and addresses of companies, in a well-organized and easily searchable format. A popular database, ABI/INFORM, contains indexing and abstracts on many business and management issues for hundreds of business journals. Detailed information is available on 1,700 insurance companies through Best Insurance Reports. Compact Disclosure provides financial and management information pulled from the 10K, 20F, and other SEC registration statements for more than 12,000 public companies. The Federal Taxation Library provides an incredible wealth of tax information, including IRS codes and many other revenue acts of the government. FormSource is a complete set of tax forms on CD.

Name:	**ABI/INFORM Global; ABI/INFORM Research; ABI/INFORM Select**
Vendor:	UMI
Cost:	$6,825, Global; $5,825, Research; $2,760, Select; check with vendor for backfile prices
Hardware requirements:	IBM PC and compatibles, 1MB RAM (490K free RAM), 2MB hard-disk space per ProQuest database installed plus 10MB hard-disk space to run after installation, DOS 3.3, 1.44MB floppy
Comments:	The ABI/INFORM database, in its various versions, covers business and management issues, including business conditions and trends, corporate strategies and tactics, management techniques, and competition. Each citation contains a 25- to 150-word abstract and full bibliographic data. Three editions are available. The differences among these allow libraries to select a price and a product that best suit their needs. ABI/INFORM Global contains citations and abstracts of

1,000 journals from 1987 to the present. Of these, 350 titles are English-language journals from outside the U.S. ABI/INFORM Research contains indexing and abstracts of 800 journals. More than 200,000 citations include material starting from 1987. ABI/INFORM Select contains indexing and abstracts of 350 frequently requested business titles plus citations from the most recent six months of the *Wall Street Journal*. A second disc of ABI/INFORM Select, which covers from 1980 to 1985, is also available. ProQuest Searchware is convenient for use by people with little or no search experience. A search may be made using the fields that are readily available or using AND/OR/NOT for search terms. Truncation, field limiting, and proximity search are also permitted. Any search set may be saved for reuse or combined with other sets. The results screen for titles shows source, publication date, location of the article in the publication, and availability of the source material.

Name:	**Accounting and Tax Database**
Vendor:	UMI
Cost:	$1,500 to $2,100
Hardware requirements:	IBM PC and compatibles, 1MB RAM (490K free RAM), 2MB hard-disk space per ProQuest database installed plus 10MB disk space to run after installation, DOS 3.3, 1.44MB floppy
Comments:	The database contains complete indexing and abstracting for approximately 300 U.S. and foreign publications related to accounting, auditing, banking, bankruptcy, compensation, consulting services, finance, fiscal and monetary policy, law, taxation, etc. Additional information is gleaned from more than 800 newspapers, dissertations, business journals, and news magazines. Information is from 1990 forward. Abstracts range from 25 to 400 words each. ProQuest Searchware is convenient for use by people with little or no search experience. A search may be made using the fields that are readily available or using AND/OR/NOT for search terms. Truncation, field limiting, and proximity search are also permitted. Any search set may be saved for reuse or combined with other sets. The results screen for titles shows source, publication date, location of the article in the publication, and availability of the source material.

Name:	**Best Insurance Reports**
Vendor:	A. M. Best
Cost:	$2,500, including one year of *Best's Review*
Hardware requirements:	IBM PC and compatibles
Comments:	Best's Insurance Reports is a CD-ROM service of Best, an agency that rates the financial condition of insurance companies. While the interface is DOS, not Windows, it is quite adequate and easy to use. There are two distinct volumes of information contained in this database. The first is the Property/Casualty edition. It contains information on more than 1,700 companies. The Life/Health edition contains information on more than 2,400 companies. Details provided about each company include important statistics such as capital and surplus, assets, and net premiums written in the year of the evaluation. A narrative contains operating comments and investment data followed by a ledger sheet containing assets and liabilities as of December 31, summary of operations, summary of premium income, distribution of premium income, capital surplus account, cash flow analysis, distribution of bonds by maturity, separate account data, investment yields, significant operating ratios, management and operations, new business issued, insurance in force, company development, and profitability tests. Any company may be searched by name, AMB (A. M. Best) number, group name, group number, index name, company type, market code, report code, and company level. The search interface supports the logical connectors of OR, AND, and WITHOUT. When users are unsure of search information, they can employ a browse function that allows them to go through the list by name, number, etc. The last chapter in each volume contains a listing of company mergers, voluntary liquidation and retirements, conservatorships, receiverships, and conversions and name changes during the previous five-year period.

Name:	**BID Disc Weekly**
Vendor:	Panatech
Cost:	$45 for five-week trial, $495 for six-month subscription, $950 for annual subscription
Hardware requirements:	IBM PC and compatibles
Comments:	As its name implies, BID Disc Weekly is published weekly on CD-ROM. It is based on *Commerce Business Daily* and is licensed by the U.S. Department of Commerce. Its primary purpose is to provide information to potential contractors who

wish to bid on government contracts, including "U.S. Government procurement invitations, contract awards, subcontracting leads, sales of surplus property, and foreign business opportunity." The edition of this product reviewed here was a DOS, not Windows, version. However, the interface uses a mouse cursor in a Windows-like environment, which is quite acceptable. Each weekly edition contains between 500 and 1,000 such notices that are printed only once and are not cumulative. The interface makes it easy to locate any word within the text of any notice. If the word isn't known exactly, it can be guessed or the database can be browsed. Searches can be made using Boolean operators OR, AND, NOT. A search may also be performed using group name (hardware and abrasives, lighting fixtures, furniture, etc.). Other search features also exist. For example, any text within the database can be blocked (selected) and used as a search criteria. Results may be saved to disk or printed out. Users have full control over screen colors, save-file locations, etc.

Name:	**BoardLink**
Vendor:	The Taft Group
Cost:	$995, single user; $1,200, 2–8 single-site version
Hardware requirements:	286 or later IBM PC and compatibles, 640K RAM with 500K available, 2MB free hard-disk space
Comments:	The BoardLink database contains information on more than 112,000 nonprofit, corporate, and foundation board members in 1,000 top U.S. companies, top 5,000 U.S. nonprofit organizations, and top 6,000 philanthropic corporations and foundations. Home and contact addresses of 50,000 board members are also included. Organizational information includes the address, telephone number, and full names and titles of all listed board members. Organizations may be searched by geographic location or type.

Name:	**Business Library, Volume 1**
Vendor:	Allegro New Media
Cost:	$59
Hardware requirements:	IBM and compatibles, 2MB RAM, Windows 3.1
Comments:	Easy to use for finding your way to essential business information, Business Library contains twelve excellent and useful business books: *Business to Business Communications Handbook*; *How to Get People to Do Things Your Way*; *International Herald Tribune Guide to Business Travel: Europe*; *Joyce Lain Kennedy's Career Book*; *Meetings Rules*

& Procedures; *State of the Art Marketing Research*; *Successful Direct Marketing Methods*; *Successful Telemarketing*; *The Feel of Success in Selling*; *Finance & Accounting for Nonfinancial Managers*; *How to Make Big Money in Real Estate in the Tighter, Tougher '90s Market*; and *Total Global Strategy: Marketing for Worldwide Competitive Advantage*. The books provide a good collection of quality business information that may be searched for specific topics, and each has a table of contents and index. A search for information may encompass all twelve volumes or one or more specific volumes, and it may be limited to all text or topic titles only. Search includes Boolean logic AND, OR, NEAR, NOT and truncation. A special adjustable cruise control feature allows for documents to scroll on the screen automatically for faster and more-convenient reading. Information may be copied and pasted to the clipboard for export, and pages in books may be marked for the addition of notes. The package is highly recommended for public library business collections.

Name:	**Compact Disclosure V. 4.1J**
Vendor:	Disclosure
Cost:	Contact vendor
Hardware requirements:	IBM PC and compatibles
Comments:	The database contains financial and management information on more than 12,000 public companies gleaned from annual and periodic reports filed with the U.S. government and the Securities and Exchange Commission. To qualify for inclusion a company must have had at least 500 shareholders; had at least $5 million in assets as of August 15, 1986; and have filed 10K, 20F, or appropriate registration statements with the Securities and Exchange Commission within the past eighteen months. The database does not contain management investment companies, mutual funds, real estate limited partnerships, or oil- or gas-drilling companies. Original documents are available on CD-ROM through Laser Disclosure. The database is easy to use. A search may be made by any of the following fields: company name, type of business, geographic area, financial information, full-text fields, number of shares/employees, owners, officers, directors, stock exchange, *Fortune* 1000 number, fiscal year, SEC filings, Forbes number, or status (active, gone private, merged, bankrupt, acquired). A search may be made using the DIALOG command search: select, display, expand, print, set,

report. A mailing file utilities section will create mail labels from downloaded addresses.

Name:	**Corporate Affiliations Plus**
Vendor:	KR Information
Cost:	$2,100
Hardware requirements:	IBM PC and compatibles, 535K RAM, 10MB hard-disk space, DOS 3.1 or later
Comments:	Corporate Affiliations Plus is a database that contains information on more than 114,000 businesses throughout the world with annual sales of $10 million or more. It includes 15,000 parent companies; 97,800 subsidiaries, divisions, affiliates, manufacturing plants, and joint ventures; 286,000 company officers and other personnel; and 62,000 brands and products. Information comes from National Register Publishing. A special and exciting feature of this CD is its "Family Tree" that makes it easy to determine which company owns or is owned by another company. It also gives information on who reports to whom and who is responsible for what. Data may be retrieved by using any of twenty-eight search criteria, for example, company name, SIC code, sales, revenue, earnings, city, state. Boolean logic can be used to combine or refine search terms (AND, OR, ANDNOT). Truncation helps to search successfully when complete data are uncertain. You can choose display or print options from a variety of record formats: brief, standard, detailed, customized, hierarchical, and company mailing label. There are quite a few indexes that may be browsed: company name, parent company name, outside service firm name, classification/type, outside firm class/type, personal name, job title/function, product type, city/state/ZIP, country/zone, state of incorporation, keyword, database, ticker symbol, SIC codes, SIC text, and company number.

Name:	**The DRI/McGraw-Hill Encyclopedia of World Economics on CD-ROM**
Vendor:	DRI/McGraw-Hill
Cost:	$345, published every six months; 5-country, 3.5-inch demo disk available free
Hardware requirements:	IBM PC and compatibles
Comments:	This economic world encyclopedia contains the following information for 80 countries that comprise 99.5 percent of the world economy: prices, labor and earnings, production and sales, other principal indicators, interest rates and yields,

monetary aggregates, foreign exchange, government finance, merchandise trade, balance of payments, and national accounts. The main menu is divided into Africa, Americas, Western Europe, Eastern Europe and the former Soviet Union, Far East and Oceania, Middle East, and South and Southeast Asia. Each country also has an economic overview that contains country, economic, and trading profiles. Much of the data can be traced back through successive years to the 1960s and 1970s. Statistics may be transferred (copied) to spreadsheets or word processors for additional analysis.

Name:	**Federal Taxation Library**
Vendor:	West Publishing
Cost:	$4,500
Hardware requirements:	IBM PC and compatibles, 400K of available RAM, DOS 3.3 or later, 5MB hard-disk space
Comments:	The Federal Taxation Library is a massive collection of tax-related information that is available as one complete package or as separate sets.

Code and Regulations sets include *The Internal Revenue Code* (annotated, with historical notes), *Code of Federal Regulations* (Title 26, Part 10 of Title 31), and indexes to *Internal Revenue Code and Regulations*. It also contains abstracts from 1982 to the present of *Revenue Rulings and Revenue Procedures* from the Bureau of National Affairs, Inc. (BNA), such as *Letter Rulings (Private Letter Rulings and Technical Advice Memoranda)*, *General Counsel Memoranda*, and actions on decisions. Other information includes the *Rules of the Tax Court and Claims Court*; *International Tax Agreements, 1955 to Present*; and federal taxation legislation: *1986 Tax Reform Act, Technical Corrections Acts of 1987 and 1988, Technical and Miscellaneous Revenue Act of 1988*, and *Revenue Reconciliation Acts of 1989 and 1990*. Federal taxation legislative history can be obtained as well with the *Congressional Committee Reports on the 1986 Tax Reform Act*, the *Blue Book General Explanation of the 1986 Tax Reform Act*, *BNA Detailed Analysis of the 1986 Tax Reform Act*, *Congressional Committee Reports on the 1989–90 Revenue Reconciliation Acts*, *Conference Report on TAMRA of 1988*, and *Descriptions of the Technical Corrections Act*. Also found is the *Federal Tax Code and Regulations, 1984–91*.

Other sets available are: Administrative Materials Set, Letter Rulings Set, and the Taxation Cases Set.

The system is easy to use and to install. West's CD-ROMs use Premise Research Software 2.1 for DOS as a search engine. Premise provides excellent search capability. Case law may be searched by citation, title, or issue, and a specific case may be retrieved by citation or title. A search by issue may be by word, topic, key number, or field. A field search may be restricted by any field: citation, title, synopsis, topic, headnote, digest, court, date, judge, attorney, or text. Premise may also be used to retrieve references to case law or references to statutes. Statutes and rules may be searched, and wild cards (*, !) can be used as well as proximity searching. Books in the database and search results may be browsed or scanned. Information from a search may be downloaded to a file or printed out.

Name:	**FormSource**
Vendor:	Prentice Hall Professional Software
Cost:	$495
Hardware requirements:	IBM PC and compatibles, 2MB RAM, DOS 5.0 or later, 2MB hard-disk space; Windows version requires 4MB RAM, Windows 3.1, and 8MB disk space; HP LaserJet series II, III, or LaserJet 4; Novell and Lantastic network compatible
Comments:	Here's a solution or alternative to the many boxes of federal and state tax forms that many libraries make available each tax season. With FormSource all forms are all in one convenient location. Included are 20,000 pages of both forms and instructions for the Internal Revenue Service and all 50 states that cover individual, corporate, partnership, fiduciary, gift and estate, payroll, and tax-exempt statuses. However, in addition to the convenience and quantity of material, FormSource offers some other real differences between this service and the usual boxes of forms. These forms can be filled out online and then printed. The printed forms (for laser printers) look like the real tax forms and are even reproduced onscreen in the original colors. While this is all useful, it will not make the calculations for the user. Other features include adding the basic information about a client (name, address, Social Security number, etc.). This information may be added into the tax forms later. A variety of special work forms are also included: 2-, 3-, or 4-column work paper; interest-income work paper; dividend-income work paper; three bank-reconciliation forms; travel and entertainment record form; office in home work paper; multiple rental-property work paper; itemized deductions work paper; things

to do; individual income tax organizer; and many others. Context-sensitive instructions are available at every step and for every form. The program will also print IRS and state mailing labels and envelopes. The interface is DOS only. No mouse or pull-down screens are available, but the system is so simple and easy to use that the lack of a Windows environment will not slow the user down.

Name:	**INSPEC Ondisc**
Vendor:	UMI
Cost:	Call for current pricing; updated quarterly
Hardware requirements:	IBM PC and compatibles, 1MB RAM (490K free RAM), 2MB hard-disk space per ProQuest database installed plus 10MB disk space to run after installation, DOS 3.3, 1.44MB floppy disk drive
Comments:	This database, from the Institution of Electrical Engineers, contains abstracts and indexes to 7,000 publications that cover computers/computer science, electronics, electrical engineering, physics, and information technology. The publications include 4,200 technical journals plus 3,000 conference proceedings, reports, dissertations, and books. Three editions are available. INSPEC Ondisc contains the complete database. INSPEC Physics and INSPEC Electronics & Computing may be purchased separately. The current subscription covers the preceding three years of citations (approximately 250,000). Separate backfile discs are available for 1989, 1990, and 1991. ProQuest Searchware is convenient for use by people with little or no search experience. A search may be made using the fields that are readily available—including chemical and numerical searching—or using AND/OR/NOT for search terms. Truncation, field limiting, and proximity search are also permitted. Any search set may be saved for reuse or combined with other sets. The results screen for titles shows source, publication date, location of the article in the publication, and availability of the source material.

Name:	**Leadership Directories on CD-ROM**
Vendor:	Chadwyck-Healey
Cost:	$385 to $500 each
Hardware requirements:	IBM PC and compatibles, 640K RAM, hard-disk drive, printer
Comments:	This series of eleven CD-ROMs provides wide access to names of leaders in state government, congress, law firms, news media, associations, and corporations. Corporate Lead-

ership contains two directories: corporate and financial. The corporate directory provides the names of 45,000 executives and 11,000 corporate board members. Information includes business descriptions, product lines, annual revenues, and telephone and facsimile numbers. It is indexed by state, industry, and individual's name and company/subsidiary/division/job function. The financial directory lists 42,000 financial executives, 9,000 board members, and information on more than 1,100 financial institutions. Government Leadership contains five CD-ROMs: Congressional, Federal, State, Federal Regional, and Municipal. The congressional CD contains information on both houses of congress, staff and committees, and support agencies such as the Congressional Budget Office and General Accounting Office. The federal directory contains information on more than 35,000 federal officials and aides in the executive branch and the cabinet and 700 independent agencies. The Federal Regional CD contains information on more than 20,000 decision makers in 8,000 regional offices of the federal government. Included are judges, librarians, district courts, military installations, and service academy administrations.

Name: **Microsoft Office; Office Pro for Windows 4.0; Microsoft Office for Macintosh 3.0**

Vendor: Microsoft

Cost: $250, Office; $359, Professional; $750, Macintosh

Hardware requirements: IBM PC and compatibles, 4MB RAM required, 17MB hard drive, Windows 3.x; Macintosh, 1MB RAM

Comments: Individual modules of this program include Microsoft PowerPoint V.4.0, Microsoft Excel 5.0, Microsoft Word 6.0, and work station license for Microsoft Mail V.3.2. Individual products work together in classic integrated software format, making them easy to learn and use. Features such as tool bars, menus, dialog boxes, and screen layouts are the same in each. IntelliSense technology makes repeated chores easy. The word processor automatically corrects typos and can be used for mail merge of personalized form letters for bulk mailings. Grammar and spell checkers are included. The spreadsheet module includes Rich Cell Editing for typing directly into spreadsheet cells. Other tools are AutoFilter, AutoSort, AutoOutline, and AutoSubtotal for collapsing, expanding, and viewing data. PowerPoint version 4.0 can be used for creating presentation graphics. Microsoft Mail version 3.2 is a PC network electronic mail program. Charts, graphs, sounds, and other data can be added directly to mail messages.

Further information: "Software Suites: Integrated Software Grows Up," *Computer Shopper*, Apr. 1994, 522.

Name: **Microsoft Small Business Consultant**

Vendor: Microsoft

Cost: $124.95

Hardware requirements: IBM PC and compatibles, 512 K RAM

Comments: This package is an excellent collection of small business resources. It includes 220 documents published by the Small Business Association, Department of Commerce, Department of Veterans Affairs, Department of Defense, General Services Administration, and the accounting firm of Deloitte, Haskins & Sells. Coverage includes personnel management skills, business finance and loan regulations, procedures for conducting business with the federal government, accounting and record keeping, marketing and selling, planning and starting businesses, and even importing/exporting practices.

Name: **Microsoft Word for Windows and Bookshelf, Video and Sound Edition**

Vendor: Microsoft

Cost: $595

Hardware requirements: IBM PC and compatibles, Windows 3.x, 2MB RAM

Comments: This comprehensive writer's tool provides the popular word processor Microsoft Word and a host of reference books. Word is an excellent word processor. In addition to the many editing features, it can be used to play and edit videos and sound effects for inclusion in documents. A video library is included, and others are available for purchase (including the Gateway Video Collection from Firstlight Productions). The reference library contains *Roget's II Electronic Thesaurus*, *World Almanac and Book of Facts*, *Bartlett's Familiar Quotations* (with 22,500 quotes), *Concise Columbia Dictionary of Quotations* (6,000 quotes), *Hammond Atlas*, *American Heritage Dictionary*, and the *Concise Columbia Encyclopedia*. Multimedia aspects of this package include 65,000 pronounced words in the dictionary and animated help files.

Microsoft Word contains a graphics editor, and it will import major file types.

Further information: J. Scot Finnie, *PC/Computing*, Sept. 1992, 36.

Name: **Million Dollar Disc**
Vendor: Dun's Marketing Services
Cost: $3,800, special library price; contact vendor for local area network pricing
Hardware requirements: IBM PC and compatibles, 640K RAM required, 2MB hard-disk space
Comments: This disc, with quarterly updates, provides access to information on the largest U.S. public and private companies with a tangible net worth of $500,000 or more. Information includes biographies of 500,000 senior executives, the corporate name, trade name, private or public status, "ticker" symbol, trading exchange, year started, state of incorporation, DC-U-N-S Number, geographic data (address, SMSA, county, city, state, ZIP and area codes), industry information (standard industry codes, line of business, import and export status), key business relationships with banks and accounting firms, and number of employees. A search may be created using just the name of a company or any number of fields. For instance, information about companies in a certain geographical region, perhaps by state, can be further defined by limiting it to companies with a certain sales volume. The resulting search data may be sorted and arranged as needed within the program, and results may be printed out. Specific search criteria may be saved to disk to speed future searches. Boolean operators are supported.

Name: **Money in the 90's**
Vendor: Laser Resources
Cost: $29.95
Hardware requirements: IBM PC and compatibles, Windows 3.1 or later, sound card optional; Macintosh, System 6.0.5 or later
Comments: The database contains the full text of *Money Magazine* from January 1990 through the 1994 Forecast issue. Topics cover many financial concerns, including certificates of deposit, stocks, mutual funds, banking, etc. Two indexes make it convenient to use. The subject index can be viewed for any year or for all years collectively. Hypertext is used to skip from article to article. A second index contains all of the tables of contents from all magazines. A full-text search may be conducted on the entire database or only on specific sections.

The operators AND, OR, NOT, and NEAR may be used. A wild-card (*) search is also supported. More than 1,000 charts and graphs that appeared in the print version are included in this CD edition. Each graphic is brought up as a separate window; therefore, charts and graphs may be kept on the desktop while roaming around the disc.

Name:	**Moody's Company Data; Moody's International Company Data**
Vendor:	Moody's Investors Service
Cost:	$995 year's subscription (monthly updates)
Hardware requirements:	IBM PC and compatibles
Comments:	Moody's Company Data database contains information on more than 10,000 public companies and includes Securities and Exchange Commission documents—6K, 8K, 10K, 10Q, 10C, 13D, etc. Contents include 29 text variables (such as SIC codes, area codes, county or region, number of employees, bond rating, auditor, general counsel, newsworthy events), 98 income statement variables, and 42 balance sheet variables (such as detailed assets, liabilities, capital and shareholder's equity). Company information includes its history, business, properties, subsidiaries, officers, directors, long-term debt, capital stock, letter to shareholders, notes to financial statements, income statement, balance sheets, statements of cash flows, auditors, general counsel, stock exchange and symbol, number of employees, number of shareholders, address, telephone, fax and telex numbers, shareholder relations contact, stock price ranges, dividends report of independent auditors, transfer agents, history of stock splits, and annual meeting date. Monthly updates include interim earnings, mergers and acquisitions, new products, new contracts, management changes, new stock issues, rating changes, financing, joint ventures, call notices, name changes, and other significant events. A search may be conducted on any word or phrase, including more than 140 financial variables. The data may be ranked or sorted by any variable and exported to spreadsheets. Output may be printed as a full or custom-designed report. Boolean logic may be used to refine a search. Moody's International Company Data contains information on more than 7,500 non-U.S.-based companies in 90 countries. Both it and Moody's Company Data also use MoodEASE software for searching, reporting, and printing data.

Name: **Morningstar Mutual Funds OnDisc**
Vendor: Morningstar
Cost: $259 to $795
Hardware requirements: IBM PC and compatibles, 520K RAM required, 4MB hard-disk space, DOS 3.3 or later
Comments: This DOS program is easy to install and use. It provides a wide range of information about mutual funds that is especially useful to investors and brokers. Finding useful and relevant mutual fund information of any complexity can be done in moments. Historical and current data on more than 4,600 mutual funds are included. Users may graph performance of each. Funds analysis, profiles, and more than 200 information fields are available for each fund. Also available are 94 criteria for screening funds, such as percent of assets in the financial sector, ten-year average annual returns that place in the top 10 percent of their investment objective, etc. There are 47 benchmarks, including *Standard and Poor's 500*, *Wilshire 5000*, and T-bills, that may be used to measure fund performance. Information may be printed out or exported to other graphics and word processing programs. Other features allow users to locate the funds that hold a specific stock or bond (such as Philip Morris or a five-year U.S. Treasury note paying 7.125 percent); to compare total returns for a single fund or for a group of funds over any of eighteen time periods; to create, save, and print customized screening formats; and to export data, reports, or graphs for use in other software programs. The program has up to eighteen months of historical monthly data. Special analysis tools include Morningstar Ratings, Investment Style-Box coordinates, Morningstar Risk and Return scores, Potential Capital Gain Exposure, and Shareholder Report Ratings.

Name: **PlanIt Earth**
Vendor: Media Vision
Cost: $14.95
Hardware requirements: IBM PC and compatibles, 4MB RAM, 15MB hard-disk space minimum (32 to install all entertainment features), Windows 3.1, 8-bit Windows-compatible sound card, CD-ROM with minimum 150K/second transfer rate, SVGA (256 colors)
Comments: This multimedia program is a fun-filled way to get organized. Produced by the National Wildlife Federation, it contains more than 400 beautiful nature pictures of animals in action

(whales breaching, bears roaring, etc.). Photos complement this feature-filled, push-button notebook. Additionally, a voice recognition feature (microphone required) allows for direct voice command of the tool by the user. This system can be used to keep track of daily scheduling and to create an address book and a calendar. A special section maintains a to-do list for the user. Photo CD can be used to import personal images to dress up the address book. Other fun materials that are included feature quotes from Isaac Asimov's *Book of Facts*, and daily jokes from the *National Lampoon*. Additional titles include alternate sets of images: PlanIt Paradise and PlanIt Adrenaline.

Name:	**SmartSuite for Windows**
Vendor:	Lotus Development
Cost:	$299
Hardware requirements:	IBM PC and compatibles, 6MB RAM, Windows 3.1 or later
Comments:	This full office package contains a wide range of useful programs: 1-2-3 Release 5, a spreadsheet program; AmiPro 3.1, a word processor; Approach 3.0, a database management system; Freelance Graphics 2.1, a full-featured graphic system; and Lotus Organizer, a computerized schedule/appointment book. The 1-2-3 Release 5 is an easy-to-use spreadsheet for Windows. It has many advanced features, including "drag-and-fill" for moving data between cells in the work sheet. All of these products work together seamlessly in an integrated environment.

Name:	**Thomas Register of American Manufacturers**
Vendor:	Thomas Online/KR Information OnDisc
Cost:	$1,495 per year with semiannual updates ($897 for public and academic libraries—40 percent discount)
Hardware requirements:	IBM PC and compatibles; Macintosh; NEC-9800 series computer
Comments:	The register contains important product information for more than 194,000 North American companies with 50,000 product classifications and 110,000 trade names. Each record also includes the officers of the company, the number of employees, a company description, products, and codes. Searching is permitted by company name, product name, city, state, ZIP code, telephone area code, trade name, SIC code, asset rating/sales assets, number of employees, geographical regions, and name and company type (manufacturer, dis-

tributor, broker). A search may be conducted using a menu selection, or a command-line search may be used by more-experienced searchers. The menu-driven option uses a word wheel, which makes it easy to browse to find a product or company name, even if only part of it is known. This product is extremely easy for anyone to use.

Name:	**TurboTax Deluxe CD-ROM Edition**
Vendor:	Chipsoft
Cost:	$39.95
Hardware requirements:	IBM PC and compatibles, up to 15MB hard-disk space, depending on which or how many of the program modules are installed
Comments:	Several products are contained on this CD to assist in the preparation of income tax forms: tax planner, tax savings guide, J. K. Lasser's *Your Income Tax*, Marshall Loeb's *Video Tax Guide*, state tax software, TurboTax 1040 for Windows, and electronic IRS instructions and software documentation. The easy-to-use program helps to explain and to properly fill in the blanks of yearly tax forms. It even provides different bar and pie charts to give users a sense of where their money is going.

Name:	**Wilson Business Abstracts; Business Periodicals Index**
Vendor:	H. W. Wilson
Cost:	$2,495, Wilson Business Abstracts; $1,495, Business Periodicals Index
Hardware requirements:	IBM PC and compatibles, 640K RAM, 3MB free hard-disk space, DOS 3.1 or later, Hayes compatible modem optional
Comments:	Wilson Business Abstracts contains abstracts (from June 1990) of 50 to 150 words and indexes (from July 1982) for 350 of the most important, significant business periodicals plus the *Wall Street Journal* and the *New York Times*. Service is updated monthly with 8,000 new records. Business Periodicals Index does not contain abstracts. Three search levels make it easy for beginners to use but possible for more advanced researchers to effectively search as well. A single-subject search mode (browse) will locate authors by searching on author's name or title of a work. Multiple-subject searches can be made by using the Wilsearch mode. A command-language search can also be implemented. This system, the same one used by Wilsonline, supports nested

Boolean logic, proximity searching, free-text and controlled-vocabulary searching, online thesaurus, truncation, ranging, multifile searching, saving of data and of search, and more. In addition, subscribers to any of Wilson's CD-ROM services also have unlimited online access time to the same service. This provides the latest information when needed.

Children's Literature

Multimedia and CD-ROM technology have combined to create some truly spectacular children's software. These packages range from reading skills improvement programs, such as learning the ABCs or counting, to traditional children's classics that have been illustrated and animated with sound and graphics. An outstanding multimedia title is the Early Learning Center that combines five educational titles on one CD. One of the most enjoyable titles, Just Grandma and Me, is based on the storybook of the same title. Kids can read the story just as they would a real book, then explore the pictures to discover surprises and excitement. The products in this chapter skim the surface of CDs that encourage and teach reading skills.

Additional products available:

> The Berenstain Bears: Learning at Home, volumes 1 and 2 (Compton's NewMedia)
>
> Book Brain Book Whiz (Social Issues Resources Series)
>
> The Adventures of Huckleberry Finn (BookWorm)
>
> The Adventures of Tom Sawyer (BookWorm)
>
> Frankenstein (BookWorm)

Name:	**Children's Reference Plus**
Vendor:	Bowker-Reed Reference Electronic Publishing
Cost:	$595 annually
Hardware requirements:	IBM PC and compatibles
Comments:	This excellent tool provides instant access to children's materials in many Bowker databases. It has a broad scope and is extremely useful for researching or selecting children's materials. Books in Print Subject Guide to Books in Print provides access to 97,000 currently active children's and young adult titles. *Books Out-of-Print* contains information on 56,000 children's and young adult titles out-of-print or

out-of-stock indefinitely since 1979. El-Hi Textbooks in Print has some 48,000 texts, text series, workbooks, tests, programmed learning materials, teaching aids, professional books, posters, and other resources for 21 subject categories and 307 subcategories. Fiction, Folklore, Fantasy & Poetry for Children 1876–1985 has bibliographic information on more than 133,000 children's titles. These are from the Library of Congress classification numbers PZ5-10. Subject tracings cover poetry, plays, legends, and songs. Some 3,900 other titles date prior to 1876. Ulrich's listings include some 3,500 children's periodicals and irregular publications and listings from professional journals in the children's field. *Bowker's Complete Video Directory* lists 19,000 home and educational videos. *Words on Cassette* combines Meckler's *Words on Tape* and Bowker's *On Cassette* and includes 49,000 listings. Additionally, many full-text book reviews are included from such professional sources as *Library Journal*, *Kirkus Reviews*, *Booklist*, *Publisher's Weekly*, and *School Library Journal.* Plot summaries, critical reviews, and annotations are also included from many titles such as *A to Zoo*, *Beyond Picture Books*, *Books for the Gifted Child*, *Fantasy Literature for Children and Young Adults*, *Science & Technology in Fact & Fiction* (Children and Young Adult editions), *Juniorplots 3*, *School Librarian's Sourcebook*, and many others. Using this tool is very simple. A search for information may be conducted by title, name (authors or contributors), subject/genre, keyword and keyword within title, price, publisher/manufacturer, year published or produced, audience, grade level, language, ISBN, LCCN/LC Class, special index, database, or status. Videos may also be searched for by awards, order number/UPC number, hue, MPAA rating, or year released. Serials may be searched by country code, Dewey Decimal number, ISSN, or online/CD-ROM availability.

Name:	**Early Learning Center**
Vendor:	Orange Hill/New Media Schoolhouse
Cost:	$69
Hardware requirements:	IBM PC and compatibles, 2MB RAM; Macintosh, 2MB RAM
Comments:	This set for prekindergarten through fourth grades contains five separate packages, none of which require more than elementary computer skills. Talking Clock (K–3) teaches

how to tell time using analog clocks (both numberless and Roman numerals) and digital clocks. Exercises include typing the time while reading the clock face. Using Money & Making Change (2–4) is an additional program with exercises on using money. If You Ran a Cookie Shop is a small business simulation in which kids buy the ingredients for cookies, make the cookies, and then sell them to customers. As young entrepreneurs they make change and add up their profits as the end of the work day. Pink Pete's ABC's helps children to recognize the alphabet. Four separate units contain games and exercises for Recognizing Letters and Finding Letters, as well as Alpha Board and Alpha Story. Vocabulary Builders emphasizes an expanded vocabulary with homonyms, antonyms, synonyms, and contractions. Talking U.S.A. Map (4–12) teaches the locations of states and capitals. Clicking on any state will bring up facts of history, land, industry, and political characteristics. It also contains a quiz on state capitals. All programs in this package use a digitized human voice as part of the format.

Name:	**Harry's StoryDisc and Coloring Book**
Vendor:	Laser Resources
Cost:	$25
Hardware requirements:	IBM PC and compatibles
Comments:	An outstanding children's work, Harry's StoryDisc contains 150 different stories, including fables and animal stories; adventure stories; magic and the supernatural; princes and princesses; and elves, trolls, and fairies. Many Aesop's fables are included, plus Hans Christian Andersen's fairy tales, *Peter Pan*, *The Wizard of Oz*, *Alice in Wonderland*, *Robinson Crusoe*, *Grimm's Fairy Tales*, *Rip Van Winkle*, *Kim*, *The Legend of Sleepy Hollow*, *The Sea Wolf*, *Heidi*, *Kidnapped*, *Twenty Thousand Leagues Under the Sea*, and many traditional fairy tales. These stories are all full text. Many have one or more children's drawings attached to them. A full-text search may be conducted on the entire database or only on specific sections. The operators AND, OR, NOT, and NEAR may be used. A wild card (*) is also supported. The Coloring Book contains the same 200 drawings that are attached to the stories, and they may be printed out and colored. This is an ideal disc for young people. It contains a wide variety of outstanding literature with computer searching.

Name:	**Just Grandma and Me**
Vendor:	Broderbund Software
Cost:	$49.95
Hardware requirements:	IBM PC and compatibles with Windows 3.1 or later, 2MB RAM; Macintosh, 4MB RAM
Comments:	This is computer software for very young children at its very best. The program has as its screens the pages from the book by the same title. Kids will have lots of fun with it. The plot is a simple one; we are going to the beach with our grandma for the day. We leave the house and wait for the bus. We arrive at the beach and spend some time. We then ride the bus to go home. At each stop, however, there is lots of fun. The words are displayed on the screen and are spoken by the two characters. The real fun, though, is exploring every nook and cranny of the screen. By moving the mouse cursor and clicking on objects, various things happen. For instance, click on a seashell and a little critter gets up and does a dance, click on a beach umbrella and it may shoot into the air like a rocket. There are dozens of these effects throughout the program. You need only go to the next page when you are ready by clicking on the corner of the page (you can go forward or backward). The best way to sum up this book is "cute." It can be played in Japanese, English, or Spanish.
Further information:	*MacUser*, Dec. 1992, 89; *PC Magazine*, Dec. 22, 1992, 353.

Name:	**Oregon Trail for MPC**
Vendor:	MECC
Cost:	$69.95
Hardware requirements:	Multimedia IBM PC and compatibles, 4MB RAM required
Comments:	Oregon Trail as a computer game has been around for a long time. This latest CD effort makes it as interesting and lively as ever. In the role of a pioneer heading West in the nineteenth century, players must purchase resources, manage their health, and make numerous decisions to make it to Oregon. Failure can lead to death by disease, starvation, snakebite, wagon fires, or other equally sad endings. One is left with an appreciation of how rough and difficult early pioneer life was without freeways or supermarkets. Players may go hunting when their food runs low. They may also trade whatever they accumulate with other travelers to get what they need. Multimedia CD offers stereo music, pictures, and digitized speech. This is a highly recommended purchase for public access or circulation by public libraries or for student use in schools.

Name: **Tale of Peter Rabbit**

Vendor: Discus Knowledge Research

Cost: $59.95

Hardware requirements: IBM PC and compatibles, 2MB RAM, DOS 5.0 or later, SoundBlaster or compatible sound card; Macintosh, 2MB RAM, System 6.0.4 or later

Comments: This classic children's tale is told once again but with a few innovations. Peter's tale has the same storyline, and the pictures are pleasantly drawn. Children can hear the story as well as read it. They may also proceed at their own pace or go directly to any page. By moving the hand (cursor) around on the screen the program will also explain what everything is, including the characters, objects, etc.

Computers and Software

Many CD-ROM databases give information about computer hardware and software. The majority contain only the most basic information such as title, vendor, and price. Computer Select, however, provides a wealth of information extracted from 77 journals and includes a catalog of products for both IBM and Macintosh and a glossary of computer terms. It is also the most expensive of these information sources. Other CD-ROMs contain information on computer security (Hacker Chronicles) or provide a pathway to the Internet (Internet Madness). Virtual Reality Madness and More! and Multimedia Madness offer an educational look at the workings of two wildly popular topics. The SelectWare System contains dozens of running demos of CD packages that may be transferred to a hard disk. For Macintosh users, the Macintosh Product Registry is quite good but is not updated monthly as is Computer Select.

Additional product available:

New Rider's Official Internet Yellow Pages (New Rider's Publishing)

Name:	**CD-ROMs in Print on CD-ROM**
Vendor:	Mecklermedia
Cost:	Free with purchase of $129 print version
Hardware requirements:	IBM PC and compatibles, 1MB RAM, DOS 3.0 or later (Windows version requires 2MB RAM with 4MB recommended and Windows 3.1 or later)
Comments:	CD-ROMs in Print contains information on more than 8,000 CD-ROM titles, 4,000 CD-ROM publishers, and 350 reviews. Special OptiSearch2 retrieval software will work with Windows or DOS. A new edition is released each spring and fall.

Name: **CD-ROM of CD-ROMs**

Vendor: Resource International Publishing

Cost: Available as a subscription: $75.90, semiannual; $191.76, bimonthly; $143.90, quarterly

Hardware requirements: IBM PC and compatibles, minimum 286 CPU, Windows 3.1, 2MB RAM; recommended configuration is 386 CPU and up, multimedia (SVGA, sound card), 4MB RAM, no hard-disk space required

Comments: This handy database contains more than 7,000 CD-ROM titles, of which 500 are reviewed, albeit briefly. Each entry contains the product's name, price, category, release date, publisher, platform, version, and description. Address information is also given for 5,874 companies that produce CD-ROMs. Information available varies from company to company; many fields are simply empty. Nearly all, however, contain the name, address, and telephone number. Some also include an 800 number, CompuServe electronic mail address, and the fax number. Despite the inconsistency of information for many items, this is still a formidable and inexpensive database. Because of its serial nature, it remains current. Entries may be searched by eight separate fields, including title. It supports Boolean logic operators of OR, AND, NOT, <, and several wild-card arrangements for words and letters.

Name: **Computer Select**

Vendor: Ziff Communications

Cost: $1,250 annual subscription, includes 12 monthly updates

Hardware requirements: IBM PC and compatibles, 2MB RAM

Comments: Computer Select is an excellent research tool for computer hardware and software technology. A single disc gives access to some 200,000 documents. To keep the database current, a new disc replaces the old one each month. Computer Select can be used by anyone who wants to research computer hardware and software. It is divided into four sections: software descriptions, hardware descriptions, vendor profiles, and literature and a glossary of 13,000 computer terms. Its 77,000 journal articles from a wide selection of computer magazines provide an excellent view of the computer world. These include popular journals such as *MacWorld* and *PC World* and more esoteric journals such as *Computer News*. Most articles are presented full text or abstracted. From the main menu there is a choice of Titles, Browse, Find, Edit, Section, Copy, Print, Utility, Info, Quit.

The search functions have been well thought out. The main menu requires the selection of one of the main categories (literature, hardware, software, vendor, user's guide). Unfortunately, there is no way to search more than one category at a time; each must be treated in a separate database. A search may be by text located anywhere in the document or in a variety of categories, such as product type, name, etc. It is easy using Boolean operators (AND, OR, and NOT) or proximity operators (WITHIN) to expand or narrow the search. Searching for material in the hardware, software, and glossary sections involves consulting a word wheel, a revolving list of all entries. This technique makes it easy to browse for useful terms. Search results may be saved to disk or printed out, either by title or by full entry. Each entry may be marked for further processing (batch printing, etc.) as required during the browse routine. Items may be browsed by title or by complete entry.

Documentation for this program gets high marks. Computer Select is quite simple to use so the instructions will rarely be needed. For users with little or no search experience, it would benefit them to consult either the hard copy or the online version (help file) for things that are not readily apparent. The book contains several examples of search strategies and information about function keys, etc., that are not highlighted in the menu choices. An index and a section on troubleshooting are also included. Some articles have special attachments such as batch files, screen shots, charts, buyers guides, etc.

Name:	**Hacker Chronicles: A Tour of the Computer Underground**
Vendor:	P-80 Systems
Cost:	$79.95
Hardware requirements:	IBM PC and compatibles, 2MB RAM, DOS 4.0 or later
Comments:	Hacker Chronicles contains a history of the hacker underground as presented in a collection of underground magazines, such as *Phrack, Cult of the Dead Cow*, and others, which will give the honest person lots of interesting reading. Would-be system crashers, however, may get other ideas when reading about credit card fraud, ATMs, and dirty tricks with computers. While of questionable value in the wrong hands, it does contain information, including a security tool kit, that can be considered useful to those trying to thwart system breakers and increase computer security.

The information was compiled by Scott Higginbotham, a computer security specialist.

Further information: Peter Stephenson, "Going Underground for Security," *LAN Times*, May 23, 1994, 56.

Name: **The Internet CD**

Vendor: PTR Prentice Hall

Cost: $49.95

Hardware requirements: IBM PC and compatibles

Comments: This excellent CD provides many information tools to use with the Internet. Included is INFOPOP, IPWIN, a popular e-mail product (Eudora 1.4), SLIP, WINPKT, TCPMAN, LView, Gopher, WAIS (wide area information server for natural-language searching of the Internet), Trumpet, and WINFTP. These tools provide a wide range of Internet utilities. INFOPOP, for example, is a good general popup reference that contains a glossary, WAIS sites, library catalog sites with numbers and a listing of library-related computer conferences and electronic journals, campus-wide information systems, bulletin board systems on the Internet (with user information), and much more. All of the available tools, however, cannot be accessed by just running an install program; each must be installed separately. Directions are located in the book that comes with the CD. In addition to the software information, the book contains a lot of basic introductory material about how the Internet works, so people new to the Internet will find this useful as well. The book part of this package also contains a glossary, a list of service providers (Internet access providers) listed alphabetically and geographically, and a list of providers that offer the SLIP (Serial Line IP) Internet access. A bibliography of books about the Internet is also appended.

Name: **Internet Gizmos for Windows**

Vendor: IDG Books Worldwide

Cost: $39.99

Hardware requirements: IBM PC and compatibles, 8MB RAM, 9600 baud modem or TCP/IP network connection, Windows 3.11 or later

Comments: This is one of the best add-on packages available to Internet users. The CD-ROM contains more than 40 commercial, shareware, and freeware packages for making the most of the Internet. These may be loaded into your computer (a one-time process that takes just a couple of minutes) and used immediately. One, Wincode, is a popular tool for encoding and decoding uuencode and uudecode files. Without such a tool, people downloading encoded graphics files would have to perform this function manually, one file at a time. With Wincode an entire directory of files may be encoded or decoded in just a few minutes with little or no intervention by the operator. Some of the other tools included are: Spry Mosaic (a World Wide Web browser), Distinct TCP/IP Sampler (data transfer tools), CompuServe WinCim (the front-end software package for accessing CompuServe), PowerBBS (a system for setting up and linking a local bulletin board service to the Internet), Trumpet WinSock V. 1.0, Pipeline, WHAM, View Pro 1.8 (an excellent graphic file viewing program), and many others. The book (more than 900 pages) contains step-by-step instructions and hints for using the programs.

Name:	**Internet Info CD**
Vendor:	Walnut Creek CDROM
Cost:	$39.95
Hardware requirements:	IBM PC and compatibles; Macintosh
Comments:	The inclusion of 15,000 documents from the Internet makes this a wide-ranging and extremely useful disc for anyone wishing to learn more about and explore the Internet without actually spending the time online. Contained in it are many "answers to frequently asked questions"; bibliographies; technical book reviews; documents and standards from IEEF, ISO, NIST, and ANSI; FTP site lists and descriptions of archives, Usenet technical archives, Internet Network maps, computer security documents, and much more. While this disc will never substitute for actually being online using the Internet and other systems, it is a way to learn a lot quickly without a modem. Since the disc is updated several times each year, the information is kept up-to-date with the purchase of newer discs.

Name:	**Internet Madness (Netcruiser)**
Vendor:	Aristosoft
Cost:	$25
Hardware requirements:	IBM PC and compatibles
Comments:	The Internet Madness CD provides an easy and inexpensive way to access the Internet. Registered users get 40 hours of prime time and 400 hours of nonprime time each month on the Internet for a monthly fee of only $19.95. Any time over the 40 hours is billed at $2 per hour. An excellent help

file is also provided to answer questions about the Internet, including what it is, how it is used, etc. Specific information about how to use e-mail, the World Wide Web, Mosaic, etc. is also included. Its Windows-interface push buttons make it easy to logon, to find services, to download, and to navigate through the maze of Internet possibilities.

Name: **Lending Library #1 and #2**
Vendor: Compton's New Media
Cost: $1,456, #1; $1,827.68, #2
Hardware requirements: IBM PC and compatibles, Macintosh, Windows and DOS
Comments: Two offers make package deals available for library CD-ROM collections. Offer #1 contains *Compton's Interactive Encyclopedia*; *Dictionary of the Living World*; *Wild Places*; *World View*; *USA Today: The '90s, volume 1*; *Bible Lands*; *Bible Stories*; *American Heritage Illustrated Dictionary*; *Greatest Books Collection*; *Library of the Future*, first edition; and *Lyric Language/CDM: Spanish.*

Option #2 contains all titles in the first option plus *The Mega Movie Guide, The KGB/CIA World Factbook, U.S. Presidents, New Basics Electronic Cookbook, Jazz: A Multimedia Storybook, USA Wars: Civil War, The Doctors Book of Home Remedies, The Electronic Library of Art,* and *Lyric Language/CDM: French.*

Name: **Macintosh Product Registry**
Vendor: Redgate Communications
Cost: $39.99
Hardware requirements: Macintosh
Comments: The Macintosh Product Registry contains 7,700 hardware and software product specifications along with their descriptions, including 2,000 multimedia products. Also included on this disc are 50 product demos.

Name: **Multimedia Madness**
Vendor: SAMS Publishing
Cost: $44.95
Hardware requirements: IBM PC and compatibles
Comments: Multimedia Madness is a book/disc combination. Its primary purpose is to teach users about the various components for creating their own multimedia. This is an excellent CD for people who are starting with little knowledge of, but high interest in, multimedia. The book provides tips and techniques for creating visual effects with video, morphing,

and animation, including large numbers of actual examples with pictures and screen shots included. Programs on the CD include Winjammer, a full-featured music sequencer; Graphics Workshop, a graphics utility for converting between graphics formats; Wave Editor, a program that facilitates recording, editing, modifying, and playing new or existing sound files; and Microsoft Media Player (Version 2), a program for playing many different types of media. Users of this package will learn the details of multimedia, how to make the most of it on their machines, and how to create their own.

Name:	**PC Intern, 5th Edition**
Vendor:	Abacus
Cost:	$59.95
Hardware requirements:	IBM PC and compatibles, 4MB hard-disk space, Windows 3.1 or later
Comments:	This book and CD-ROM combination goes a long way toward answering many of the frustrating questions that plague many computer users. In the book are the basics of PC hardware plus many important problem areas such as software and hardware interrupts, memory layout, support chips, the bus, and ports. The level of information is quite high, of interest to system troubleshooters, hackers, and computer hobbyists. Contained within this mass of data (more than 740 pages with illustrations and diagrams) are a lot of good diagnostic and purchase suggestions. It includes information on CD-ROM technology, sound cards, DOS, memory configuration, processor types, etc. On the disc is the entire text and all illustrations from the book. The search function makes it possible to locate any relevant material quickly. Also on the disc are hundreds of working program examples in C, QuickBASIC, Turbo Pascal, and Assembly language.

Name:	**ROMfinder**
Vendor:	Design Publishers
Cost:	$19.95 per 2 issues for subscribers
Hardware requirements:	IBM PC and compatibles, 4MB RAM, Windows 3.1, 256-color card, and sound card suggested for multimedia demos
Comments:	This database lists more CD-ROMs (approximately 10,000) than others do. However, the amount of information about each is limited to basic vendor information and hardware specifications with limited or no notes about product performance or quality. Some product demos are included. New

editions are issued each summer and winter. According to ROMfinder, new product information is included in each issue four months prior to its release.

Name:	**SelectWare System**
Vendor:	SelectWare Technologies
Cost:	$49.95, annual subscription; $24.95 for current issue only
Hardware requirements:	IBM PC and compatibles, 450K RAM, DOS 3.0 or later, sound card
Comments:	SelectWare is a "magazine on a disc." It provides an inexpensive way to look at demos of new CD-ROM and multimedia products. Each issue contains several hundred software listings. Each listing has a "snapshot" that contains basic facts; an overview of each product that provides more in-depth features and information; technical information about the name, address, and phone of the vendor; price; memory and other hardware requirements; and other details. Information may be sorted by company, category, or name, though there is no way to search for specific listings. The demos are fun, and many give the would-be buyer some insight into the nature of the product, especially the games. By seeing actual screen shots and other features, it is often possible to determine a game's interest and quality. Major categories of software covered are MS-DOS, Windows, OS/2, multimedia, and new multimedia hardware products. As a bonus, contained on the CD is optiDigest, a CD-ROM magazine that contains columns (including reviews of CD-ROM hardware and software products), articles about the trends and future of CD-ROM/multimedia technology, and CD-ROM news and announcements.

Name:	**Shareware Bonanza**
Cost:	$69.95
Hardware requirements:	IBM PC and compatibles
Comments:	This set of four CDs contains 25,000 shareware and public-domain programs which can be freely copied and distributed (with the usual shareware restrictions and requirements). The programs are compressed, so the discs contain almost a gigabyte each. Extracting them, however, is automatic. When a program has been selected, the Unzip program expands and copies it to the hard drive. When the user is finished, the system automatically deletes it. This interface is quite excellent, being almost invisible to the user. Programs may also be transferred permanently to a floppy for transfer to

other computers. Categories of programs include computer assisted design, games, graphics, printer utilities, clip art, spreadsheet utilities, Windows programs, database management, educational programs, desktop publishing, ham radio programming utilities, business, word processing, and computer program.

Name:	**Support on Site**
Vendor:	Ziff Communications
Cost:	$1,295, annual subscription
Hardware requirements:	IBM PC and compatibles, 640K (500K free), DOS 3.1 or later
Comments:	As its name implies, this CD provides technical support for major software such as AmiPro, Paradox, Symphony, WordPerfect, MS-DOS, Windows, Lotus, Q&A, and others. Information is gathered from manufacturer's data and journals, and the disc contains more than 50,000 documents. Included are drivers, macros and utilities for programs, and technical discussions. These may be downloaded to any PC. Thousands of error messages, often the source of much mystery to users, are identified in this product and explained, and methods are given to overcome the problems causing them. There is also a great deal of attention given to interactions between programs (e.g., multiple caches losing data). A search may be made by a description of the problem or symptom, product/application, publication type, publisher, software drivers/add ins, date range, etc.
Further information:	M. Keith Thompson, *PC Magazine*, Jan. 12, 1993, 48.
Name:	**Virtual Reality Madness and More!**
Vendor:	SAMS Publishing
Cost:	$44.95
Hardware requirements:	IBM PC and compatibles
Comments:	Virtual Reality Madness and More! is an excellent book/disc (two CD–ROMs are included) to provide to the public, since more and more people wish to learn about virtual reality. This is an excellent CD for people who have little knowledge of, but high interest in, virtual reality. The book is an overview of various virtual reality possibilities (defined by the author as "anything that isn't real, but does a good job of faking it," including an explanation of the goggles and the power glove sometimes used to enhance virtual reality. The book provides tips and techniques for creating visual effects with video, morphing, and animation, including large numbers of

actual examples with pictures and screen shots included. In fact, nearly every page of the more than 500 pages in this book contains two or more visuals. Sometimes the same image is shown six different ways. The purpose of this is to demonstrate the effect of different techniques on images. The major software package contained on the two discs is Vistapro, a three-dimensional landscape simulation program. Other software on the disc includes a variety of excellent demos that illustrate some aspect of virtual reality. One of the more sensational demos is Fly the Grand Canyon, a complete 3-D tour by plane. (Yes, you can wear your 3-D glasses for true 3-D effect.) Stunt Island Movies (Disney), Superscape VR (Dimension International), and PhotoMorph (North Coast Software) are other examples of VR software that are included. Two other demo programs are of interest to amateur astronomers. Distant Suns is a demo of a planetarium of the night sky. Users can look at the sky from any location from 4137 B.C. to A.D. 10,000. The only limitation with this demo program is that it permits dates for only one year to be used. The other demo is Mars Explorer, a program that simulates travel over the entire Martian surface. Using the mouse cursor, any coordinate may be picked and then zoomed to for close inspection. The full package allows for zooming from 4× to 64×. The demo version only allows for 8×. A truly spectacular 3-D effect is watching the Martian globe rotate on its axis. Mate (VRontier Worlds), Megatron (John Dee Stanley), Ken's Labyrinth (Epic Megagames), Wolfenstein 3-D (Apogee), and Alone in the Dark (Interplay) are also included as demos.

Cookbooks

For the many people who like to cook, CD-ROM technology opens up a tremendously exciting world. The biggest volume of recipes is Cookbook USA with more than 1.1 million recipes (more than 8,000 for brownies alone!). But these volumes do more than just list endless numbers of recipes that can be searched in many ways. Some will create a recipe for an exact number of people, provide lists of nutrients, develop a shopping list of ingredients, or even include short videos on how to beat eggs or perform other cooking chores correctly. Some are multimedia with sound, music, and slides. A few of the programs are DOS-based with no fancy features, just lots of recipes. While no library with cookbook CDs will want to discard any of its print cookbooks, the CDs make a useful addition to a collection.

Name:	**Cookbook Heaven**
Vendor:	Most Significant Bits
Cost:	$39.95
Hardware requirements:	IBM PC and compatibles, multimedia
Comments:	This exciting CD will be the envy of everyone who likes to cook. With its many useful features, Cookbook Heaven is more than just a cookbook; it's even more than just one cookbook. Recipe sources include *Edna's Cookbook*, *Grandma's Greatest Recipes*, and others—thousands upon thousands of recipes. A search for one specific recipe may return a number of variations. One interesting, specialized database contained within the disc is Brewbase, a buying guide and fact book about the world's best beer. Meal-Mate is a food and recipe analysis program—simply type in a specific food for a quick analysis of fat, protein, and carbohydrates. Type in a whole meal selection to receive a report on total calories and other important nutrition facts.
	New recipes may be added to the database as desired. Recipe Processor automatically adjusts the ingredients of a recipe according to how many servings are required. Recipes

may be added by the user or imported from other files. The program will also print out the recipe list and a shopping list. The Medical and Health Menu provides a battery of useful programs, including weight loss (Slimmer), PC Nutri-Diet, Personal Nutritionist, Diet Analyzer, 6 Steps to Stress Control, and Cardio-Vascular Risk. Personal Nutritionist is an outstanding program that gives comprehensive nutritional information about hundreds of foods and lets the user indicate personal exercise choices and how many calories each exercise burns during a specified number of minutes. By browsing through the food lists, it is easy to get a picture of which foods are high in fats or cholesterol or which are good sources of amino acids. Special sections include Chef Tell's Cooking School and Health Cooking. Each section of the program contains its own manual.

Anyone interested in cooking or food will want to browse and explore this database for hours on end. The program runs directly from the CD, requiring no hard-disk space. This collection of programs on a single CD is shareware and may be copied, but users must send an additional fee to the author if they desire to register the product.

Name:	**Cookbook USA**
Vendor:	J & D Distributing
Cost:	$49.95
Hardware requirements:	IBM PC and compatibles; Macintosh
Comments:	DOS-based Cookbook USA contains 1,094,579 recipes in 52 chapters. It is advertised as being twenty-five times larger than the nearest electronic competitor. Recipes were drawn from 200,000 cooks represented in 4,700 cookbooks. The contents are quite astounding, though it contains no multimedia pictures, video clips, animations, sounds, or "how-to-cook" instructions. Categories (chapters) represent all of the usual cooking areas, such as desserts, seafood, side dishes, main dishes, fruit dishes, breads, eggs, rice, etc. Special areas of interest include children's favorites, diabetic cooking, holiday meals, microwave cooking, outdoor cooking, south-of-the-border cooking, and VIP meals. There is even a chapter on wild game. It is not until you do a search that you realize just how huge this cookbook is and how much information it contains. For instance, a search for the word "brownie" in the title of a recipe returns 8,882 hits. A search for "bear meat" as an ingredient returns 8 hits, including one for "Pioneer Winter Stew." Recipes can also be searched

by "words describing preparation" (e.g., stew, which returns 3,458 hits). However, the same characteristic that makes this cookbook so interesting—its large number of recipes—also makes it hard to use. A good example of this is the "Foreign and Ethnic" chapter, which contains 22,379 recipes. Short of paging through thousands of recipe titles, there is no shortcut. The search feature has limited usefulness, since a search for "African-American" returns 0 hits (though a search for African does return 13 hits), but a search for "Mexican" in the description field returns 514 recipes. If a person is familiar with certain ingredients that are "ethnic," the ingredients can be entered for a specific search. Also, all recipes have a specific number that can be used later for identification and retrieval. Recipes can be printed out in an 8.5 × 11-inch page format or in a 3 × 5-inch recipe card format.

Name:	**Healthy Cooking**
Vendor:	Multicom Publishing
Cost:	$39.95
Hardware requirements:	IBM PC and compatibles
Comments:	People just learning to cook will enjoy this CD. Its Windows interface and multimedia elements make it easy to access the right food selection in several ways. Foods are grouped by general categories such as side dishes, meatless main dishes, microwave main dishes, and take-along lunches. An alphabetical listing contains hundreds of foods by convenient push button. A calorie index sorts foods into seven different groups, from less than 50 calories to more than 300. A nutritional index groups foods by the five categories of low or no cholesterol, low fat, and low or no sodium. By choosing preparation time as a field, users can select from lists of foods that takes less than 15 minutes, 15 to 29 minutes, 30 to 59 minutes, 1 to 2 hours, 2 to 4 hours, and more than 4 hours. Once a food selection has been made, a picture of the dish becomes the center of a new menu. At this point in the program users have access to a full-screen photograph, recipe, and a shopping list of things to buy to prepare the meal.

The program also contains a host of short videos that demonstrate cooking skills. These may be viewed as desired from the main menu. To help with each individual menu, pertinent videos are recommended with each food selection, and the videos may be accessed directly from within the selected food menu. The contents of these videos are some·

of the most unusual, including beating egg whites, boiling water, shredding, shaping meat into ring, and many others.

Other features of the program include a tantalizing food slide show. The user selects a food category, and the foods in that category are displayed full screen with the number of calories in big friendly letters at the top of the screen. The screen can then be advanced to the next or previous food in that category by pressing a screen arrow or by going directly to the recipe. A "What's for Dinner?" feature lets the user specify the ingredients and the cholesterol, fat, and sodium content (low, none, doesn't matter), and the calorie count of the foods to create a customized food list. Another feature, "Calorie Count," will give the calories, fat, fiber, cholesterol, sodium, potassium, protein, and carbohydrate of each ingredient. This is a very well-thought-out CD-ROM on cooking. It will make every PC user go to lunch early after viewing it.

Desktop Publishing Accessories

The storage capability of CD-ROM technology has made possible vast libraries of fonts and clip art. Competition has brought the prices down to where any library staff can own as much clip art as it could ever possibly use. Perhaps the biggest is DeskGallery, which contains 120,000 images. Fonts also come packed on a CD-ROM. While most of us are satisfied with only a few fonts, anyone who wants to can select from among a thousand or so fonts on a single disc.

The famous desktop publishing package Print Shop Deluxe Ensemble now comes on a CD. It is probably the best all-purpose, low-cost desktop graphics tool, with its fonts, clip art and capability of making posters, flyers, cards, and more. Since the program is all on one CD, there is no longer a struggle to use or change floppy disks, and installation takes just a few minutes.

Name:	**Announcements 3.0 for Windows**
Vendor:	Parsons Technology
Cost:	$49
Hardware requirements:	IBM PC and compatibles, Windows
Comments:	Announcements is an easy-to-use graphics program that creates posters, announcements, calendars, invitations, banners, and postcards. It includes 200 graphics such as borders, backgrounds, and people for general-purpose work. Sets of additional graphics for this program are also available: Borders & Backgrounds, Business Images, Christian Images, Family Images, Holiday Images, Kids & Education Images, and Sports & Leisure Images. Custom graphics may be imported into the system. A variety of tools can be quickly used to zoom, stretch, shrink, rotate, or copy and move graphics.

51

Name: **Clip Art CD-ROM**
Vendor: Educorp
Cost: $49.95
Hardware requirements: Macintosh Plus
Comments: This CD contains more than 90 megabytes of images for general-purpose desktop publishing. Topics include animals, people, automobiles, sports, maps, and more.

Name: **CorelGallery**
Vendor: Corel
Cost: $69.95
Hardware requirements: IBM and compatibles, 4MB RAM, Windows 3.1; Macintosh 4MB RAM, System 7.0 or later
Comments: This extraordinarily fine collection of clip art is a low-cost way to obtain a large collection. The disc contains 15,000 images, many of which are in color. The Visual Clipart Manager that comes with the package is easy to use and arranges clip art into broad categories: 3-D, animals, aircraft, arrows, birds, celebrations, children, communications, computers, crests, crustaceans, designs, electrons, fantasy figures, fires, fish, flags, floods, holidays, insects, insignia, justice, landmarks, leisure, men, maps, medical, miscellaneous, money, music, people, plants, portraits, reptiles, ships, signs, space, sports, tools, vehicles, weapons, weather, women. There are also two categories of borders—simple and themes—and subcategories within each category. For example, within theme borders there are separate areas for business, gardening, etc. Most categories have more than one, sometimes four or five, sources of the clip art. While much of it is Corel, the CD also contains clip art from 3G Graphics, Archive Arts, Cartesia Software, Image Club Graphics, One Mile Up, TechPool Studios, and Totem Graphics.

The clip art manager will preview up to four images at one time (though they are all reproduced in color in the manual that comes with the CD). An image may be enlarged or shrunk to fit within the current window. A handy button will instantly expand or shrink an image to the size in which it was originally drawn. Art may be exported to a variety of word processors and desktop publishing programs, including WordPerfect, Word, AmiPro, PowerPoint, Freeland, Harvard Graphics, Microsoft Publisher, and Ventura Publisher.

The quality of the clip art and its usefulness to librarians doing newsletters, flyers, and other such projects is quite high. It contains many graphics that can be used with children's programs (insects, animals, kids on skateboards, etc.), a wide variety of illustrations for use with adult programming, and a lot of general-purpose, generic materials (signs, people pointing, etc.).

A search utility is useful in handling the large volume of clip art available. Searching is permitted by keyword or name and may be modified by more than one term with Boolean operators AND and OR. A search may be made of all directories or only the current one.

Further information: Kristin L. Parkinson, "Clip-Art Releases Include Borders, Cartoons and Ornate Initial Caps," *MacWeek*, Sept. 5, 1994, 24.

Alan J. Fridlund, "Clip-Art Kit on CD-ROM Is a Bargain," *InfoWorld*, May 2, 1994.

Name: **Designer's Club**
Vendor: Dynamic Graphics
Cost: $49.50 per month subscription
Hardware requirements: IBM and compatibles; Macintosh
Comments: Each month's CD contains more than 55 encapsulated PostScript (EPS) images. Of these, 20 percent are in both color and black and white. A special export file, Fetch, comes with the CD and will add each month's clip art to a database for quick retrieval. A printed monthly catalog provides a second way to locate useful images. Many of these images are "layered" or have elements that can be manipulated separately from the rest with an EPS drawing program. Also included is a monthly CD-ROM magazine, Idea Source, that helps subscribers make the most of the illustrations by providing tips on good newsletter development (initially available for Macintosh versions only, to be announced for IBM later). This magazine is multimedia and interactive. A printed monthly magazine, *Options*, is full color and gives sample layouts, how-to instructions for designing articles, and electronic tips and tricks.

Name: **DeskGallery**
Vendor: Zedcor
Cost: $149.95
Hardware requirements: IBM PC and compatibles (Windows or DOS); Macintosh
Comments: This colossal collection contains 120,000 clip art images in four major categories: people, nature, pictorial designs, and sports. Each category has hundreds of subcategories. From the pens of dozens of different artists, clip art is

available in three separate formats: EPS, PICT, and TIFF. It is compatible with Photoshop, PageMaker, Illustrator, Freehand, QuarkXpress, ClarisWorks, Corel Draw, Corel PhotoPaint, Painter, Canvas, Microsoft Word, DeskPaint, MS Works, Microsoft PowerPoint, MS Publisher, AmiPro, WordPerfect, Printshop, MacDraw, and Harvard Graphics as well as other graphics and word processing packages.

Name: **Electronic Clipper**
Vendor: Dynamic Graphics
Cost: $67.50 per month
Hardware requirements: IBM PC and compatibles; Macintosh
Comments: This monthly subscription service provides a CD-ROM containing more than 70 high quality TIFF and EPS images plus a 24-bit, full-color illustration. Many of these images are "layered" or have elements that can be manipulated separately from the rest with an EPS drawing program. A special export file, Fetch, comes with the CD and will add each month's clip art to a database for quick retrieval. Also to aid retrieval, the *Clipper 5-Year Index* is a printed supplement that contains illustrations of all of the images on the CD. The system comes complete with storage binders. A monthly multimedia and interactive CD-ROM magazine, Idea Source, helps subscribers make the most of the illustrations by providing tips on good newsletter development (initially available for Macintosh versions only, to be announced for IBM later). A printed monthly magazine, *Options*, is full color and gives sample layouts, how-to instructions for designing articles, and electronic tips and tricks.

Name: **GIFs Galore**
Vendor: Chestnut Software
Cost: $39.95
Hardware requirements: IBM PC and compatibles; Macintosh
Comments: The GIFs Galore program contains more than 6,000 GIF (the CompuServe Graphics Interchange Format) images such as photographs, drawings, and cartoons that span a wide range of interest. Categories include art; flying machines; birds; buildings; boats; military weapons; flowers and plants; fantasy creatures such as wizards, goblins, and unicorns; fish; food; landscapes; maps and geography; space exploration; sports; science fiction; science and technology; TV shows; the Vietnam War; locomotives; dinosaurs; scenery; and even some clip art. Purchasers of this material can probably find

a lot of uses for it, including as a slide-show screen saver. Many of the pictures have bulletin board system numbers on them, appearing to have been designed originally as ads for bulletin board operators. Pictures come in all sizes and colors (from 2 to 256 colors).

Users can identify a useful image by consulting a file for each category containing postage-stamp-sized miniatures. Images may be viewed using any of the many viewers that come with the product. These work for the Commodore Amiga, Atari ST, DecStation, Macintosh, MS-DOS, Windows, neXT work station, OS/2, Silicon Graphics Irix work station, Sun SparcStation, and the x11 Window System. Some of the viewers will convert images from one format to another (for example, GIF to BMP) for greater flexibility in their use. All viewers are shareware and must be registered if used for an extended period of time.

Name:	**International Graphics Library**
Vendor:	Educorp
Cost:	$99
Hardware requirements:	Macintosh; IBM PC and compatible; 2MB RAM
Comments:	As its name implies, this is an international collection of images of currency symbols, stocks, maps, flags, outlines of the fifty states, and U.S. presidents.

Name:	**Print Shop Deluxe CD Ensemble**
Vendor:	Broderbund
Cost:	$79.95
Hardware requirements:	IBM PC and compatibles, Windows 3.x
Comments:	Print Shop Deluxe CD Ensemble contains The Print Shop Deluxe plus a lot of add-on products that are normally purchased separately. The now-classic Print Shop is an excellent program to produce greeting cards, envelopes, certificates, calendars, banners, signs, business cards, posters, letterheads, and postcards. To anyone who hasn't seen the Print Shop since its early Apple II days, it has changed a great deal. The Windows format makes the selection and viewing of graphics easy and quick. The system comes complete with more than 1,000 clip art graphics of all types, including Business Graphics (125 in color), Comic Characters and Amazing Animals Graphics (100 animals of all types), and Sampler Graphics (125 graphics) of theme graphics for parties, education, etc. Text can be changed to meet the occasion as well, since there are 73 fonts included.

The Graphics Exporter is another program that is included; it lets Print Shop graphics be exported in any of seven different file formats: EPS, EPS with Preview, CGM, TIFF, PCX, Adobe Illustrator 88, and Windows MetaFile. Once exported, graphics may be used with other desktop publishing and word processing programs. Calendars may be created in English, French, German, and Italian for the year, month, week, or day. The Print Shop Deluxe Companion contains many special text and graphics effects for arching, squeezing, ballooning, and otherwise distorting text into terrific eye-catching shapes. All fonts may be rotated, stretched, or scaled. Any of The Print Shop projects can be completed in just a few minutes. To do advance planning and screening, graphics or fonts may be viewed in the handy reference booklets that come with the program. Once staff members have become familiar with the program's many capabilities, they will use it every day for library publicity.

Further information: Dan Miller, "Print Shop Deluxe CD Ensemble 2.0," *PC World*, Oct. 1994, 274.

Adam A. Hicks, "Adding on to Print Shop, CD-ROM Style," *PC Magazine*, May 17, 1994, 13.

Name: **Publique Arte**
Vendor: Quanta Press
Cost: $99.95
Hardware requirements: IBM PC and compatibles; 1MB hard-disk space
Comments: This large collection of line drawings contains 2,500 PCX-compatible images. The disc contains its own viewer for quick examination of potentially useful drawings. The quality of the images varies, but the main thrust is newsletter enhancement. All images are simple, many with a humorous tone. Specific categories are aircraft, animals, borders, cards, cartoons, farming, flowers, food, holidays, insects, maps, military, people, plants, religion, sports, symbols, travels, trees, tools, and vehicles. A miscellaneous category and two categories labeled extra1 and extra2 provide many additional images. The names of most of the images provide at least a hint as to their content. Some, however, are a puzzle until they have been viewed (take, for example, ten files all labeled "truck" 1 through 10). Also, the files in the extra categories are labeled with only numbers, making them a complete mystery until viewed. A complete directory listing is included that,

happily, contains all clip art grouped by category with a clear one-line description of each file's contents.

Name:	**Quick Art Deluxe Vol.1; Quick Art Deluxe for Windows; Quick Art Lite; Quick Art Lite for Windows**
Vendor:	Wheeler Arts
Cost:	$349.99, single user; $1,149, five user; $119, Quick Art Lite V. 1
Hardware requirements:	IBM PC and compatibles (Windows version available); Macintosh; 512K RAM required
Comments:	The Quick Art Deluxe collection of clip art includes more than 3,200 images in 300 dpi. Categories of interest include animals, borders, buildings and landscapes, celebrations, clothing and sewing, education, farming, food, gardening, health and medicine, people, plants, sports, science, travel, offices, etc. Images are in TIFF format. A smaller collection of clip art, Quick Art Lite, containing only 1,600 images, is also available.

Name:	**TrueType Font Axcess 2.0; TrueType Font Axcess 2.0 for Windows**
Vendor:	Quantum Axcess
Cost:	$16 each
Hardware requirements:	IBM PC and compatibles, DOS 5.0 or later, Windows 3.1 or later, 2MB free hard-disk space.
Comments:	More than 1,000 TrueType fonts for Windows are contained on this CD-ROM. They are all shareware or freeware, which explains the extremely low price of the disc. After an initial trial period, users should send in registration money for those fonts that they intend to continue using. (Try as I might, however, I could find few actual addresses to which to send money for registration.) To make selecting fonts from such a large collection less difficult, an excellent browser is included. A sample of each highlighted font is viewed in the text box. Any font may be added to the Windows operating system as desired. Fonts range from A to Z (Alexuss Heavy Hollow to Zinco ExtraBlackCondensed), from useful to comical, and from bold to italic to thin. Others include WociDings (which make no sense at all in the sample), Wedgie (an interesting propped-up-looking style), USPS Bar Code (which, yes, looks something like a bar code), and many others. Each font may be scaled up or down to just about

any required size for viewing and may appear in bold, italic, or underlined. The screen sample may be full justified or right or left justified for viewing. A full character map may be displayed for any font. Most of these features are push-button accessible. Help files are all online; there is no paper documentation.

Dictionaries

Dictionaries have made their way to CD-ROM in a spectacular way. The CD for the *Oxford English Dictionary* contains all the information in the printed volumes. The real advantage of many of these products is their flexibility and convenience for word processing. Without quitting the word processing program, a writer may access and search a dictionary with many capabilities and features. In some cases, information may be copied directly from the dictionary into a document.

Name:	**American Sign Language Dictionary on CD-ROM**
Vendor:	HarperCollins Interactive
Cost:	$79.95
Hardware requirements:	IBM PC and compatibles; Macintosh
Comments:	This multimedia dictionary is based on the *American Sign Language Dictionary* by Martin Sternberg. It provides a convenient way to learn sign language. More than 2,600 video simulations of signs allow users to watch and practice. There are also more than 200 animated explanations. The program can be used in English, Spanish, German, French, and Italian. Special features that enhance understanding include zooming in or out to better see the actions on the screen and signing in slow motion. Audio is available for hearing the signs while they are being displayed on the screen. Browse and search features make it easy to practice specific phrases or words.
	Signs and finger-spelling characters may be printed out as needed. The program is divided into the dictionary, a skills section, a finger-spelling section, an overview, and a guided tour.

Name:	**Dictionaries & Languages**
Vendor:	Chestnut Software
Cost:	$29.95
Hardware requirements:	IBM PC and compatibles

Comments: Dictionaries & Language provides a variety of tools for working with foreign languages. The disc is a huge collection of shareware programs. Dictionaries are included for Chinese, Czechoslovakian, French, German, Greek, Hebrew, Italian, Japanese, Russian, Spanish, and Esperanto. Programs consist of translation programs, flashcards to learn vocabulary, and tutorials. A foreign language word processing program called Intext is also included. It comes with a variety of add-on modules that make it possible to do word processing in a number of foreign languages, including Albanian, Croatian, Serbian, Macedonian, Russian, Hebrew, Greek, Farsi, Urdu, Chinese, Arabic, Dutch, French, German, Danish, and Finnish.

Many other included word tools are worth exploring. Three dictionaries, for example, contain add-on spellcheck legal and medical lexicons for WordPerfect. The Devil's Dictionary, a humorous collection of definitions, will add a chuckle to anyone's day. A telecommunications dictionary provides definitions to 400 communications-related terms. Glossaries of terms are provided for general PC knowledge, graphics file extensions, jargon, and MIDI terms. Two other glossaries, of interest to anyone who has a sarcastic wit, are "a glossary of terms for those who strive to be politically correct" and "a glossary of slurred English terms." Both of these will have readers rolling in the aisles. Two separate programs will assist anyone trying to solve a crossword puzzle or cryptogram.

The interface for all of this is not a fancy Windows variety, but it does provide for various options. Programs may be copied to a hard drive or (sometimes) run directly from the CD. Instructions on how and where to send any required registration fees for programs are included on the disc. Since it is shareware, it is an excellent disc to loan without fear of copyright infringement. Patrons can decide if they wish to keep a particular program, load it into their own computers, and the burden of sending in any fees is transferred to them.

Name: **Merriam-Webster's Collegiate Electronic Dictionary**
Vendor: Merriam-Webster
Cost: $79.95
Hardware requirements: IBM PC and compatibles, 17MB hard-disk space if entire dictionary is installed, Windows; Macintosh
Comments: The Merriam-Webster is an impressive dictionary containing 160,000 entries; 3,000 abbreviations; 600 foreign words and phrases; 6,000 biographical entries; and 9,000 geographic

entries. A search may be conducted by any of seven fields, Boolean logic, and wild cards. Special features, including "Jumble Option," "Cryptogram Option," "LetterBank Option," and "Crossword Option," perform a variety of functions relevant to puzzle solving. The dictionary may be installed completely to hard disk (requiring 17 megabytes) or run completely from the CD if space is unavailable.

Further information: Patrick McKenna, *Newsbytes*, Nov. 23, 1994.

Name: **Microsoft Bookshelf**

Vendor: Microsoft

Cost: $295

Hardware requirements: IBM PC and compatibles

Comments: This set of seven hypertext reference volumes (*Word Almanac, Concise Columbia Encyclopedia, American Heritage Dictionary, Hammond Atlas, The Concise Columbia Dictionary of Quotations, Bartlett's Familiar Quotations*, and *Roget's II Thesaurus*) is suitable for library or home use. Its Windows environment is an outstanding example of a user-friendly interface. The American Heritage Dictionary contains some 200,000 definitions for more than 65,000 words and is self-pronouncing. Many words are accompanied by illustrations. Roget's II Thesaurus is easy to use and can be searched either by topic or by all text. It contains definitions and synonyms for 16,000 words. Bartlett's Familiar Quotations has more than 6,000 quotes from famous people through history. The Concise Columbia Dictionary of Quotations has more than 22,500 modern quotations. The Concise Columbia Encyclopedia is a wealth of multimedia elements, including pictures, drawings, animations, and spoken text. Users of the Hammond Atlas will enjoy the ease with which countries can be located and the fact that their names are pronounced on disc and that many national anthems can be played. Flags of all countries are also prominently displayed and can be copied to the Windows clipboard. Another exciting feature about the Atlas is a direct interface with the Columbia Concise Encyclopedia. Topics about countries in the encyclopedia can be pulled up from within the Atlas. Users can also jump directly into the encyclopedia as well for a more extensive search. The Atlas also has a topographical map corresponding to each political map. Quotes from famous people can be looked up in The Concise Columbia Dictionary of Quotations by topic, such as vanity, actors/actresses, science, honor, hope, etc.

Name:	**Oxford Compendium on CD-ROM**
Vendor:	Lotus Development
Cost:	$59
Hardware requirements:	IBM PC and compatibles, 6MB RAM, Windows 3.1 or later
Comments:	Oxford Compendium on CD-ROM contains four highly useful tools to assist writers. The Concise Oxford Dictionary (120,000 entries), the Oxford Dictionary of Quotations, the Oxford Thesaurus (275,000 synonyms) and the Oxford Dictionary of Modern Quotations. The system is easy to use and provides a wide range of useful information for composing and editing papers or stories.

Name:	**Oxford English Dictionary**
Vendor:	Tri-Star Publishing
Cost:	$895
Hardware requirements:	IBM PC and compatibles
Comments:	The Oxford English Dictionary on CD-ROM is a researcher's or lover-of-the-arcane's dream come true. The entire twenty volumes of the print version fit neatly onto one disc. The CD version is useful in every way and exciting and is on a par with the paper version in quality. The text is easy to read. Users can control both the font and the intensity and color of the parts of each entry. Great control over other displays is also possible; the etymology, definition, and quotations may all be limited as desired. A search may be conducted in many ways, depending on the needs of the user. Proximity searching can be used to find terms that are within five words of each other. Wild-card searching uses asterisks and question marks. The asterisk can be used to substitute for one or more characters in an arrangement of letters. The question mark matches a single character. Wild-card searches are also only for the determined scholar since it can take up to 15 minutes to return a result. Other search fields include quotation, work title, language, cited form, and author. The date filter is restricted to the quotation sections of entries. Adding dates to limit quotations, however, is not recommended, since it slows down the search process. The maximum number of hits for a search is 8,000. Results can be sorted or saved to disk.

One reviewer has found the dictionary to have "Inexcusably poor design; can't guess misspelled words; search results and some program functions are unreliable; complex searches require a form of programming; occasionally crashes; poor manual; no tech support" (Eckhardt, 1994). Despite this, the CD-ROM version provides orders-of-magnitude better search capability and ease of use than the paper edition. Researchers and nonresearchers alike will find it a delight to use.

Further information:	Robert C. Eckhardt, "The Oxford English Dictionary," *Mac-World*, Apr. 1994, 77.

Cameron Crotty, "Oxford English Dictionary Second Edition," *MacWorld*, Dec. 1993, 44.

Name:	**Random House Unabridged Dictionary, Second Edition**
Vendor:	Random House Reference and Electronic Publishing
Cost:	$79
Hardware requirements:	IBM and compatibles, 2MB RAM, 1MB hard-disk space, Windows 3.1 or later; Macintosh, System 6.03 or later, 1MB RAM, 1MB hard-disk space
Comments:	The Random House Unabridged Dictionary contains 315,000 entries, including biographical and geographical names as well as foreign terms and abbreviations. Information may be pulled from the dictionary and copied into the user's document. Search features include wild cards. In addition to the usual features of online dictionaries, the Random House Unabridged has some very clever and useful features not found in print or other online dictionaries. The use of the Boolean operators AND, OR, and NOT make it easy to find information indirectly. For example, "wall AND paper" will list half a dozen terms, including decoupage. The only drawback to combining search terms in this way is that it slows down the process, taking a minute or more on average to complete. Another special search feature produces a list of anagrams for any word. The system makes it possible to limit the amount of information displayed on the screen for any definition. Both the pronunciation and etymology may be eliminated, if desired. Font size may be set from 12 to 25. This dictionary loses a few points for not being a self-pronouncing dictionary. However, it remains a powerful and useful tool for writers of all kinds.
Further information:	Rubin Rabinovitz, "$79 Random House Dictionary: Look It up under Bargain," *PC Magazine*, Jan. 25, 1994, 56.

John Gliedman, "Random House Dictionary on CD-ROM Is an Unabridged Delight," *Computer Shopper*, Mar. 1994, 784.

Education and Careers

Students will find several databases in this section useful in seeking career and educational opportunities. For example, CollegeSource lists colleges, financial aid, and related information. Peterson's College Database and Barron's Profiles of American Colleges also provide much the same information with some variations. In all cases, however, users may fine tune their search for information by keying in specific criteria or needs, such as tuition, academic standards, campus life, study body size, and geographic location.

Name:	**Barron's Profiles of American Colleges**
Vendor:	Laser Resources
Cost:	$199
Hardware requirements:	IBM PC and compatibles with Windows 3.x, 256 color graphics adapter, sound card optional; Macintosh, 256 color graphics adapter
Comments:	Contains the information in *Barron's Profiles of American Colleges*, twentieth edition, of approximately 1,650 colleges. It is a multimedia production, including photographs and videos in addition to descriptive text. Included are advice and suggestions for finding a college suitable for the user, improving scores on entrance exams, finding financial aid, and surviving the freshman year. A section called Barron's Step by Step Guide to College Acceptance is a useful guide to college applicants. Additional sections include an index of college majors, specialized data, a closer look at the colleges, and the main section, Profiles of American Colleges. Also included is educational and career information in nine broad fields of study. A full-text search may be conducted on the entire database or only on specific sections. The Boolean operators AND, OR, NOT, and NEAR may be used. A wild card (*)

is also supported. Colleges may also be selected according to their admissions competitiveness. Hypertext makes it easy to move from section to section. Eighteen colleges have included promotional videos. A push button will activate a map of a state with the location of the college circled. Other convenient push-button features include immediate access to the college's admission application, the college catalog, and photographs of the campus. While the videos and photographs may give the program an interesting multimedia spark, they are often just groups of students standing around or someone talking about the virtues of a particular school. The information in the catalogs and other text, with the ability to search, is the real utility of this product.

Name:	**Beacon**
Vendor:	Macmillan New Media
Cost:	$59.95
Hardware requirements:	IBM PC or compatibles, 640K RAM, 3MB free hard-disk space, DOS 3.1 or later
Comments:	This program lets students search for two- and four-year colleges and career information, graduate studies, financial aid, and scholarships. The database contains information on more than 3,200 undergraduate colleges and 1,100 graduate schools. Approximately 900 career paths are available from which to choose. Using the interactive exercises that are provided in this program, students begin to narrow their choices. They may, for example, choose athletics and campus activities, tuition and fees, or student population or from among some 200 other criteria for choosing a school. For financial assistance information, there are some 2,100 scholarships, grants, and loan programs listed. A user-friendly interface makes the program simple to use for beginners.
Further information:	Stuart Silverman, "Keeping Good Counsel: Software for School Counselors to Help Students Down College and Career Paths," *Electronic Learning*, Feb. 1994, 34.

Name:	**Capitol Hill**
Vendor:	Software Toolworks (MindScape)
Cost:	$49.95
Hardware requirements:	IBM PC and compatibles; Macintosh
Comments:	This CD-ROM provides an educational experience by letting the student play the role of congressperson. It is just after the election, and they assume the office. The program takes them

through the steps of organizing their work, deciding what to do, working with staff, keeping appointments, etc.

Name: **CD School House 9.0**
Vendor: Wayzata Technology
Cost: $25
Hardware requirements: IBM PC and compatibles (Windows or DOS); Macintosh
Comments: The Windows version of this program provides easy access to and installation of more than 1,500 educational programs, games, and utilities. Many of these are shareware requiring a registration fee for continued use. It is a marvelous way to allow library patrons to try out programs prior to purchase. There is a wide range of educational material included: business, finance, food, science, math, language, music, religion, Windows utilities, and more. Games include arcade, adventure, cards, classics, puzzles, space, strategy, and more. Each program entry contains its name, a paragraph describing it, the registration fee, and a rating. Clicking on "Play Me" will install the program to the hard disk. Some of the educational programs include Name the States, Music Flashcards, Origins of Mythology, Kiddie Puzzles, and others. A search may be conducted using Boolean logic (AND, OR, NOT, ANDNOT, XOR, ORNOT), phrases, or proximity. Wild cards may be employed for truncation (*) or single letters (?).

Name: **CollegeSource**
Vendor: Career Guidance Foundation
Cost: $798, national; $348, regional; network per-station charges extra
Hardware requirements: IBM PC and compatibles
Comments: This Windows-based product gives basic catalog information for 3,600 colleges in its national edition. Regional editions for the Eastern, Western, Southern, and North Central United States are also available. Coverage includes two- and four-year institutions and graduate schools. The Windows interface makes it extremely simple to use. Data for each school include course descriptions, academic policies, faculty information, financial aid information, and academic calendar. The search utility is the package's greatest benefit. Simply clicking on fields makes it easy to customize the selection process for schools based on specific criteria: tuition, majors, enrollment, type of degree, affiliation (public, religious, etc.), and state. Information about a college is displayed with push-button ease: accreditation, admissions,

costs (including room and board, transportation, per-hour charge, books and supplies, and miscellaneous), financial aid (including types of grants available), programs, and majors. The actual catalog for each college is reproduced, and they may be searched separately. Information may be printed out or saved as a disk file. Restrictions on use of information may be added with password protection. This disc is highly recommended for any library that makes college catalogs available. The CD should save enough time and space to quickly pay for itself.

Name:	**DISCovering Careers & Jobs CD**
Vendor:	Gale Research
Cost:	$495
Hardware requirements:	IBM PC and compatibles
Comments:	This outstanding package will be useful in any library that offers a career center or career information to students or other patrons. It contains the complete *Occupational Outlook Handbook* and the *Dictionary of Occupational Titles*, career information on more than 1,200 job titles, and information on more than 41,000 potential employers. Job profiles includes salary and licensing information and more than 1,000 full-text articles, abstracts, and excerpts taken from trade and professional journals. Approximately 1,000 of the companies are described in essays of up to 2,500 words. Company information may be accessed by name, geographic region (state, ZIP, or area code), industry group (SIC codes), or occupations employed. The system operates with a user-friendly Windows interface. Multiple methods can be used to access job information. By first selecting a job title, the searcher will receive a job description, current trends and advice, projected job growth and employment outlook, wages and salaries, job qualifications, licensing rules and requirements, helpful publications and guides, helpful organizations and services, and potential employers.

Name:	**ERIC on CD-ROM**
Vendor:	National Information Services Corporation
Cost:	Free with purchase of any other NISC disc costing more than $500
Hardware requirements:	IBM PC and compatibles, 512K RAM available
Comments:	The database of the Educational Resources Information Center (ERIC) is a vast collection of educational materials. It contains more than 840,000 bibliographic records of

documents and journal articles. Quarterly updates add 8,000 additional citations. Indexes and abstracts include research papers, dissertations, conference proceedings, literature reviews, syllabi, curricula, and articles from 800 education-related journals. Coverage is on two discs. Disc I is from 1966 to 1979. Disc II is from 1980 to the present. The database also contains approximately 1,200 full-text ERIC digests on major topics in education. A list of more than 10,000 official index terms, The Thesaurus of ERIC Descriptors, is used to locate keywords quickly. A standard NISC-disc interface provides search modes for novice, advanced, and expert levels with full use of Boolean operators, proximity searching, and field-specific retrieval capabilities.

Name:	**Lovejoy's College Counselor**
Vendor:	InterMedia Interactive Software
Cost:	$59.95, standard edition; $199, professional edition
Hardware requirements:	IBM PC and compatibles, 4MB RAM, 256 color VGA, sound card (8-bit WAV-compatible), DOS 3.1 or later, Windows 3.1 or later
Comments:	Lovejoy's College Counselor is an outstanding source of college profiles, financial aid sources, and other college-based information. It is a tool for learning about and choosing a career, comparing colleges (1,600 four-year colleges represented), and locating financial aid (2,500 financial aid sources described). There is also information about 4,000 technical and trade school programs. College information may be viewed alphabetically, by region, or by state. The college profiles contain all information in the print edition of Lovejoy's, such as telephone numbers, student body statistics, admissions requirements, campus life activities, and financial data. Performing a search for special criteria is made simple by the search application. Admissions, majors, characteristics, costs, location, athletics, and special services may be tagged for special consideration. Each area has a list of criteria that can be tagged as "must have," "can't have," "shouldn't have," or "should have." This makes it possible to perform a highly sophisticated search with a minimum of effort or skill. The search for financial aid is as effortless as is the search for college information. A selection of choices (athletic aid, ethnic-specific aid, government aid, national merit, union affiliation, vocation/technical aid, and others) is available as push buttons.

In the general index to the CD there are also profiles for 120 important careers. Each contains a synopsis about future prospects for the career plus some vital statistics.

Name:	**Peterson's College Database; Peterson's Gradline**
Vendor:	SilverPlatter Information
Cost:	$595, College Database; $695, Gradline
Hardware requirements:	IBM PC and compatibles, 640K RAM, 3.2MB hard-disk space
Comments:	Peterson's College Database contains information on 3,100 accredited, degree-granting colleges in the United States and Canada, including a profile, housing, campus life, athletics, majors, special programs, financial aid, expenses, SAT and ACT score ranges and admission requirements, ethnic and geographic mix, student enrollment, etc. Peterson's Gradline contains 27,000 profiles of graduate and professional programs for 300 academic disciplines in more than 1,500 U.S. and Canadian colleges and universities. Information includes names and addresses of schools, faculty, research specialties, degree levels, financial aid, etc.
Further information:	Alfred Poor, "Spin Doctor: CD-ROM Titles to Help Students Prepare for College," *Computer Shopper*, Sept. 1994, 542.

Name:	**Vocational Search**
Vendor:	EBSCO Publishing
Cost:	$2,399, school year, with quarterly updates; $2,799, academic year (August through May); $3,199, monthly subscription, per year
Hardware requirements:	IBM PC and compatibles, 2MB RAM, 5MB hard-disk space, DOS 5.0 or later; Macintosh, System 6.05 or later, 1.5MB RAM (2MB with System 6.05; 4MB with System 7.0 or later), 1MB hard-disk space
Comments:	The Vocational Search database contains 500 indexed and abstracted magazines and journals of use to libraries that serve a technical or vocational curriculum. Almost 100 of these journals are also presented full text. The software will allow local collection holdings to be tagged in the database and marked with up to ten lines of text for quicker identification and location of library materials. Menu-driven search software makes it easy for first-time or inexperienced users to search. Advanced users may conduct a more-sophisticated search using truncation, wild cards, and proximity/phrase searches.

Encyclopedias

CD-ROM encyclopedias represent a clean break from their print counterparts. Most now contain many multimedia elements, including videos, slides, and sound clips. At least one survey names Grolier's Encyclopedia as the number one CD-ROM in use by libraries. The price of these reference tools has dropped in recent years. The majority can be purchased for less than $100. The CD-ROM encyclopedias usually contain the same text as a print encyclopedia plus additional visual and auditory information in the form of videos, speech, and music—all searchable—making them an excellent value. Kids and adults can enjoy learning using any of them.

Additional products available:

> Compton's Interactive Encyclopedia (Compton's NewMedia)
>
> Grolier Encyclopedia Americana (Grolier; due out soon)
>
> The Multimedia Encyclopedia of Science Fiction (Grolier)
>
> Webster's Interactive Encyclopedia 1995 (Attica Cybernetics)

Encyclopedias for Children

> Heinemann Multimedia Encyclopedia (Reed Technology & Information Services)
>
> My First Encyclopedia (Knowledge Adventure, Inc.)
>
> Microsoft Explorapedia: World of Nature (Microsoft)
>
> Random House Kid's Encyclopedia (Random House Reference and Electronic Publishing)

Name:	**The American Indian: A Multimedia Encyclopedia**
Vendor:	Facts On File
Cost:	$295
Hardware requirements:	IBM PC and compatibles, 640K RAM, DOS 3.x or later

Comments: The American Indian multimedia encyclopedia covers 150 American tribes from approximately A.D. 1000 to the present. Included are their locations, migrations, contacts with white people, wars, social structure, means of subsistence, housing, tools, agriculture, clothing, arts and crafts, transportation, religious and spiritual beliefs, legends, and rituals. The encyclopedia contains the full text from four references that include rare maps, treaties, land grants, letters—250 historical documents. It also includes more than 1,100 VGA illustrations such as original photos and drawings. Recordings of authentic American Indian songs make this a full multimedia experience. Biographical text is included on more than 1,000 persons in Native American history. Menus make it easy to jump from one subject or area of interest to another—from history, biography, tribes, legends, and documents to tribe location. Another good feature includes the five separate time lines that include biographies, history, documents, photographs, and explorers. Legends may be looked up by tribe or by region. Throughout, users have immediate access to sounds, maps, photos, and drawings. Also available are 34 separate guided tours that range from Standing Bull to Wounded Knee. A search may use the Boolean operators AND, OR, NOT, and NEARBY. Text may be sent to printer. It is quite a spectacular production.

Name: **Britannica CD 1.0**

Vendor: Encyclopaedia Britannica

Cost: $995, if purchased separately; $495, if purchased with print version

Hardware requirements: IBM PC and compatibles, Windows; Macintosh (due out soon); LAN version requires a gigabyte of disk space and is packed onto two CDs (non-LAN version is packed onto one CD)

Comments: This CD product contains the entire 44 million words from the print encyclopedia plus the yearbook—some 82,000 articles, 16 million references, and 70,000 definitions from the Merriam-Webster's Collegiate Dictionary. Hypertext links move the user from article to article. For it to work, a special parallel port adapter is required (included). While impressive in its volume of information, this CD version of Britannica does not completely replace the print edition; it is all text. This is to be remedied with the introduction of 2.0 in the near future.

Name: **Compton's Interactive Encyclopedia**

Vendor: Compton's NewMedia

Cost: $149.95

Hardware requirements: 386SX/16 or later, 4MB RAM, multimedia 256 color card, sound card

Comments: Compton's is a fully multimedia encyclopedia. It contains more than 35,000 articles; 8,000 photographs and illustrations; more than 100 full motion videos; 3-D animations and presentations; and 15 hours of sounds of music, nature, and history. Students will especially enjoy the many special features such as the interactive world atlas, idea search, time lines, and even a quick-search capability called InfoPilot. Also included is an online Webster's dictionary that contains more than 150,000 entries. Two separate search modes, easy and expert, make the encyclopedia accessible to beginners and challenging enough to assist advanced students.

Further information: Carol S. Holzberg, "Compton's Encyclopedia 2.0 Is Packed with Dynamic Data," *Computer Shopper*, Feb. 1994, 834.

Name: **Countries of the World**

Vendor: Bureau of Electronic Publishing

Cost: $395

Hardware requirements: IBM PC and compatibles, 640K RAM; Macintosh, 1MB RAM

Comments: Countries of the World contains the full text of 106 handbooks in the U.S. Army Country Handbook Series plus maps, full-color flags, and actual audio recordings of national anthems. Text for each entry includes the country's history, society, environment, economy, government, national security, and politics. High-resolution color maps (by Hammond, Inc.) provide additional insight into agriculture, ocean bottoms, climate, energy, mining, population, etc. Access is provided by browsing through the country study books or other sections or by keyword searching.

Name: **Encarta**

Vendor: Microsoft

Cost: $79

Hardware requirements: IBM PC 386SX or later, 4MB RAM, 2.5MB hard-disk space, Windows 3.1 or later, DOS 3.1 or later, sound card

Comments: Microsoft's Encarta is an outstanding reference and learning tool for all grades and age levels. It is multimedia in its approach, containing text, pictures, sound, animation, and video. Encarta has developed the online multimedia encyclopedia to a new high, taking most of the space on the 673MB of data on the CD. It has eight hours of sound bytes. It also has nearly 8,400 images, 100 animation and video clips, 798 maps, 100 interactive charts, and the 29-volume *Funk and Wagnalls*. Hypertext lets users hop from one article to other related articles. To put all of this knowledge into perspective, from any point users can click on the "Timeline" button for a visual linear representation of human and nonhuman events from 15 million B.C. to A.D. 2000. The "Category Browser" divides knowledge into nine areas of interest. These may be further defined by checking off any or all subheadings provided for it. For example, the topic of geography lists as subheadings, islands, countries, oceans and seas, maps and map making, etc. This system makes it easy to zero in on specific topics quickly. Topics may also be selected with an *A* to *Z* contents feature. Two special search features are Find Wizard and Gallery Wizard. Find Wizard asks the user to define a search by filling in the blanks and clicking on certain choices. This feature is intended for newer and more inexperienced users. The Gallery Wizard helps users to find specific media, including sounds, slides, etc. More-conventional searching can be applied using the Find utility. Operators OR, NOT, AND are permitted. Also, the proximity operator NEAR (with specified number of words) can be used. A search can be limited to current or all topics, to exclude certain media types, or even to include only certain years or geographical locations where relevant. An always-ready atlas provides world-search and zoom-in/zoom-out options for pinpointing and learning about any area on the globe. Encarta is a masterful production that will engross student or casual reader alike for hours of searching and reading and learning.

Further information: Kirsten L. Parkinson, "Top Microsoft CDs Crossing over to Mac: Encarta, Cinemania Slated for Spring," *MacWeek*, Jan. 3, 1994, 170.

Michael Goodwin, "Golf to Stravinsky, and Everything In Between," *PC World*, May 1994, 305.

Name: **Encyclopedia of Associations CD-ROM**
Vendor: Gale Research
Cost: $1,095 subscription, updates in June and December
Hardware requirements: IBM PC and compatibles, 640K RAM (500K available), DOS 3.1 or later, 1MB hard-disk space or diskette drive

Comments: This reference tool contains the information from three titles: *National Organizations of the U.S.* (descriptions of 23,000 U.S.-based associations), *International Organizations* (more than 10,000 international and multinational associations and national associations headquartered outside the United States), and *Regional, State and Local Organizations* (48,000 U.S. associations of regional, interstate, city, or local scope or membership). Information about each listed organization includes everything in the print volumes: scope and activities, size, budget, publications, committees, chief official, services, conventions and meetings, and contact data. The search process is through a menu for less-experienced users or an advanced search option for experienced users. The menu search allows for organization name, budget size, and membership size. Proximity searching with truncation and Boolean logic are also supported.

Name: **The New Grolier Multimedia Encyclopedia**
Vendor: Grolier Electronic Publishing
Cost: $395
Hardware requirements: IBM PC and compatibles; Macintosh
Comments: This superior product can be made available to adults or children for browsing or research with good results. The multimedia package contains sound, video, animation, and text. Thousands of articles can be accessed in a variety of ways, including some special features. The Knowledge Tree, for instance, divides human knowledge into the arts, geography, history, science, society, and technology. Each is further subdivided into more-specific categories (museums, areas of technology, etc.), finally resulting in articles for the user to read. A simple search tool also makes it possible to find information on any topic quickly using the operators of AND and NOT in up to four separate search fields. A search for "Henry VIII," for example, finds 73 articles, including one specifically on Henry VIII and 72 others on related topics. When a specific article is selected, a button bar across the top of its window tells whether or not a picture, animation, or other special feature is available. A bookmark may be placed at any point in the encyclopedia for quick retrieval later. Another exciting feature is the "Timeline," which is a running history from 40,000 B.C. to the present. Animations include the human body, inventions, Earth, and the climate. The video list contains clips from U.S. presidents, famous world leaders, plants, animals, space exploration, and science and

technology. A handy button bar across the top of the screen is a quick way to jump from search to title index, the Knowledge Tree, sound, pictures, or to perform other functions. An atlas button provides maps of the world accessible by country.

Name: **World Book Multimedia Information Finder**

Vendor: World Book Educational Products

Cost: $395

Hardware requirements: IBM PC and compatibles, 386 processor or later, Windows 3.1 or later, DOS 3.1 or later, 4MB RAM, 256 color capability, sound card, 5MB hard-disk space; Macintosh (any color model), System 6.07, 4MB RAM, 5MB hard-disk space, CD-ROM drive with 150K/second transfer rate or better

Comments: This exciting product contains all of the 17,000 articles in the traditional and popular *World Book Encyclopedia*. There are also 1,700 tables; 150,000 index entries; 225,000 dictionary entries; 5,000 pictures; and 260 maps. The multimedia elements provide users with animations and videos of important events and concepts. This reference work provides users with a great many opportunities to find information by browsing or jumping from entry to entry with hypertext links. Infotree is a special tool for viewing information in broad ranges of topics and subject areas. Timeline provides a history of the world from 570 million B.C. to the present. Children will love seeing what happened when the dinosaurs ruled. The many maps can be used interactively as well, by clicking to get from any spot to any spot on the globe. If users don't have multimedia, a text-only version of this product is also available at the same price.

Entertainment, Games, and Humor

Computer games are always popular. Any library can stock up on large collections of shareware games for circulation without fear of copyright infringement. Entertainment comes in all types, including adventure, classic board games (chess, etc.), role playing, and educational. In Sherlock Holmes, Consulting Detective, players take the role of Sherlock and, within an exciting multimedia world, take off after the villains. With regard to the popular and more expensive games, a library may consider the purchase of inexpensive demos for circulation or use.

Within the more traditional role of reference, the Speaker's Encyclopedia provides a highly useful database to assist in selecting just the right quotations for speaking events.

Name:	**House of Games**
Vendor:	Hi-Tech Productions
Cost:	$79.95
Hardware requirements:	IBM PC and compatibles, 512K RAM
Comments:	House of Games is an outstanding and inexpensive collection of high quality games. Most are shareware, so patrons or other users will bear the responsibility of registering and sending in their license fees. The disc and programs may be freely used. Most, though not all, of the hundreds of games will play directly from the CD. They may be copied to a hard drive if desired. The games on the disc are well balanced, with certain specific categories: board, adventure, educational, logic, casino, card, and miscellaneous games. There is also a collection of painting programs. These include Electronic Coloring Book, Kid Paint, Mega Paint, Turbo Paint, Bert's Dinosaurs, and others. Usually in such a large collection many things don't work without some effort; however, all of the games that I tried out worked immediately. The range

of games is excellent. They span from Jill of the Jungle to Classic Star Trek. Board games include two excellent versions of mah-jongg (mouse version), Chinese checkers, and others. Card game buffs will go wild with twelve versions of solitaire to play. As for adventure games, don't get too excited, since most of them are actually arcade games, though some are quite good. Gambling games include Black Jack, Las Vegas Craps, Friday Night Poker, Five Card Draw, poker, and various forms of slot machines. Educational games include word games, astronomy, geography, mathematics, and chess. About 60 other games are represented in the miscellaneous section.

Name:	**Interactive Game Madness**
Vendor:	SAMS Publishing
Cost:	$29.95
Hardware requirements:	IBM PC and compatibles, 2MB RAM, Windows 3.1 or DOS 5.0 or later, sound card, 256 color graphics card; Macintosh, System 6.0 or later, 2MB RAM
Comments:	Interactive Game Madness is a way to provide more than 80 interactive demos. This book and disc combination is especially useful and exciting to people who are new to computer games or multimedia. It is a good way to see and hear the style of a game prior to its purchase. While some of the games can be run from the Windows menu created by running the Install program, most must be invoked directly from the disc. No particular game type prevails, but there are adventure games, quiz games, flight simulation games, and some arcade games. The disc includes a few nongame selections such as Distant Suns (an astronomy program) and Movie Select (a movie database). Some truly educational programs teach music and art. Old favorites are represented with Jeopardy and Wheel of Fortune, the TV quiz games, and Star Trek: Judgment Rites. Battle Chess provides for a look at one of the more recently popular incarnations of this game. Some of the other programs on this CD are Alone in the Dark (1 & 2), Body Blows, Chess Maniac Five Billion and One, Civilization, CyberRace, Dark Legions, Detroit, Eagle Eye Mysteries, Fatty Bear's Birthday, Gabriel Knight (interactive murder mystery), Gateway 2, Impressionism and Its Sources, Iron Helix, Lenny's Music Toons, Lunicus, Masque Blackjack, Masque Video Poker, Master of Orion, MechWarrior 2, Mowgli and His Brothers, Multimedia Music: Mozart, My First World Atlas, Peter Pan's

Story Painting, Rags to Riches, Renaissance Masters #1 & #2, Rex Nebular, Silverball, Sitting on the Farm, Spectre VR, Super Tetris, The Four Seasons: Vivaldi, The Lost Vikings, The Ugly Duckling, Time Out Sports, Tornado, Total Distortion, Video Jam, and more. Even if you never buy any of the full versions of these games, the demos alone would provide many hours of outstanding entertainment. Included with the disc is an excellent, oversized book filled with color images of the programs on the disc. A text narrative is also provided for each, making it easy to review and select potentially interesting demos prior to using the disc. The package includes 3-D glasses (not necessary for most of the programs).

Name:	**Sherlock Holmes, Consulting Detective, Vols. I, II, and III**
Vendor:	Viacom New Media
Cost:	$69.95 each volume
Hardware requirements:	Multimedia IBM PC and compatibles, 640K RAM; Macintosh, 2MB RAM
Comments:	Each disc contains three mysteries and pits the player as Sherlock against the bad folks. This game is quite spectacular and worthy of applause by fans of this great detective of literature. A video introduction gives users the lay of the land and a bit of turn-of-the-century ambience. As detective, the user has a number of tools at his or her disposal, including the Baker Street irregulars to track down additional clues. Users move around London in a carriage to check out their latest hunches or to gather information and sort out witnesses. Volume I includes "The Case of the Mummy's Curse," "The Case of the Mystified Murderess," and "The Case of the Tin Soldier." The disc contains 90 minutes of color video, as well as audio clips of Holmes and others talking. Included is a hint book containing private Holmes files. Volume II includes "The Two Lions," "The Pilfered Paintings," and "The Murdered Munitions Magnate." Volume III has the cases of "The Solicitous Solicitor," "The Banker's Final Debt," and "The Thames Murders."

Name:	**Speaker's Encyclopedia**
Vendor:	Interactive Multimedia Pursuits
Cost:	$19.95
Hardware requirements:	IBM PC and compatibles, 386 minimum, Windows, 5MB RAM

Comments: The Speaker's Encyclopedia is a useful compendium of riddles, puns, jokes, proverbs and quotations, and an "Alternative Dictionary." The dictionary is full of witticisms that can be used for public speaking, but its contents are also lots of fun to just browse. (It is filled with stuff like, "Absurdity: Fact that is explicitly inconsistent with your own opinion.") The Windows interface is a pleasure to use. Push buttons for the major categories are quick and convenient ways to access the materials. While the categories divide the database into types of information, the best way to search for information on any of the 1,600 topics included is through the index. This may lead to any or all of the categories. A search may be specified in any or all of the categories and may use AND, OR, NEAR (within eight words), or NOT (i.e., the search may include puns and quotes but leave out other categories). While many of the puns and jokes are "family value" stuff, there are many that are more "adult" in nature.

Film

Many good CD-ROM–based film databases exist, usually at reasonable prices. Some are specialized, but most provide access to the whole spectrum of movies. They are useful in several ways. Their principal use is reference; they satisfy requests for film information. For this sort of data, the larger the database—the more movies contained within it—the better. To find out what a movie is about or to have it reviewed in some detail requires additional text. For this kind of reference, pictures are not particularly useful; they are usually added for amusement.

Additional products available:

> Art on Screen on CD-ROM (G. K. Hall)
>
> The Complete Guide to Special Interest Videos (Quanta Press)
>
> Halliwell's Interactive Film Guide (Updata)
>
> Precision One MediaSource (Brodart Automation, produced by the Consortium of College & University Media Centers)

Name:	**Baseline Motion Picture Guide to Horror and Science Fiction**
Vendor:	ScanRom Publications
Cost:	$19.95
Hardware requirements:	IBM and compatibles
Comments:	This inexpensive guide is an exceptional value. It is of special interest to horror and sci-fi addicts. Being one myself, I used it for several weeks prior to making any judgments about its usefulness. I have a small collection of science fiction and horror film books of my own, so it was also useful to compare it to a print collection. I can report that I am a happy user of this tool. It can be used in several ways, including to search directly for information and for browsing. Each entry contains and may be searched by title, credits for cast and production, parental ratings, star ratings, producing country, genre, running time in minutes, releasing

company, producing company, MPAA rating, color/BW, producer, director, writer, music composer, music director, music and lyrics, art director, set director, special effects, stunts, costumes, makeup, choreography, technical adviser, and animation. The main search menu contains all of these individual fields, thus making it very user friendly. Each entry also contains a synopsis and a review that vary in quality and length. Selected entries contain one or more visual images, usually still publicity shots of actors and occasionally stills from the movie, in black-and-white or color. My impression is that my books contain far more information about the films. The CD, however, has search features not found in books. An added bonus on this CD is three books: *Horror Film Stars*, 2nd edition, by Michael R. Pitts; *Science Fiction Films of the Seventies* by Craig Anderson; and *Vintage Science Fiction Films* by Michael Benson. Information in the book ends at 1991. Another title of interest from ScanRom is Hollywood: The Bizarre, a catalog of 5,000 of the greatest Hollywood stars, with extensive data on 140 of them, such as Elvis, Marilyn Monroe, and Jayne Mansfield.

Name:	**Cinemania**
Vendor:	Microsoft
Cost:	$59.95
Hardware requirements:	IBM PC and compatibles, 2MB RAM, 4MB hard-disk space, Windows 3.1; Macintosh
Comments:	Cinemania is a small reference library of film books plus multimedia that will be of interest to all film buffs. Included is *Leonard Maltin's Movie and Video Guide* with its more than 19,000 movie reviews, *Roger Ebert's Video Companion* with more than 1,300 reviews, and Pauline Kael's *5001 Nights at the Movies* with more than 2,500 reviews. Other books with reviews include *The Picture Guide*, *The Encyclopedia of Film*, James Monaco's *How to Read a Film*, and Ephraim Katz's *The Film Encyclopedia*. Another reference feature is a complete listing of all Academy Awards since 1927.

The main database is accessible through a list of film titles, actors' names, and subject headings that may be searched collectively or by category. Users interested in science fiction may simply type in that subject heading and a long essay will be displayed. The many references to specific science fiction films are in hypertext, permitting users to jump immediately to any of them.

The information for each film includes one or more brief reviews from the above sources and the film's length, director, cast, and rating and whether it is in color or black-and-white. Most cast members' names are also in hypertext. There are good black-and-white portrait photos of the actors along with birth dates, filmographies (also in hypertext), and brief biographical sketches. Some film entries have a still included, but most do not. Pictures may be pulled out separately from entries for slide show viewing.

Aside from delightfully browsing this mass of film data for hours on end, there are other useful ways to engage it. A search for any word in any or all of the areas of the database can include AND, OR, NOT, and NEAR terms. ListMaker is a feature that will create the user's personalized list or library of favorite or owned movies. The Multimedia Gallery contains hundreds of black-and-white as well as color stills of movies and cast. It also contains musical themes, dialog, and even film clips. (Watch as Obewan and Darth Vader battle it out in *Star Wars* right on your computer screen.) Although it is perhaps the best movie guide on CD yet produced, Cinemania multimedia items are interesting and fun, but most are as abbreviated as the movie reviews.

Further information: Rebecca Rohan, "Microsoft's Cinemania Brings Screen Gems to CD-ROM," *Computer Shopper*, Mar. 1994, 780.

Mike Langberg, "Cinemania Makes Microsoft the Star of CD-ROM Movie Reviews,"*San Jose Mercury News*, Nov. 14, 1993, 4.

Name: **Magill's Survey of Cinema**
Vendor: EBSCO Publishing
Cost: $99
Hardware requirements: IBM PC and compatibles, 640K RAM, 5MB hard-disk space
Comments: Magill's Survey of Cinema contains a broad range of more than 15,000 classic and contemporary films. Each record lists full credit data, careers of actors, directors, producers, and cinematographers. The information has been compiled from the following books: *Magill's Survey of Cinema: English Language Films*, 1st Series, 2nd Series; *Magill's Survey of Cinema: Silent Films*; *Magill's Survey of Cinema: Foreign Language Films*; and *Magill's Cinema Annual*. Approximately 4,000 of the films listed also have full-text reviews and story-line abstracts. The software will allow local collection holdings to be tagged in the database and

marked with up to ten lines of text for quicker location and identification of library materials. Menu-driven search software makes it easy for first-time or inexperienced users to find what they need. More-advanced users may conduct a sophisticated search using truncation, wild cards, and proximity/phrase searches.

Name:	**Mega Movie Guide**
Vendor:	Infobusiness
Cost:	$59.95
Hardware requirements:	IBM PC and compatibles, Windows
Comments:	The movie reviews in this collection are *TV Guide* fare, just a line or two to sum up the plot. The scope of the work, however, is outstanding. Some 56,000 movies are compressed into a highly useful and easy-to-use database. It includes made-for-TV films, international films, and documentaries. Information about films is accessible in several ways. A search may be made by country, director, length, MPAA, stars, title, or year. Boolean operators AND, OR, NOT, and XOR may be used. A search may also be limited to a specific field, note, level, or group. For the person just wanting to browse, the database offers a quick push-button approach with immediate access to the movie listings, stills, star profiles, video clips, and greatest hits (a list of the best movies for each decade beginning with the 1920s). Each entry also contains the language the movie is in, and whether or not it is available as a videotape. The Academy Awards section lists best picture, director, comedy director, actor, actress, and writing (for an adaptation or for an original story). There are dozens of film star biographies that provide hypertext access to the film references in each biography. More than 75 still pictures and 115 video clips of favorite movies are included. But don't rely on these for too much visual information since both are reduced to postage-stamp size in the center of the screen. Approximately 5,000 of the movies are given more-extensive reviews. Users of this database may append their own notes, reviews, or comments to the movie entries. Information in the guide may be highlighted and color coded for easier reference later. A convenient button bar makes it easy for users to find their way around and gives direct access to features such as print, search, highlight, backtrack, bookmark, etc.
Further information:	Ron White, "New on CD-ROM: Flicks, Fractals, and Fine Art," *PC Computing*, Dec. 1993, 148.

Name:	**Roger Ebert's Movie Home Companion**
Vendor:	Quanta Press
Cost:	$44
Hardware requirements:	IBM PC and compatibles, 640K RAM, DOS 3.1 or later; Macintosh, 1MB RAM, System 6.0 or later
Comments:	This CD can be run entirely from the CD-ROM drive, requiring no hard-disk space. The database contains more than 27,000 lengthy movie reviews written since 1986 by the popular critic Roger Ebert. It also contains Ebert's many interviews with actors and actresses, as well as the full introduction to each edition of the printed volumes. Movie buffs will appreciate the ease with which they can find detailed opinions about many movies. Predetermined fields can be used to search by cast names, title, MPAA rating, Ebert's rating, or director. Using the word wheel makes it easy to search for categories, keywords or subjects. A search can involve Boolean terms (AND, OR, NOT, EXCLUSIVE OR). A proximity search can be used to define within how many words search terms must be found. Areas of the database can be searched separately; titles, credits (directors and actors), essays, book introductions, and interviews. When a search has been completed, the program will print out results if desired. Custom screen colors can be chosen to accommodate different tastes. This CD is a lot of fun, and especially useful when searching for specific films or stars and directors and when a critical opinion is desired (though you only get one—Ebert's).

Name:	**Videohound**
Vendor:	Visible Ink Software
Cost:	$79.99
Hardware requirements:	IBM PC and compatibles, Windows 3.x
Comments:	This is an outstanding database for research and entertainment. While print products may provide as much information, Videohound makes it possible to access videotapes quickly by keyword, format, title, color, critical review, year of release, closed caption, and MPAA rating or to combine search categories and criteria to produce specialized lists. The database is quite large: more than 30,000 cast members; 15,000 images of the cast; directories; 1,000 categories; and sound effects. For example, in the horror or science fiction category users can select and play sound effects for friendly or unfriendly aliens and many others; the effect is multimedia. Images include many in full color, including

movie posters. Award-winning films can also be found, including some 1,700 movies that have won some honor. The database contains basic biographies of many specific cast members and a videography of films by year in which the cast member appeared. A picture is appended to each cast member's information sheet. Regarding the films themselves, they are rated by "bones." Four bones, three bones, etc., all the way through W-O-O-F! (so bad it may be good). A brief synopsis of each film gives the general plot. Other details include cast, director, etc. A file listing just the movies a user owns can be created by customizing the database using the List Maker feature. This list, as well as most of the selections mentioned in this review, can be printed out.

Further information: Harry McCracken and Richard Popko, "Movie Buff's Best Friend," *Multimedia World*, Aug. 1994, 48.

Health, Medicine, and Nutrition

CD-ROMs on health are now very popular. These take the form of databases of treatment information, such as Doctor's Book of Home Remedies, and traditional prescription drug information, such as the Physician's Desk Reference. A few, such as Family Doctor, provide general assistance to consumers in making decisions about their health. Health Reference Center on InfoTrac is a periodical index that provides full text and abstracts of many health-related periodicals. Patrons can use this reference tool to find articles about ailments, cures, drugs, etc.

Additional products available:

Comprehensive MEDLINE (EBSCO Publishing)

CORE MEDLINE (EBSCO Publishing)

Personal Medical Advisor (EBSCO Publishing)

Hazard Awareness Health and Safety Library (On-Line Computer Systems)

HEALTH: Planning & Administration (EBSCO Publishing)

MDX Health Digest (SilverPlatter Information)

MEDLINE (SilverPlatter Information)

Physician's MEDLINE Plus (EBSCO Publishing)

Name:	**Child Abuse and Neglect CD-ROM**
Vendor:	National Information Services
Cost:	Free to libraries and qualified institutions
Hardware requirements:	IBM PC and compatibles, 512K RAM available
Comments:	Designed to help people who work to prevent and treat child abuse, this database contains more than 18,000 bibliographic citations and abstracts of professional books, journals, government reports, conference papers, state annual reports, curricula, and unpublished papers. Materials include court

cases, family violence reports, and editorials and letters to the editor. Physical abuse, sexual abuse, emotional and psychological abuse, and child neglect are covered. Areas of importance are the definition and etiology of child abuse and neglect, social and economic factors, ethnicity and cultural competency, legal issues, federally funded research projects, abuse and developmental disabilities, training programs for service personnel, service programs, prevention programs, and effects on children and on adults who were abused as children. A full-text search may be conducted on the entire database or only on specific sections. The operators AND, OR, NOT, and NEAR may be used. A wild card (*) is also supported.

Name:	**Doctor's Book of Home Remedies 2.0**
Vendor:	Compton's NewMedia
Cost:	$39.95
Hardware requirements:	IBM PC and compatibles
Comments:	Home Remedies contains thousands of hints and helpful ideas for relieving the pains and misfortunes of daily life, growing older, and just plain bad luck. As its name implies, it is a collection of home remedies recommended by doctors. Created by the editors of *Prevention Magazine*, it was written as a series of articles by MDs. As many as half a dozen doctors listed at the end of each chapter coedited each section. There are three main parts to this reference work: the idea search, the articles, and the dictionary. It is not multimedia, so there are no pictures, diagrams, videos, animations, or sounds. The idea search lets users look for words or phrases in both the articles and the dictionary databases. It does not support Boolean logic searches, although the system does keep track of previous searches and allows them to be repeated quickly. The average patron looking up some complaint for recommended treatments will have little trouble finding the information quickly and efficiently. A term or phrase can be highlighted in any of the articles and copied into the search windows to expedite a search.

The articles database covers hundreds of useful topics listed alphabetically by title. It includes remedies for headaches ("40 Hints to Head off the Pain"), acne ("Know When to Squeeze"), allergy relief, pain relief of many kinds, and insomnia and tips on problems associated with breast-feeding, diets, exercise, bedwetting, bites, menopause, stress, over-the-counter medication, and much more. The remedies can be done at home with materials bought from a drugstore or grocery store. In addition, there is also helpful advice for using inhalers, aspirin and other pain relievers, etc. correctly to make them work better. The dictionary component contains a Merriam-Webster dictionary, thesaurus, and foreign words and phrases. This section also contains the dictionary tables, such as information about the planets, weights and measures, books of the Bible, chemical elements, etc.

Further information: David Kolker, "Is There a Cyber Doctor in the House?" *Los Angeles Times*, Sept. 23, 1994, E2.

Name: **Dr. Schueler's Self-Health for Windows**

Vendor: Pixel Perfect

Cost: $69.95

Hardware requirements: 386 PC or later, 256 color graphics adapter, 4MB RAM, 6MB hard-disk space

Comments: This software acts as a personal health manager, including multimedia elements of sound, photos, and videos. The system contains modules for disease prevention for adults, care of infants, health cost analysis, and monitoring an individual's health with graphs and charts. My favorite reference-like feature is the health cost analysis. Here, parameters of geographic location (city, state) and type of procedure can be entered to return a range of costs one should expect to encounter when obtaining services. Videos in this system include baby care, breast- and bottle-feeding, picking up, holding, burping, and many more important baby care skills. Drug interactions may be searched. For instance, problems with taking both Prozac and caffeine are included. The personal medical manager will keep track of medical records, legal documents (living will and durable medical power of attorney), and entries for routine medical tests such as blood pressure.

Name: **Family Doctor**

Vendor: Creative Multimedia

Cost: $79.95

Hardware requirements: IBM MPC and compatibles, Windows 3.x

Comments: Family Doctor consists of several publications on one CD-ROM. It consists of two programs in one: Consumer Guide to Prescription Drugs and Questions and Answers, and includes illustrations, health update booklets, anatomy of the human body, and addresses of educational and support groups. The information is useful for general reference work. Information is in easy-to-follow language and is intended for the layperson. Twenty-three major areas are covered, such as pregnancy and childhood, accidents, aging and the elderly, doctors and hospitals. Each is subdivided into numerous subcategories that quickly pinpoint a subject. The Questions and Answers section handles 2,000 topics. The Consumer Guide to Prescription Drugs contains an outstanding introduction to drug use and knowledge, including such basics as understanding a prescription (with illustration), administering medication correctly, coping with side effects and understanding how drugs work, Canadian brand names, and tablet/capsule identification. The drug section is fully searchable and contains the brand name, type of drug, ingredients, dosage forms, storage, uses, treatment, side effects (major and minor), interactions with other food and drugs, and warnings for each of 1,600 drugs. Health update booklets cover diabetes, aging, the heart, arthritis, and colorectal cancer. Each area has several extensive essays of general interest.

The Windows version makes hopping through all sections with the mouse cursor very simple. The search facility covers the entire database, including drugs. Even beginners will find it easy to use, with Boolean operators conveniently supplied from a popup menu. A number of drawings provide some good visuals for some areas, including surgical procedures, hip replacement, biopsy, etc. Point and click anywhere on the human anatomy with the mouse to zoom in or out on a particular part of the body. By clicking the right mouse button on a word in this section, the program will "speak" the body part (e.g., "legs"). I found this feature amusing at best.

Name:	**Food/Analyst; Food/Analyst Plus**
Vendor:	Hopkins Technology
Cost:	$99, Analyst; $199, Plus
Hardware requirements:	IBM PC and compatibles, 512K minimum RAM
Comments:	Food/Analyst provides nutritional analysis of foods and meals. The database contains 80 nutrients and more than 5,000 foods. Meals may be entered and tracked as long as desired for maintaining a running analysis of diet. Output includes recommended daily allowances graphs. Food/Analyst Plus also includes USDA food composition database. Users have access to *Handbook No. 8*, USDA survey database, USDA *Home Economics Research Report 48* on sugars, and *Canadian Nutrient File 1988* plus information on more than 8,000 foods from 150 companies.

Name: **Health and Drug Information Library**

Vendor: SilverPlatter

Cost: $1,295 annual subscription, semiannual updates

Hardware requirements: IBM PC and compatibles, Windows

Comments: This database contains a variety of health-related information, including 400 reviews of health articles from the American Academy of Family Physicians Foundation. More than 1,900 articles contain patient advice that spans some 6,000 medical procedures, conditions, and drug products. Approximately 200 pediatric articles are in English and Spanish, and 100 images provide supplemental illustrations of anatomy and health conditions. This guide for the layperson provides information on the symptoms and causes of conditions, tips for when to call a doctor, treatment instructions, medication descriptions, and prevention advice. It covers adult health, women's health issues, and child and adolescent health. Hypertext allows users to jump from section to section for immediate access to related information and images. The Windows interface is easy to use with pull-down menus and point-and-click push-button features.

Name: **Health & Medical Industry**

Vendor: American Business Information

Cost: $49

Hardware requirements: IBM PC and compatibles, DOS or Windows

Comments: This disc is a directory of health services in the United States and Canada. Information is grouped under 60 headings. Health professionals can be searched for by physicians (439,000), dentists (171,000), pharmacies (58,000), psychologists (42,000), physical therapists (18,000), retirement homes (17,000), health clubs (12,000), and more than 280,000 other listings. A search may be conducted by type of business, professional specialty, ZIP code, city or state, or business or professional name. Each detailed record contains the name, partial address, city, state, ZIP code, and telephone number. A total of 1.1 million listings are contained in this database.

Name: **Health Reference Center on InfoTrac**

Vendor: Information Access

Cost: $2,500

Hardware requirements: IBM PC and compatibles, 640K RAM

Comments: This is an easy-to-use medical database, though it is limited in its search capability. It will be of excellent use to the general public looking for information about medical problems, medical alternatives, medications, and research. The text covers 150 health and medical periodicals, 300 references from general-interest periodicals, and 500 medical education pamphlets. The material is dated from September 1991 to the present. Also included on the disc are dictionary definitions from *Mosby's Medical, Nursing and Allied Health Dictionary, 4th Edition, 1994*; *Columbia University College of Physicians and Surgeons Complete Home Medical Guide*; *The People's Book of Medical Tests*; *USP DI-Volume II Advice for the Patient: Drug Information in Lay Language*; and *Consumer Health Information Source Book*.

The database search screen is the traditional InfoTrac single-line search box that will accommodate a 32 alphanumeric character search. A search is made of an alphabetical list of subjects, corporate and product names, place names, personal names, titles of books, etc. When a term is chosen, it will return a number of hits from which to choose. These may contain full text, subject headings, or cross references. The system is convenient, easy to use, and easy to read. Results of any search may be printed to hardcopy.

Name: **Health Source**

Vendor: EBSCO Publishing

Cost: $1,995, 12 monthly; $995, 6 bimonthly issues; $495, one issue every four months

Hardware requirements: IBM PC and compatibles, 2MB RAM, 5MB hard-disk space, DOS 5.0 or later; Macintosh, System 6.05 or later, 1.5MB RAM (2MB with System 6.05; 4MB RAM with System 7.0 or later), 1MB hard-disk space

Comments: The Health Source is a collection of the full text of 57 rotating (changed from year to year) health-related journals for three years and the index and abstracts for 200 other periodicals and more than 500 health-related pamphlets. Some of the journals included are (full text) *AIDS Weekly*, *Cancer News*, *Harvard Health Letter*, *Health Facts*, *Hospital Topics*, *Issues in Law & Medicine*, *Obesity & Health*, *Psychology Today*, *Runner's World*, *Total Health*, and many others; (indexed and abstracted) *Aging Today*, *American Baby*, *Arthritis Today*, *Backpacker*, *Bicycling*, *Black Health*, *Business & Health*, *Contemporary Drug Problems*, *Food & Nutrition*, *Inside MS*, *Muscle & Fitness*, *New Scientist*, *RN*, and many others. The *New England Journal of Medicine* appears full text and is indexed and abstracted. Abstracts are approximately 50 words each. Topics covered include sports, drugs, consumer products, medical self-care, psychology, environment, nutrition, safety, and exercise. Some charts and graphs are also included with the articles. The software will allow local collection holdings to be tagged in the database and marked with up to ten lines of text for quicker location and identification of library materials. Menu-driven search software makes it easy for first-time or inexperienced users to search. Advanced users may conduct a more sophisticated search using truncation, wild cards, and proximity/phrase searches.

Name:	**Herbalist 2**
Vendor:	Hopkins Technology
Cost:	$49.95
Hardware requirements:	Multimedia IBM PC and compatibles, 2MB RAM required, Windows 3.x
Comments:	This multimedia production is for the health care worker or patient interested in herbal medicines and a holistic perspective. It contains 171 color slides of herbs, voice narratives, and even some music. The program uses the Windows interface and is well organized with multiple access points for most information. The material is well written with citations in most topic areas to MEDLINE and other sources. The database contains introductory materials on the principles of holistic medicine, including classification of medicinal plants, the formulation and preparation of herbal medicines, sources of phytotherapeutic information (bibliography and contacts), and selection criteria to use when choosing herbs. The human organism is covered system by system: digestion, cardiovascular, lower respiratory, upper respiratory, urinary, reproduction, musculoskeletal, infections, skin, and immunity, and special attention is given to problems of children and the elderly. Additional information includes a glossary, *Materia Medica* with citations, English-to-Latin names, Latin-to-English names, prefixes and suffixes, herb names and plant taxonomy, herbal poetry by Jim Duke, and a narrated 30-minute walk through an herb garden. The software offers full-text search capability with Boolean operators OR, AND, NOT, and NEAR. The Windows interface permits bookmarks to be placed anywhere for later reference. Printouts can be produced of both text and pictures.

Name:	**Home Medical Advisor Pro 3.0; Home Medical Advisor Pro 3.0 for Windows**
Vendor:	Pixel Perfect
Cost:	$88
Hardware requirements:	IBM PC and compatibles, 512K RAM, 4MB hard-disk storage; Windows version requires 4MB RAM and 4MB hard-disk storage
Comments:	This multimedia disc has a wealth of material about health-related matters. Approximately 70 quite excellent short videos are informative and exciting to watch. One video about radial keratotomy shows exactly how the procedure is performed. More than 1,000 still images in color are also on the disc. These show a wide variety of medical phenomena, including medical procedures, symptoms and conditions, and health-related matters. Some of these contain material of a powerful or graphic nature, including gunshots, genital warts, etc. Such material is prefaced with a warning prior to viewing. Separate features cover prescription drugs, 500 common household poisons (aspirin, acids, beer, bleach, etc.) and instructions for what to do if they are ingested, injuries, diseases, 150 medical tests, symptoms, multiple symptoms, and health and diet. The injury file has information on more than 150 common injuries with first-aid help to advanced-care instructions. Exercises for recovering from sports-related injuries are also included. The program also has the capability for storing 14 different types of medical histories (medical, surgical, allergy, etc.) that may be printed out.

Each section contains a number of topics that may be viewed separately. Essays contain hypertext that may define more-difficult terms or may hop to a related topic. The push-button Windows interface makes it easy to backtrack after skipping from concept to concept. A search may be performed in any of the major topic categories. The program also has a drug-interaction feature in which the user can choose any of the 2,400 prescription drugs from the list, and the program will analyze them for interactions.

The information in this program is useful and easy to follow. Adult patrons will find it a wonderful tool for browsing and learning about their medical conditions. Kids may find it appealing because of the goodly number of truly gross pictures one might expect in a medical guide (spider bites, injuries, etc.). It is highly recommended. Other products from Pixel Perfect Software include Self-Health, a personal health counselor for preventive medicine and longevity, and Your Medical Records.

Further information: Michael Goodwin, "Doctor on a Disk," *PC World*, June 1994, 315.

Name: **Mayo Clinic Family Health Book on CD-ROM; Mayo Clinic—The Total Heart; Mayo Clinic Family Pharmacist**

Vendor: Interactive Ventures

Cost: $95, Family Health Book; $34.95, Mayo Clinic Total Heart; $59.95, Mayo Clinic Family Pharmacist

Hardware requirements: IBM PC and compatibles; Macintosh

Comments: Intended for the general public or nonmedical community, the Mayo Clinic Family Health Book has information on approximately 1,000 medical conditions, first aid, and disease prevention. All are explained in easy-to-follow lay terms. The guide contains animations and videos for many of the topics it discusses; there are 500 full-color illustrations and 90 minutes of sound. Included with and complemented by these multimedia elements is the full 1,372 pages of the print edition. The Windows format makes it simple and easy to find any condition or topic very quickly.

Mayo Clinic—The Total Heart is also heavy on multimedia elements, including 145 full-color illustrations and 3-D visualizations as well as 60 minutes of audio to explain the inner workings of the human heart and its diseases and treatments.

The Mayo Clinic Family Pharmacist contains important data about more than 7,600 prescription and over-the-counter drugs, including full-color illustrations of each. Its 68 video and animation segments will walk the patron through dosages, early disease detection, and first-aid treatments.

Name: **Physician's Desk Reference Library on CD-ROM**

Vendor: Medical Economics Data

Cost: $575 to $995, depending on options; subscription includes initial disc and three updates during year

Hardware requirements: IBM PC and compatibles, 640K RAM, DOS 3.1 or later

Comments: This impressive electronic database includes *Physician's Desk Reference*; *PDR for Nonprescription Drugs*; *PDR Guide to Drug Interactions, Side Effects, Indications*; *PDR for Ophthalmology*; and *PDR Supplements*. A search for information may be by product, indication, therapeutic category, manufacturer, interactions and side effects, or word.

Name:	**The Pill Book**
Vendor:	Compton's NewMedia
Cost:	$39.95
Hardware requirements:	IBM PC and compatibles
Comments:	The Pill Book is a CD version of the book by the same name. It contains essential information about the 1,500 most frequently prescribed drugs in the United States. The CD, like the book, is easy to use. Although useful and interesting, it won't take the place of the more thorough volume, *Physician's Desk Reference.* An article or a photo of a particular drug can be found either through the table of contents or by a search. In addition to the generic or chemical name, the text contains various brand names, a classification of the type of drug, uses prescribed for, general information, cautions and warnings, pregnancy/breast-feeding information, information for seniors, possible side effects, drug interactions, food interactions, usual dosage, overdosage, inhalation, tablets, and any special information. A search using a generic name such as aspirin will result in many choices listed under various brand names. To assist in understanding the text there is a complete English-language dictionary online with definitions and pronunciation. The disc also comes with a color supplement booklet that pictures all of the drugs. A list of the 200 most widely prescribed drugs is also included. Whenever a searched-for drug is included in it, a reference is made to this list. Also included are some online help files.

Name:	**Sante (for Good Health)**
Vendor:	Hopkins Technology
Cost:	$99.95
Hardware requirements:	IBM PC and compatibles, 512K RAM, 2MB hard-disk space
Comments:	Sante is a multifunction database of health and nutrition. It contains diet-control information, weight-control help, an exercise system, and a menu-preparation aid. For the person simply trying to toss off a few pounds, this program is definitely overkill, but for the person wanting to begin a good exercise, diet, and lifestyle regimen and keep track of it all on a daily basis, it is ideal.

Users begin by entering their personal data: name, sex, ideal weight, etc. Numerous people may be entered into the same database. Up to eight different meals may be entered into the system for each day. The program provides detailed lists of foods and portion sizes. Once entered, nutrients, calories, etc. for each meal and a grand total for that day are calculated. Meals may be revised, deleted, added to, and even graphed. Graphing the meal creates a bar graph of the protein and vitamins in the food. Additional foods may be added to the database, if desired, for special diets. There are also 415 recipes on the disc that may be imported to the program to use in the meals. If the user enters the cost of each individual food, a special utility will calculate the cost of a meal or recipe. There is also a section of advice from a dietitian. It covers dozens of topics, from diabetes, calories, and weight loss to shopping hints. It is quite good and provides information in a question-and-answer format.

The daily exercise section provides a Daily Exercise Worksheet, a Calorie in/out Report, and a History Graph of results. This section provides a complete list of exercises from which to add to the work sheet. There is also a very good manual with this program. It contains explanations and tips on getting the most from Sante. This program is DOS-based, but uses a mouse and pull-down menus.

History and Genealogy

People of all ages will find suitable CDs within the history category. Ancient Lands is specifically designed for young people, including stories of young people living in ancient, far-away lands. The Constitution Papers brings together all of the major state and federal documents that have figured into the development of the United States since the beginning of the republic. The Story of Civilization is the full text of the magnificent print volumes and has many pictures squeezed onto one disc.

A number of genealogy CDs exist, including the outstanding FamilySearch, which contains information on some 300 million people.

Additional product available:

Landmark Documentaries in American History on CD-ROM (Facts On File)

Name:	**Ancient Lands**
Vendor:	Microsoft
Cost:	$59.95
Hardware requirements:	IBM PC and compatibles, Windows 3.x
Comments:	Ancient Lands is a multimedia encyclopedia of history complete with guided tour or independent travel through the ages. The program is rich in sights and sounds as well as in opportunity for learning. It can be used successfully with all age groups, though young people and younger students will find it particularly educational. There is a main index that quickly lets users find specific areas of interest such as battles, countries, generals, weapons, writing, and mummification. Most of these subject entries, however, are intended to lead users to interesting or organized browsing rather than to be used as a serious reference tool. Selections may be made geographically by pointing and clicking on any area of a map of the ancient Mediterranean area. Once a land has been

selected, Egypt, for example, specific areas of interest about it may be chosen: work and play, people and politics, and monuments and mysteries. All lands also provide tour guides. Egypt provides six: a woman pharaoh, an Egyptian boy, an embalmer's daughter, a priestess, a craftsman, and Melvin, a world-traveling accountant. Each tells about ancient Egypt from his or her own perspective, providing a marvelous way for young people to learn. The pictures and images are quite splendid, and together with many sounds of exotic music, animals, and other effects make for an outstanding and captivating atmosphere by which to understand civilizations that flourished long before our own. There is a total of more than 1,000 articles. Three separate screen savers are also provided; an Egyptian theme, a Greek theme, and a Roman theme. Another exciting feature is the ability to transfer on request any of the many images in the program to a hard-disk drive for use as wallpaper. Maps and time tables of each ancient area and epoch are available throughout the program. Topics can also be found using a find command and hotkeys. Some outstanding animated movies demonstrate topics such as ancient ship development and the history of plates.

Name:	**Atlas of U.S. Presidents**
Vendor:	Applied Optical Media
Cost:	$39.95
Hardware requirements:	IBM PC and compatibles
Comments:	The Atlas of U.S. Presidents is an excellent historical tutorial of the presidents of the United States from George Washington to George Bush. Its push-button interface makes it easy to use, and elementary school children will find it fun and useful. The CD is moderately multimedia, though no video or animation is included. At the main menu, there are separate buttons for displaying the presidential flag, seal, song, and oath. The White House is represented as a large detailed cutaway map. A good color portrait or photograph of each president is the centerpiece of each entry. The program includes some basic biographical information about each president: ancestry, religion, parents, birth place and date, date of death and place of burial, and age at inauguration. Users can explore the listings of presidents by browsing through them. Each entry also contains quick access to other presidential and educational information, such as a map of the election results. An outline historical map shows the most-significant events and trends in the United States at the time of

each presidency. A biography of 500 to 600 words discusses the highlights of each presidency, and a somewhat smaller entry discusses each first lady. Sound clips of the actual voices of more-recent presidents during their inaugurals or other events are included; for earlier presidents, actors recite some work or speech by the president.

Good help files are available online, but the system works so well, with no hidden surprises, that they are unnecessary. There are no search features. Presidential entries are in alphabetical order or chronological order.

Name:	**Constitution Papers**
Vendor:	Johnston
Cost:	$99
Hardware requirements:	IBM PC and compatibles
Comments:	Early papers from American history are well represented and easily accessible in this collection. The WordCruncher software used to search the database is easy to use and menu driven. A word wheel makes it fun to look for words and concepts. Documents may be examined in the order in which they appear in the database, in a steady stream, or called up by name, chapter, or subsection. The software also permits search by an exact phrase, a partial phrase, words in the same paragraph, related words, or partial words with the same substring or ending. The interface is DOS based, without any fancy windows, hypertext, or mouse support. These shortcomings do not, however, detract from the disc's overall usefulness.

This disc will be especially useful to students doing papers but also to anyone interested in an easy way to learn more about the original documents that have formed the modern democracies over the past millennium. These include the *U.S. Constitution, The English Bill of Rights, Resolution of Independence, Declaration of Independence, Constitution of North Carolina, Virginia or Randolph Plan, Letters of a Federal Farmer, Constitution of New Hampshire, Washington's Farewell Address, Constitution of Delaware, The Magna Carta, Penn's Plan of Union, Constitution of Virginia, Constitution of Maryland, Constitution of Massachusetts, Virginia Statute of Religious Liberty, Objections to the Federal Constitution, Washington's First Inaugural Address, Jefferson's First Inaugural Address, The Monroe Doctrine, Declaration and Resolves of the First Continental Congress, Mayflower Compact, Albany Plan of Union, Virginia Bill of Rights, Report of Constitution, Massachusetts Bill of Rights, Judiciary Act of 1789, Constitution of Connecticut, Constitution of New York, Constitution of Rhode Island, The Petition of Right, Common Sense, Constitution of New Jersey, Articles of Confederation, Constitution of Vermont, Hamilton's Plan of Union, Constitution of South Carolina, Constitution of Pennsylvania, Constitution of Georgia, The Federalist Papers*, and others.

Further information: Edward L. Waldorph, "The Constitution Papers & Word-Cruncher," *CD-ROM Professional*, Nov. 1993.

Name: **Encyclopedia of the JFK Assassination**
Vendor: ZCI Publishing
Cost: $32.95
Hardware requirements: IBM PC and compatibles; Macintosh
Comments: The Encyclopedia of the JFK Assassination is a multimedia tour de force. It is both educational and entertaining for all but the most youthful students or readers. Its interface lets the user approach the subject from a variety of ways. The contents are rich, beginning with 36 minutes of music, voice, and visuals on 18 separate presentations of different aspects of the assassination. It also contains the entire text and images from a variety of pertinent works, providing the tools for anyone to become an amateur detective. Readers may examine the evidence and come to their own conclusions regarding the various problems with the original *Warren Commission Report*, which is also reproduced in its entirety. Other texts included are *The House Select Committee on Assassinations Report*, 20 essays by Jane Rusconi and Bob Harris, *National Security Action Memoranda*, and CIA documents. There are 315 photos including those of locations such as the book depository and of many documents relating to the assassination such as police reports and memos all criss-crossed by hypertext references. The whole intended effect is to stir up the reader's skepticism and interest. While it is possible to become a junior Sherlock Holmes, it is also possible to become lost in a massive maze of hypertext documents and references.

Separate indexes cover all documents, photos, and bibliography of several hundred books, government reports and documents, magazines, and other resources. A glossary is included. If all of this information isn't entertaining and intellectually stimulating enough, a huge, categorized collection of assassination quiz questions will help to evaluate the reader's assassination IQ. Also available in this series are The World Encyclopedia of Assassination, The World Encyclopedia of Organized Crime, and The Encyclopedia of Western Lawmen and Outlaws.

Name:	**FamilySearch 2.18**
Vendor:	GeneSys
Cost:	$2,150
Hardware requirements:	IBM PC and compatibles, 4MB RAM, 566K free conventional memory, 933K expanded memory, DOS 5.0 or QEMM, 30MB free hard-disk space, 400ms minimum access time
Comments:	The Church of Jesus Christ of Latter-day Saints developed the software and data files for FamilySearch. FamilySearch, Ancestral File, International Genealogical Index, and The Family History Catalog are trademarks of The Church of Jesus Christ of Latter-day Saints. The CD-ROM includes International Genealogical Index, Ancestral File, The Family History Library Catalog, the Social Security Death Index, and a Military Index. Each section may be ordered separately. Ancestral File contains more than 15 million records of individuals' names that are linked into family groups and pedigrees. File information may be conveniently downloaded to a patron's disk. Genealogical Index contains more than 200 million records, with some of names in this file going back as far as the Middle Ages. This is a world listing, divided by disc into the following geographic areas: British Isles and Wales; Continental and Southwest Europe; Germany; Mexico; North America (U.S. and Canada); Scandinavia (Norway, Sweden, Denmark, Finland, Iceland); and South and Central America, Africa, Asia, Australia, New Zealand, Pacific Islands, and miscellaneous World. The Family History Library Catalog is a description of the Family History Library in Salt Lake City, Utah, a comprehensive genealogical library that assists many people in doing research. It has extensive census, church, immigration, military, probate, and other vital records from many countries, states, counties, and towns. The Social Security Death Index contains names of some 39.5 million people who became deceased from 1962 through 1988. This index helps people find birth and death dates, last place of residence, where death benefit payments were sent, and an individual's social security number. A help file gives directions on how to order a civil death certificate from a state. The Military Index contains information about 100,000

U.S. military service men and women who died in the Korean conflict and Vietnam War.

Name: **Multimedia U.S. History for Windows**
Vendor: Bureau of Electronic Publishing
Cost: $395
Hardware requirements: IBM PC and compatibles, 640K RAM; Macintosh, 1MB RAM
Comments: More than 1,000 images plus the text of 107 history volumes are in this U.S. history database. Some of the books are *Air Force Combat Units of WWII, American Home Front, At Home in the Smokies, Big Bend: A History of the Last Texas Frontier, Cowpens, Exploring the American West, Ford's Theatre, Glacier Bay, Golden Spike, Iran-Contra Affair, Our Country* (volumes 1–8), *U.S. Budget in Brief,* and *Wright Brothers.* Information may be searched or browsed by word, event, book, picture, or article. Search results may be printed out.

Name: **Multimedia World History for Windows**
Vendor: Bureau of Electronic Publishing
Cost: $795, single user; $2,495, network of 2–9 users; $3,996, network of 10 or more users
Hardware requirements: IBM PC and compatibles, 640K RAM; Macintosh, 1MB RAM, System 6.0.4 or later
Comments: All history buffs will enjoy this enormous collection of works. Approximately 700 books, letters, and articles cover the history of the world from ancient times to modern, making this a convenient and comprehensive source of material for research or pleasure. The contents include the Bible and other religious texts, including the Apocrypha, Koran, and the Egyptian Book of the Dead; texts by many ancient authors, such as Plutarch, Tacitus, Plato, and Xenophon; well-known works of history, such as *Rise and Fall of the Roman Empire*; and hundreds of other works, great and small, that document history, such as *Communist Manifesto,* Luther's *95 Theses,* Darwin's *Descent of Man,* Benjamin Franklin's *Experiments With Electricity, Great Plague at Athens, History of Early Rome, History of Europe during the Middle Ages, History of the Conquest of Mexico, Destruction of Pompeii, The Discovery of Neptune, The First Combat Between Modern Ironclads,* and *The Laying of the Atlantic Cable.*

The database is easy to work with as it is arranged in useful sections. Themes available are economics; religion;

exploration; discovery and travel; people and letters; science; technology and inventions; politics; society; culture and arts; wars, conquests, and battles; and philosophy. There is also a section of overviews and narratives. The user can select from the main menu to go directly to any book title, theme, region, time period, picture, map, illustration, speech, or eyewitness account. More than 700 photos and illustrations give readers a fuller appreciation of the material presented in the texts. Several dozen sound clips of speeches or famous recorded moments (e.g., the moon landing) also provide a rich sense of history.

The most interesting feature is the full-text search. Finding a single event or person can be done in seconds and pinpointed directly to a particular text. In the case of a word search, the specific occurrence is highlighted within the text. In the case of a theme inquiry, for instance, a bibliography of works from which to choose is presented. Text and works can be printed out. Most public and academic libraries will find this CD useful as a resource for anyone who is a serious student of history or for students doing term papers.

Name: **The Revolutionary War: Gallery of Images**
Vendor: National Archives
Cost: $49.95
Hardware requirements: Macintosh, System 6.0.7 or later, 4MB RAM, color monitor
Comments: Smaller than many databases, The Revolutionary War contains 140 public domain and royalty-free historical images from the National Archives arranged in 14 categories. Scenes depict battles, famous historical figures, etc. The program stores images in a HyperCard stack in PICT format. Two resolutions for each image allow for screen display or printing.

Name: **The Story of Civilization**
Vendor: World Library
Cost: $49.95
Hardware requirements: IBM PC and compatibles, 640K RAM, Windows 3.1 or later, 2MB RAM, SoundBlaster or compatible audio card, 16-bit video card, MPC-rated CD-ROM drive with 150K or faster transfer rate
Comments: This program is available in DOS or Windows. Thirty minutes of video documentary about Will and Ariel Durant provides important insight into the authors' lives. The CD includes all eleven volumes of the original massive volume

of world history. Each section contains an audio preface (40 minutes total). Included are 800 original illustrations, maps, and photos. A search may be conducted by word, phrase, or date. Special user features include bookmarks and user notes. Different works may be examined simultaneously on the screen, including up to eight in the Windows version but only two in DOS. User-selected font typefaces and font size and cut-and-paste make it a flexible program. All material may be printed out as partial or whole volumes as well as saved in ASCII files. This is a magnificent and well-organized work that most public libraries will want to own. Its low price makes it an attractive CD to consider loaning out to patrons for home use.

Name:	**Time Table of History: Science and Innovation**
Vendor:	Software Toolworks (MindScape)
Cost:	$59.95
Hardware requirements:	IBM PC and compatibles
Comments:	This is a simple, yet effective, program to assist students of history in learning about the long march of time. As its name implies, a key feature of the program is a time line that stretches from 5000 B.C. to A.D. 1990. The period of human history is divided into eight sections, which are then subdivided into shorter units of time. Events covered in this program are scientific discoveries and innovations, not political history. Many events or innovations make available a relevant picture, though many do not. Nor are there any video clips in this package. Relevant books are recommended at every step by displaying the covers on request. Aside from a time line and time table (two forms of the same thing), there is a highly useful and interactive periodic chart of the elements. Also, to make a point about the vastness of space and astronomy, one routine displays a sequence of slides starting with a building and gradually moving farther into space until reaching a point in space where the earth is completely lost in the vastness of the galaxy. Other products in this series include Time Table of History: Arts and Entertainment and Time Table of History: Business, Politics, and Media.

Name:	**USA Wars: Civil War; USA Wars: Desert Storm; USA Wars: Korea; USA Wars: Vietnam; USA Wars: World War II**
Vendor:	Quanta Press
Cost:	Contact vendor, prices vary per disc

Hardware requirements: IBM PC and compatibles; Macintosh

Comments: This series contains spectacular coverage of America at war. USA Wars: Civil War contains images, text, and music. Statistics, bibliographies, biographies, and many other aspects of the war are presented. USA Wars: Korea contains more than 1,000 photographs of people, equipment, and campaigns of the war. Information includes biographies, statistics, and a glossary. USA Wars: Vietnam contains color and black-and-white photographs of the Vietnam War. Information includes statistics, equipment, missions, etc. Also, the entire Vietnam memorial database is included. USA Wars: World War II contains more than 1,000 photographs. In addition to photos and sounds, USA Wars: Desert Storm also contains 30 minutes of video about the Persian Gulf war.

Home and Automotive Improvement

Automotive and home repair books have long been important to library patrons. Chilton on Disc improves the traditional Chilton volumes by adding new tools and search capabilities. The Home Survival Toolkit will make a do-it-yourselfer a better-informed and more practical worker with clear instructions, suggestions, ideas, and how-to drawings and videos on even the most basic of carpentry and home remodeling routines.

Name:	**Chilton on Disc**
Vendor:	Chilton Professional Automotive
Cost:	$4,995, 7 discs for domestic and imported cars, but much less for renewal or multiple-year subscriptions; $3,500, disc for domestic cars; $3,000, disc for import cars; quarterly updates included in base price
Hardware requirements:	IBM PC and compatibles, Windows 3.1, 8MB RAM, 33MHz clock speed, 10MB hard-disk space
Comments:	Material in this set of discs has been gathered from original equipment manufacturers' (OEM) repair information, *Motor Age Magazine*, training, as well as technician- and field-validated information. The initial release of this product covers the years 1985 to 1992. All information has been organized into the following categories: component locations, customer review, technician safety, "how it works," identification placards, labor times, maintenance intervals, OEM parts, repair procedures, wiring schematics (that may be zoomed in), special tools, training/certification information, diagnostics, technical information, and technical service bulletins. The system employs a relational database. A Windows interface with hyperlinks makes it convenient to

use and search. User notes may be added to the disc content for later reference. A particular auto or truck is identified by make, model, year, and engine. Specific problems may be looked up by identifying a symptom of car trouble. Specific vehicle systems may be identified in the alphabetical index. A topic bar contains 18 different options, including component location, diagnostics, customer review, diagram, labor time, maintenance schedule, manufacturing placard, *Motor Age Magazine* (articles related to the current chosen topic), part numbers and prices, repair procedures, technical information, technical service bulletins, emission control system, technician safety, technician training, and special tools needed for repair.

This wonderful program for locating detailed information for vehicle repairs can be up and running in minutes after inserting the disc. It is, however, the only program I have seen that comes with a "dongle," a key device that plugs into the parallel port of the computer as a security system by the manufacturer. The program will not operate unless this part has been installed.

Name:	**Complete House**
Vendor:	Deep River Publishing
Cost:	$99.95
Hardware requirements:	IBM PC and compatibles, 2MB RAM required, 30MB hard-disk space
Comments:	The Complete House is a computer assisted design (CAD) database intended for use by the nonprofessional exploring the possibilities of home design. It will take the novice from initial conceptualization to finished floor plans. Included are the principles and background for designing a bath, kitchen, or the rest of the home. Beyond the CAD aspects, however, the database contains a range of additional information, including a large bibliography of further reading and an online magazine with photos and sample homes. For anyone unfamiliar with CAD, there is also a library of floor plans that help to speed up the design process. When their plans are completed, users should be ready to talk intelligently with a contractor or architect about what they want. There are no construction plans contained in this data; it is design only.
Further information:	John Blackford, "Spin Doctor," *Computer Shopper*, Apr. 1993, 532.

Name:	**Home Survival Toolkit**
Vendor:	Books That Work
Cost:	$49.95
Hardware requirements:	IBM PC and compatibles, 2MB RAM, 12MB hard-disk space
Comments:	Home Survival Toolkit is a multimedia guide for weekend handy Andys. It uses sound, slides, and animation to illustrate and explain major repair categories of around-the-house work. The interface is easy to use, making it possible to find most anything just by browsing. A search facility that uses Boolean AND, OR, NOT, and NEAR is also included. The guide is divided into units for plumbing, electrical, heating and cooling, floors and walls, windows and doors, painting, roofs, and basements. Outside work includes fences, posts, concrete posts, roofs, walks, and siding. Three Estimators, calculators, will do the math involved in estimating how much paint or concrete will be used in a project or how much material will be needed for attic venting. Additional units cover working with a professional, using rental tools, and tools in general. There are also four excellent reference tools included. A national directory of toll-free numbers gives quick help with hundreds of phone numbers to call when having trouble or needing help with installation of appliances, saunas, or dozens of other areas. A complete guide to stain removal will help users determine how to take oil stains off concrete, pet stains off carpets, and many more; a paint reference will help users select just the right paint for any job, inside or out, concrete, wood, brick, etc. One other guide helps to select and use adhesives for carpeting, masonry, or other materials.
	Sometimes even weekenders have to hire someone to do a big project. This guide provides a sample contract, ways to check for fraud, and general procedures for hiring a contractor. For beginners who are totally unfamiliar with tools, there is a unit devoted to the identification and use of most major tools. The guide also provides additional references at any point. This is one in a series of outstanding electronic do-it-yourself manuals. Others include Design & Build Your Deck, 3D Landscape, and Get Wired.
Further information:	Philip F. H. Rose, "Home Survival Toolkit Gives a Multimedia Lesson in Repairs," *Computer Shopper*, Apr. 1994, 774.

Language

Language software provides a marked improvement over traditional means of learning a foreign tongue. Using pictures and sound, these programs provide a gradual means of learning. Thousands of vocabulary words, parts of speech, and sentences may be practiced as much as desired. Key Translatorpro will automatically translate ASCII text into a foreign language. Languages of the World CD contains dictionaries for 132 languages.

Additional products available:

All-in-One Language Fun (Syracuse Language Systems)

Viva 2000 Language Series (Power Up!)

Name:	**Fundamental Japanese**
Vendor:	Knox Computer Systems
Cost:	$495
Hardware requirements:	Multimedia IBM PC and compatibles, 2MB RAM required
Comments:	This multimedia program teaches the Japanese language with sound, animation, and graphics. Three sections divide the material into manageable slices. The first section teaches Hiragana, Katakana, and basic vocabulary. Section 2 covers numbers, telling time, and calendars. Section 3 covers more-advanced levels with conversations and phrases.

Name:	**Games in Spanish**
Vendor:	Syracuse Language Systems
Cost:	$39.95
Hardware requirements:	IBM PC and compatibles; Macintosh
Comments:	This language game package is appropriate for ages 4 and above. It consists of 27 different games that promote word use and thinking in another language. Games include memory teasers, concentration, jigsaw puzzles, Simon says, numbers, bingo, build a face, dress the baby, telling time, and

others. Games teach more than 200 words. Word building covers people, food, animals, counting, and objects such as those found in a bathroom or at school. The point-and-click Windows interface makes it easy for anyone to use this program because no writing or reading is required—all words are spoken. There is no translation of any words. The user must identify items in the games that correspond with the spoken words. All games are well designed and colorful.

Additional packages in this series include: Introductory Games in French, Introductory Games in German, Introductory Games in Japanese, and Introductory Games in English. A multimedia adventure story rendition of "Goldilocks and the Three Bears" (ages 4 to 12) includes 21 more puzzles and is available in Spanish, English, and French.

Name:	**Key Translatorpro**
Vendor:	Softkey Software Products
Cost:	$39.95
Hardware requirements:	IBM PC and compatibles, Windows 3.x
Comments:	Many people need to translate from English to Spanish or Spanish to English, a time-consuming and difficult task. Key Translatorpro for Windows is an amazing and impressive program that can do most of the work. There are four separate programs in the package: Key Translator Spanish, Key Accents, Key Grammar—Spanish, and Key Bilingual Dictionary. The main program, Key Translator Spanish, supports a number of word processors: WordPerfect 6.0, Ami-Pro, Microsoft Write, Notepad, WordPerfect 5.1, Microsoft Word, Microsoft Works, Clipboard, and WordStar. When working with a document, either part of it or the entire article may be selected for translation. Once completed, the new Spanish document is loaded into the word processor. In the case of WordPerfect, for example, both the original and the new documents are viewed simultaneously in separate windows. The system is a snap to use. It took between one-half and one minute to translate a 350-word paragraph. Since I don't speak Spanish, it would be difficult for me to know how well it did the job. Therefore, I would not advise anyone to rely completely on it without access to a proofreader. But for anyone who can check for computer errors, it should cut translation times dramatically. Key Grammar—Spanish is a grammar checker program. It will check a Spanish-language file for punctuation and spelling errors. Key Accents will add the various accents to words in any Windows application. The

included bilingual dictionary contains 380,000 entries and can be used to fine-tune a translation. All three programs can be loaded into memory and accessed from a floating window. They may also be unloaded from memory at any time. A good manual that provides an overview plus detailed instructions of each component comes with the package.

Name:	**Languages of the World**
Vendor:	NTC Publishing Group
Cost:	$79
Hardware requirements:	IBM PC and compatibles
Comments:	While little information was available for this CD, I included it because it contains dictionaries in 132 languages. It provides extensive coverage for business, science, technology, and data processing terms for 12 languages, including English, French, Chinese, Japanese, Finnish, Swedish, Spanish, and others.

Name:	**Learn to Speak English; Learn to Speak French; Learn to Speak French for Windows 4.0; Learn to Speak Spanish 4.0; Learn to Speak Spanish for Windows 4.0**
Vendor:	HyperGlot Software
Cost:	$179, Learn to Speak French; $99 each, other versions
Hardware requirements:	IBM PC and compatibles, 2MB hard-disk space, multimedia; Macintosh, 2MB RAM required, approximately 9 to 10MB hard-disk space
Comments:	Each program contains between 30 and 36 lessons. They deal with a possible situation that a newcomer to another country would encounter: renting an apartment, emergencies, social events, etc. Students are introduced to more than 1,000 vocabulary words.

Name:	**Rosetta Stone; Rosetta Stone for Windows**
Vendor:	Fairfield Language Technologies
Cost:	$395; demo disk available with 12 chapters in each of 5 languages with user's guide, $9.95
Hardware requirements:	386 or later multimedia IBM PC and compatibles, 4MB RAM, Windows 3.x; Macintosh, 2MB RAM for System 6, 4MB RAM for System 7
Comments:	Rosetta Stone is an instructional language program that contains 92 chapters grouped into 8 units. This program is available in English, Spanish, German, French, and Russian. The disc consists of thousands of pictures used in different ways to teach each language. Beginning instructional units

show four pictures at one time. The program then pronounces a word or phrase. The user picks one of the pictures as the word's meaning. Study becomes progressively more challenging. The full Rosetta Stone is designed to be a language course or to accompany a course of instruction in the first two years at the university level or three years at the high school level. Ten separate Run Modes can be used for each chapter. These present information in different ways: voice and text, voice only, text only, etc. Dictation Mode presents students with four pictures, each with a speaker button in the corner. When a speaker button is pressed a text-entry window appears into which the student types the text for the phrase. Another feature of this program is the Browser's Reference Tools. With this option, users may look up specific information for practice. Within this mode the Voice Record/Playback option will allow users to record their own pronunciation, which may be compared with that of the program.

Name:	**Think and Talk; Think and Talk for Windows**
Vendor:	HyperGlot Software
Cost:	$199 each (includes 1 software CD and 6 to 8 audio CDs, depending on language)
Hardware requirements:	IBM PC and compatibles, 2MB RAM, 30MB hard-disk storage, Windows 3.x, sound card; Macintosh, System 7, 2MB RAM, sound card
Comments:	This language learning program is available in French, German, Italian, and Spanish. It employs multimedia elements to help users master 1,000 vocabulary words in everyday situations. Fifty lessons are included. An online dictionary includes more than 10,000 words. The system is completely interactive, allowing users to repeat material as many times as desired.
Further information:	John Blackford, "CD-ROM," *Computer Shopper*, May 1993, 531.
	Rubin Rabinovitz, "Reference Works on CD-ROM," *PC Magazine*, Dec. 22, 1992, 347.

Name:	**TriplePlay Plus! Spanish**
Vendor:	Syracuse Language Systems
Cost:	$99.95
Hardware requirements:	IBM PC and compatibles; Macintosh
Comments:	The TriplePlay Plus! multimedia language-skills program is appropriate for ages 9 through adult. It is available in

Spanish, French, German, Japanese, and English. Users will be exposed to more than 1,000 vocabulary words and phrases used in a variety of contexts. Users begin by choosing a subject area of interest: food, numbers, home and office, places and transportation, people and clothing, or activities. Three levels of games correspond to three levels of language usage that may be chosen. At every level, it is possible to have the computer repeat the word or phrase as often as desired. Level I games include basic vocabulary in the games of bingo, concentration, memory mania, square off, match up, city map, jigsaw puzzle, sketch artist, world map, and family tree. Level II games are slightly more involved. They include descriptions of objects that must be matched instead of just simple repetition. Level III games involve actual conversations at places such as a cafe, restaurant, market, or baseball game; or conversations when looking for an apartment, visiting a friend, shopping, playing tennis, going on vacation, and other activities. An additional feature of this program is Automatic Speech Recognition, which involves using a microphone (included) for user's input. This speech may then be played back for comparison with the computer-generated language. Also available from Syracuse Language Systems is TriplePlay Plus! Hebrew.

Law

The average person who has no legal experience can produce a will and other legal forms using CD products. However, since laws change frequently, be sure to obtain the latest versions of the CDs in this section. Complete Home and Office Legal Guide CD for DOS is a legal guide for the home user. It is simple and easy to use, providing a multitude of fill-in-the-blank forms. It can be used to make out a will, a power of attorney, etc. Lawyers, paralegals, and others will find assistance when seeking help on complex legal questions with West CD Libraries. They provide a massive amount of data for the researcher or legal professional. Complete directories for most state laws and courts and restatements of laws are available.

Additional product available:

LawDesk (Lawyers Cooperative Publishing)

Name:	**Complete Home and Office Legal Guide CD for DOS**
Vendor:	Chestnut Software
Cost:	$29.95
Hardware requirements:	IBM PC and compatibles
Comments:	This outstanding tool contains not only many legal references but fill-in-the-blank legal forms ready for patrons to use. The body of legal statutes and information is quite impressive and will be useful to many patrons. It includes selected Supreme Court cases from 1989 to May 1994 (as of this edition of the disc), uniform acts (includes uniform commercial, corporate, model penal, and model probate codes, among others), and federal statutes and regulations (copyright and patent codes, bankruptcy code, Internal Revenue code, Americans with Disabilities Act, computer-related regulations, ham radio regulations, enacted state computer crimes laws, ethical and professional rules, North American Free Trade Agreement, military justice materials and legal courses, the Immigration

Act, and general statutes). A section of tutorials (basically a series of essays) contains much useful information on issues such as community property rights, federal estate tax law, liability of parents for child's wrongful acts, etc. In addition to explanations of certain legal issues, some of the essays contain name and address files (e.g., Attorneys General of the fifty states).

Sample legal forms with fill-in-the-blank counterparts cover a wide array of everyday matters: real estate, personal and family, corporate, lending and borrowing, partnerships, torts and personal injury, sales of personal property, and service and professional agreements. There are many types of lease forms, wills, health care, powers of attorney, etc. Forms may be edited and then printed out.

The disc is updated and reissued every six months and is available by subscription. Even if the forms are not used, this disc is a treasure trove of interesting information. The computer crime laws for each state make for fascinating and interesting browsing.

Name:	**West CD-ROM Libraries**
Vendor:	West Publishing
Cost:	Contact vendor
Hardware requirements:	IBM PC and compatibles, 400K available RAM, DOS 3.3 or later, 5MB hard-disk space
Comments:	West publishes five different groups of CD-ROMs related to law: Federal Libraries, State Specific Libraries, Topical Libraries, Practice Libraries, and restatements of the law. The Federal Libraries group contains CDs for the *Supreme Court Reporter*, the *Federal Reporter*, the *Federal Rules Decisions*, *Federal Supplement*, *United States Code Annotated*, *Federal Circuit Reporter*, *Second Circuit Reporter*, *Federal District Court Reporter*, and the *Federal District Court Reporter—District of Columbia*. Topical Libraries include a CD collection on bankruptcy, court martial reports, federal securities library, Federal Practice and Procedures, Government Contracts Library, military justice library, and West's Social Security Library. The Practice Libraries contain the following informational topics: Civil Appeals and Writs, Civil Procedure before Trial, Civil Trial and Evidence, Corporations, Enforcing Judgments and Debts, Family Law, Federal Civil Procedure before Trial, Landlord-Tenant, Law Practice Management, Personal Injury, and Probate. Separate restatement of the law CD-ROM libraries are available for

agency, conflict of laws, contracts, Foreign Relations Law of the United States, Judgments, Property, Restitution, Security, Torts, and Trusts.

West's CD-ROMs use Premise Research Software 2.1 for DOS as a search engine. Premise provides excellent search capability. Case law may be searched by citation, title, or by issue. A specific case may be retrieved by citation or title. A search by issue may be by word, topic, key number, or field. A field search may be restricted by any field: citation, title, synopsis, topic, headnote, digest, court, date, judge, attorney, or text. Premise may also be used to retrieve references to case law or references to statutes. Statutes and rules may be searched. Wild cards (*, !) can be used as well as proximity searching. Books in the database and search results may be browsed or scanned. Information from a search may be downloaded to a file or printed out.

Library

Several outstanding programs described in this section may provide help for the internal functioning of the library. BiblioFile Public Access Catalogs is a complete CD-ROM public access catalog created from the library's records. Circulation systems are also available. Electronic Dewey is the Dewey decimal system on CD-ROM, which can be searched with much greater ease than the paper edition.

Available soon is R.A.L.P.H. (Retriever, Advisor, Library Patron Helper) from Gale Research. The product is designed to automate simple ready-reference questions without staff intervention. Three separate products will be available: R.A.L.P.H. Recommends, R.A.L.P.H.'s Ready Reference, and R.A.L.P.H.'s Special File. R.A.L.P.H. Recommends will provide suggestions for periodicals, CD-ROMs, movies, videos, or books from a database of more than 100,000 items. The material may be searched by name, title, Library of Congress Subject Headings, genre, media type, etc. R.A.L.P.H.'s Ready Reference will include a collection of answers to more than 5,000 questions, including trivia, sports, and all major subject areas, taken from ready reference files from libraries. Information may be searched by keyword, broad subject, specific topic, or even Boolean logic. R.A.L.P.H.'s Special File will give instant access to more than 500 pamphlets, documents, and other resources.

Additional product available:

Sneak Previews Plus (Follett Software)

Name:	**Alliance Plus**
Vendor:	Follett Software
Cost:	$295, single-site license; $1,395, district-site license
Hardware requirements:	IBM PC and compatibles, 640K RAM, 20MB hard-disk storage
Comments:	Alliance Plus is a MARC record database intended for school libraries for shelf list creation and retrospective conversion. Media types include book, AV, and serials from 1901 to the present. Since the program can interface with

the vendor's Circulation Plus and Circulation/Catalog Plus, MARC records can be saved directly into these packages. MARC records contain annotations, review sources, reading and interest levels, and subject headings (LC, LC Children's, and Sears). The menu-driven system provides bibliographic searching by LCCN, ISBN, title, author, subject, and series. Title, author, subject, and series searches may be truncated. Several special features make this an outstanding tool for schools. For instance, it will help with curriculum development. Collection development is aided by subject series and author being compared with the existing collection. An interface with the CardMaster Plus module gives access to card catalog and label production.

Name:	**BiblioFile Acquisitions**
Vendor:	Library
Cost:	$2,450
Hardware requirements:	IBM PC and compatibles, 640K RAM required, 20MB hard-disk storage
Comments:	BiblioFile Acquisitions is a full-service system for materials purchase decision making, ordering, tracking, budgeting, and reports. A special Consideration File allows items to be stored prior to order. Item File maintains one record for each item in the Consideration File. Items may then be ranked. The system will create requisitions and tentative purchase orders. Once orders have been placed, the system continues to track all materials, making it easy to check on the status of an item at any given time. Searches may be conducted by title, author, LCCN, subject, and vendor. Fund analysis and reports may be generated by the program account or department. The database comes with information for 20,000 publishers. Order forms may be created as traditional 3-by-5-inch multipart cards.

Name:	**BiblioFile Cataloging**
Vendor:	Library
Cost:	$2,250, includes software, LC MARC English-language database with latest update, and user documentation; $1,250, for software only, databases extra
Hardware requirements:	IBM PC and compatibles, 640K RAM required, 20MB hard-disk storage
Comments:	This database is used for locating cataloging information by LC card number, ISBN, ISSN, and author or title. Publications are identified by year, year range, number of

pages, or type of work. Information may be copied to a local floppy disk or hard drive and added to the local database. The system includes full MARC records, free CD mastering of local holdings, local printing of cards in filing sequence, local printing of spine and pocket labels, records export in MARC II communications format and to other automation systems, and more. Annual subscriptions are available for the following databases: LC MARC English (weekly, monthly, quarterly, annually), LC MARC Foreign (quarterly), Search Cataloging (quarterly), MedMARC (quarterly), Contributed Cataloging (school and public quarterly), Contributed Cataloging (research and academic quarterly), Canadian MARC (quarterly), Docufile (quarterly), A/V Access (monthly or quarterly), and NICEM A-V MARC (quarterly). Prices vary.

Name:	**BiblioFile Circulation**
Vendor:	Library
Cost:	$4,000 and up
Hardware requirements:	IBM PC and compatibles, 1MB RAM required, 100MB hard-disk storage
Comments:	This circulation system tracks items from checkout using bar code ID numbers or keyboard to final checkin and follow-up. All records are based on MARC format. Statistical information is maintained for collection development. A search may be made by patron name or ID number. Checkout periods, types of materials, fines, patron types, overdues, and grace periods may all be configured for the local situation. Security levels are available for different personnel. The system will print a variety of reports, notices, date-due slips, and receipts. A backup system for downtime is also provided. New patrons may be added "on-the-fly." The system will also display the shelf status of any item.

Name:	**BiblioFile Public Access Catalogs**
Vendor:	Library
Cost:	$500, software only; monthly, bimonthly, quarterly, biannual, or annual updates
Hardware requirements:	IBM PC and compatibles, 640K RAM required, 40MB hard-disk storage
Comments:	This public access catalog has a variety of features suitable for small libraries, especially school libraries. Some of the

features include optional spoken help messages, maps of the library, display of a community events calendar, a suggestion box for patron comments, an Intelligent Catalog User Manual online, and much more. Patrons may access the collection using the Find Anything, View Catalog, or Browse Topics functions. A search may be made by keyword, author, title, subject, call number classification, LCCN, ISBN, and other numbers. Information may also be looked up by language or date range. Context-sensitive help screens assist patrons when needed and may be configured according to local library needs. Boolean logic, truncation, built-in cross references, and even on-screen maps of the library can be created. Retrieved records may be displayed by full MARC record or by full or brief labeled display or full card display. A scoping feature can be employed to limit results to an individual library, by type of library, by library system, or by geographic region. Searches are automatically logged to a statistical database.

Name:	**Bibliographic Index**
Vendor:	H. W. Wilson
Cost:	$1,095
Hardware requirements:	IBM PC and compatibles, 640K RAM, 3MB free hard-disk space, DOS 3.1 or later, Hayes compatible modem optional
Comments:	The Bibliographic Index database provides librarians and teachers with important tools to assist in collection development and research and to keep abreast of professional literature. Citations are from bibliographies in books, pamphlets, and periodicals in Wilson indexes or received at research libraries with 50 or more entries in a bibliography. Users can distinguish between annotated and unannotated bibliographies. Coverage is from November 1984 to the present. Three search levels make it easy for beginners as well as more-advanced researchers to effectively search. A single-subject search mode (browse) will locate authors by searching on the author's name or the title of work. A command-language search can also be implemented. This system, the same one used by Wilsonline, supports nested Boolean logic, proximity searching, free-text and controlled-vocabulary searching, truncation, ranging, multifile searching, saving of data and of search, and more. In addition, subscribers to any of Wilson's CD-ROM services also have unlimited online access time to the latest information when needed.

Name:	**Electronic Dewey**
Vendor:	OCLC Forest Press
Cost:	$400; demo disk, free; $2,100, complete Dewey 486SX/25 work station with Electronic Dewey database and software
Hardware requirements:	IBM PC and compatibles
Comments:	Electronic Dewey contains full Dewey Decimal Classification (DDC) 20 schedules, tables, manual, relative index, and all published updates. It operates within a windowed environment. Unlike the print version, the CD-ROM Dewey contains frequently used LC subject headings that are associated with a class number. These have been taken from LC-cataloged bibliographic records. It lists the number of bibliographic subject headings and the percentage of use by the top five. A variety of techniques are offered for finding appropriate Dewey numbers. These include keyword searching for numbers, words in captions, notes, and the Relative Index. Index browsing for terms and phrases can also be performed. Boolean operations also provide flexibility. Full-text browsing of the DDC schedules is allowed. A notepad is integrated into the system for recording and building class numbers. Segmentation marks help to identify abridged numbers, help classifiers make decisions about length, and can be used by educators to teach classification.

Name:	**LaserQuest CD-ROM Cataloging System; LaserGuide CD-ROM Public Catalog**
Vendor:	SWL
Cost:	$4,300, first year; $2,600, each additional year; monthly supplements
Hardware requirements:	IBM PC and compatibles; 512K RAM required
Comments:	The LaserQuest Cataloging System contains more than 8 million MARC records on 6 discs to aid libraries with retrospective conversion and current cataloging. The subscription includes a bimonthly cumulative supplement disc. The records are from the Library of Congress, the National Library of Canada, and contributions from LaserQuest cataloging system user for more than 26 years, including 2 million records pre-1968. When a record has been found, users may print out one main entry card, a full set of cards, or a full set plus an additional main entry card to use as a shelf list card. Cards may be sorted by author, title, subject, or call number. This system will also print cards and labels of different sizes and shapes, including large-print labels. A search may be conducted by title or number.

LaserGuide CD-ROM Public Catalog is a CD-ROM-based system for accessing library records. It includes complete indexing of all words; menu-driven windows for conducting Boolean searches with AND, OR, and NOT; and field-limiting parameters for narrowing a search to specified authors, pagination, and date ranges.

Name:	**Precision One Integrated System Version 1.3**
Vendor:	Brodart Automation
Cost:	Inquire
Hardware requirements:	IBM PC and compatibles, 640K RAM
Comments:	Precision One is a complete automated library system that includes public access, technical services, and circulation control. All work stations in this system are linked together in a local area network for greater integration. The Precision One Integrated Public Access Catalog is Le Pac. Le Pac offers Browse Access to search authors, titles, or subjects, and keyword searching of author, title, or subject fields. Another feature, called Anyword, allows the search of any MARC fields that were selected by the library when the catalog was created, such as contents notes, format type, and language as well as author, title, and subject fields. Boolean logic terms NOT, AND, and OR as well as wild cards (*, ?) are supported. Precision One Technical Services module includes three ways to edit the bibliographic record for local use and prints spine and pocket labels. Precision One Integrated Circulation Control module is a complete checkin, checkout, reserve, fines, and overdue system.

Name:	**U.S. Library of Congress CD-ROM: Cataloger's Desktop; CDMARC Bibliographic—Overseas Acquisitions Subset; The Music Catalog on CD-ROM; CDMARC Bibliographic—Spanish/Portuguese Only Subset; CDMARC Names; CDMARC Subjects; CDMARC Bibliographic; CDMARC Serials**
Vendor:	Library of Congress
Cost:	Contact vendor
Hardware requirements:	IBM PC and compatibles, 5MB free hard-disk space, 530K free RAM
Comments:	Eight products provide a wide range of access to information of the Library of Congress. Cataloger's Desktop contains many cataloging publications, including *Library of Congress Rule Interpretations, USMARC Format for Authority Data*, and others. CDMARC Bibliographic—Overseas Acquisi-

tions Subset includes 500,000 bibliographic records for "rare and hard-to-get" materials. CDMARC Bibliographic—Spanish/Portuguese Only Subset includes some 337,000 USMARC records of particular use to librarians in Spain, Portugal, Spanish America, Brazil, and Portuguese-speaking Africa or anyone in the U.S. who serves Spanish- or Portuguese-speaking patrons. The Music Catalog on CD-ROM contains more than 268,000 bibliographic records from the Library of Congress collection of books, scores, and sound recordings. CDMARC Names contains more than 3,444,000 personal and corporate names plus uniform titles. CDMARC Subjects contains more than 215,000 LC-authorized subject headings. CDMARC Bibliographic has more than 5,000,000 bibliographic records. CDMARC Serials, a subset of CDMARC Bibliographic, includes more than 700,000 serials records.

Literature

Literature on CD-ROM may be divided into two convenient categories: CDs that contain actual works of literature and those that contain references and information about literature. Project Gutenberg plans to make ten thousand useful books available on one or several CDs over the next few years for only a cent or so per book. One CD, Great Literature Plus for Windows, contains 1,896 separate works plus sound and pictures. Literature products are excellent for research, but their feasibility in replacing the printed book is yet to be determined. The drawbacks are obvious. Sometimes CDs cost more than the print version, though this is not usually the case (and in the case of thousands of volumes on a single disc, the cost per individual work is slight). The major drawback is that literature on a disc requires the use of a computer, which may cost several thousand dollars; furthermore, the need for hardware limits the use of a collection of books on a CD-ROM to work stations. The old complaint that you can't curl up with a computer to read is certainly true. Some people also complain of eye strain when reading a computer screen for long periods. Nevertheless, many patrons as well as librarians will find the CD-ROM version of literature useful.

Reference CDs for research include many fine products for seeking critical reviews, author biographies, poems, plots, etc. Works such as Cumulative Book Index and Book Review Digest are databases of basic bibliographic information such as price, author, and publisher. Contemporary Authors on CD and Scribner's Writers Series on CD-ROM provide excellent sources of author information and biographical and literary notes. When translated to disc these products increase in usefulness because CD-ROM provides a convenient way to search for information quickly and efficiently. Critical notes on 300 of the most important writers in history may be found by using the DISCovering Authors series.

Columbia Granger's World of Poetry is a collection of books on disc. A quick and efficient search may be made for any poem by word, title, or Boolean logic. The complete works of William Shakespeare are contained on a single disc, not only once but twice, in the Queen's English and in American English.

Students will appreciate Monarch Notes for Windows, which contains a collection of more than 200 of the ever-popular print editions.

The most expensive of the reference CD-ROMs is English Verse Drama: The Full-Text Database, at $16,000.

Additional products available:

Canterbury Tales (BookWorm)*

Complete Dickens on CD-ROM (Bureau of Electronic Publishing)

Complete Twain on CD-ROM (Bureau of Electronic Publishing)

Great Poetry Classics (World Library)

Hamlet (BookWorm)*

Little Women (BookWorm)*

Masterplots II (EBSCO Publishing)

Masterplots Definitive Revised Edition (EBSCO Publishing)

Moby Dick (BookWorm)*

Poem Finder (Roth Publishing)

Turn of the Screw and Other Works (BookWorm)*

World Literary Heritage (Softbit)

World's Best Poetry on CD (Roth Publishing)

Name:	**Book Review Digest**
Vendor:	H. W. Wilson
Cost:	$1,095
Hardware requirements:	IBM PC and compatibles, 640K RAM, 3MB free hard-disk space, DOS 3.1 or later, Hayes compatible modem optional
Comments:	Book Review Digest contains excerpts from and citations to reviews of books, both adult and juvenile, fiction and nonfiction, from January 1983. Each year this tool covers reviews of some 6,500 English-language books taken from 90 American, British, and Canadian periodicals. Each citation contains author, title, paging, price, publication year, publisher, Dewey decimal classification, search subject headings, ISBN, LC number, descriptive note, age or grade level, review excerpts and citations, reviewer's name, and word count. Three search levels make it easy for beginners and advanced researchers to search effectively. A single-subject search mode (browse) will locate authors by searching on author's name or title of a work. Multiple-subject search using Wilsearch mode can be used to search for authors by field: genre, nationality, language, gender, century/period, birthday, and keyword. A command-language search can

---

* Note: All BookWorm titles require the Student Reader Kit in order to run.

also be implemented. This system, the same one used by Wilsonline, supports nested Boolean logic, proximity searching, free-text and controlled-vocabulary searching, truncation, ranging, multifile searching, saving of search data, and more. In addition, subscribers to any of Wilson's CD-ROM services also have unlimited online access time to the latest information when needed.

Name:	**Columbia Granger's World of Poetry**
Vendor:	Columbia University Press
Cost:	$699
Hardware requirements:	IBM PC and compatibles, 640K RAM
Comments:	Material for this CD is obtained from *Granger's Index to Poetry*, 8th Edition; *Columbia Granger's Index to Poetry*, 9th Edition; *Columbia Granger's Guide to Poetry Anthologies*, and *Columbia Granger's Dictionary of Poetry Quotations*. The product includes more than 3,000 quotations from poems; 8,500 complete classic poems; and 4,000 subjects. Anthology locations are given for 90,000 poems by 15,000 poets, and 400 recent anthologies of poems are described. Search results may be written to disk or printed as hardcopy. A poem may be found by author, title/first line, subject, or words within poems. Browsing may be done by moving up or down through field lists. A proximity search can look for words within a poem in a specific order, for example, within five words of each other. Anthologies may be searched for by title list, editor list (alphabetical by last name), subject, or a merger of these three lists. Boolean AND, OR, or NOT may be used to enhance a search.

Name:	**The Complete Works of William Shakespeare**
Vendor:	CMC ReSearch
Cost:	$49
Hardware requirements:	IBM PC and compatibles
Comments:	As the title implies, this disc contains the complete works of Shakespeare in both American English and the Queen's English and is based on public domain versions. Each work has been reformatted with rewrapped text for the computer screen; therefore, line numbers of plays may differ from hardcopy versions. Material may be accessed in several ways. The most direct is from the main menu, which provides an act-by-act and scene-by-scene access. The probable date when each piece was written is included at the beginning of each work. Also, the *Dramatis Personae* lists every speaking

part. A handy feature lets the reader list the *Dramatis* at any time by pressing the F9 function key. Stage directions are clearly visible and are separated from the dialogue. Original directions are in braces; editor's directions are in brackets. Specific access to material may be achieved by using up to seven search fields. Wild cards may be used for both single letters or truncation, and a proximity search is also allowed. Browsing through a wheel index can be done with hotkeys for words, authors, subjects, and titles.

Name:	**Contemporary Authors on CD**
Vendor:	Gale Research
Cost:	$3,650 (plus $650 for yearly updates), annual purchase stand-alone; $4,500 for 2–8 users at a single site (plus $995 for year updates); $795, annual lease
Hardware requirements:	IBM PC and compatibles; Macintosh
Comments:	Contemporary Authors on CD contains information on more than 100,000 writers. Search is permitted by fields: author name, title, subject/genre, personal data on authors (birth year, birth place, death year, nationality, education, politics, religion, addresses, career, military service, memberships, honors/awards, interests, and media adaptations), or advanced-search mode (full text). Full-text mode will permit search by Boolean logic using AND, OR, NOT, or NEAR (proximity search of words within 30 characters of each other). Search results may be displayed or printed out.

Name:	**Cumulative Book Index**
Vendor:	H. W. Wilson
Cost:	$1,295
Hardware requirements:	IBM PC and compatibles, 640K RAM, 3MB free hard-disk space, DOS 3.1 or later, Hayes compatible modem optional
Comments:	The Cumulative Book Index database contains information about English-language books worldwide from January 1982 with quarterly updates. Information follows AACR2 guidelines for descriptive cataloging and the *Library of Congress Subject Headings*. Entries contain author or editor's full name, title, subtitle, illustrator, translator, compiler, edition, series note, size if other than standard, pagination, illustrations, binding if other than cloth, price, publication date, publisher, distributor, ISBN, ISSN, and LC control number. Cataloging information is based on MARC records or on the examination of the actual book. Three search levels make it easy for both beginners and advanced researchers

to search. A single-subject search mode (browse) will locate authors by searching on author's name or title of a work. Multiple-subject search using Wilsearch mode can be used to search for authors by field: genre, nationality, language, gender, century/period, birthday, and keyword. A command-language search can also be implemented. This system, the same one used by Wilsonline, supports nested Boolean logic, proximity searching, free-text and controlled-vocabulary searching, truncation, ranging, multifile searching, saving of search data, and more. In addition, subscribers to any of Wilson's CD-ROM services also have unlimited online access time to the service for the latest information when needed.

Name:	**DISCovering Authors; DISCovering Authors: British Edition; DISCovering Authors: Canadian Edition**
Vendor:	Gale Research
Cost:	$500
Hardware requirements:	IBM PC and compatibles; Macintosh
Comments:	DISCovering Authors contains biographical and critical information on 300 most-studied authors from ancient times to the present. Many entries are taken from other Gale Research works such as *Contemporary Authors*, *Contemporary Literary Criticism*, *Twentieth-Century Literary Criticism*, and others. Some are original entries. Each author is represented by comments from five to seven literary critics, with differing opinions about the merit and quality of work. Information may be accessed by author name, title, subject, birth date, other personal data, or through a full-text search. The main menu allows immediate access to a bibliography of writings, media adaptations, and sources for further reading. Specific material may be marked to save or print. Gale Research also publishes DISCovering Authors: Canadian Edition and DISCovering Authors: British Edition.

Name:	**English Verse Drama: The Full-Text Database**
Vendor:	Chadwyck-Healey
Cost:	$16,000
Hardware requirements:	IBM PC and compatibles, 386 or later, 25 MHz, 4MB RAM, 5MB hard-disk space, Windows 3.1 or later (to avoid slow searches the publisher recommends a 486 at 33 MHz, 8MB RAM, and a CD of 200ms access time for peak performance), floppy disk drive (the database comes on two CDs plus floppies with search software)

Comments: Most suited for academic and large public libraries, this database provides a massive collection of plays in verse by British writers. More than 1,500 works by approximately 450 authors and some 230 anonymous works are included. These range in time from the late thirteenth century to the end of the nineteenth century. Based on the *New Cambridge Bibliography of English Literature*, it includes masques, short dramatic pieces written in verse, selected translations, works written for children, and even adaptations. Some of the authors included are John Skelton, John Redford, John Bale, John Heywood, Thomas Kyd, William Shakespeare, Sir William Alexander, Ben Jonson, Tobias Smollett, and Aphra.

A search may be conducted on any word or phrase in the text or title or may be restricted by field: author(s), a play, type (e.g., comedy), period, speaker, stage directions, songs, notes, epigraphs, or even commendatory poems. A search may also be conducted on the date of first performance or bibliographical information. Boolean operators, wild cards, and truncation may be employed to enhance a search. Browsing texts page-by-page, as if they were printed books, is also possible. A table of contents lists all the verse dramas. Separate lists of authors, titles, speakers, periods, genres, types of verse dramas, and a complete index of all words in the texts are also available. Search results are viewed in the context of the complete work in which they are found. Texts viewed on the screen look much like book texts. A summary or part or full text may be printed or saved as ASCII text for word processing.

Name: **Gale's Literary Index CD-ROM**
Vendor: Gale Research
Cost: $295 subscription, incudes mid-year update
Hardware requirements: IBM PC and compatibles
Comments: This DOS-based program provides a complete index to all 32 Gale Research literary series, including access to 110,000 author names and 120,000 titles. There are 675 Gale volumes represented, including *Authors and Artists for Young Adults, Authors in the News, Bestsellers, Black Literature Criticism, Black Writers, Children's Literature Review, Classical and Medieval Literature Criticism, Contemporary Authors, Drama Criticism, Hispanic Writers, Literature Criticism from 1400 to 1800, Poetry Criticism, Short Story Criticism*, and many others. Something about

the author is also included. A search may be conducted from the main menu using author name, title, birth/death years, nationality, or Gale series. The author-name field contains a name wheel that includes variant names and pseudonyms. Local titles in the series may be marked, and a note may be included on each title to indicate location in the collection.

Name:	**Great Literature Plus for Windows**
Vendor:	Bureau of Electronic Publishing
Cost:	$64.95
Hardware requirements:	IBM PC and compatibles, 25 MHz or later, MPC1 compatible, 2MB RAM minimum (4MB preferred), DOS 3.3 or later, VGA card
Comments:	This CD contains 1,896 great works selected from ancient and modern historically significant writings (all in full text), plus 449 high-resolution pictures and illustrations (some in color), 65 spoken excerpts of speeches, and 29 relevant and interesting musical excerpts from great composers. Text, graphics, and sound are combined throughout, making it a good example of a multimedia product. A study of history can be made by using the hypertext links to jump from one subject or time period to another. In additon to the text, multimedia elements provide music, narrations, art, and animations. The animations (e.g., Alice chasing the rabbit in *Alice in Wonderland*) make the disc excellent for use with younger readers. The great works of literature make an excellent small home library. They include Shakespeare (70 plays and sonnets), Charles Darwin, Martin Luther, John Milton, Machiavelli, Washington, Voltaire, Wordsworth, Browning, Emerson, Lincoln, Marcus Aurelius, Adam Smith, Jonathan Swift, Tacitus, Tennyson, Thoreau, Byron, Hamilton, Hippocrates, Oliver Holmes, Homer, David Hume, Columbus, and many more. There are also excellent minibiographies with hypertext links to each author's works.

Installation of the program is simple. This disc may be run directly from the CD, but it requires a minimum of hard-disk space if used from a hard drive in a menu program. Using the program is very simple. The main menu provides access to search routines, browsing, contents, and change/quit. Searching and browsing can use phrases, wild cards (*, ?), proximity searches, and the search terms AND, OR, NOT, OFF, and NEAR. Up to seven search terms may be used at one time. Search and browse can be used for words, authors, titles, and subjects. Hints and options are given online. This is an outstanding literary tool for high school or college students or for anyone interested in reading and studying great literature.

Name:	**Greatest Books Collection; Library of the Future**
Vendor:	World Library
Cost:	$49.95, 150 titles; $79.95, 450 titles; $99.95, 950 titles; $149.95, 1,750 titles
Hardware requirements:	IBM PC and compatibles
Comments:	Four different renditions are available, each covering more literature than the last. The first edition is called Greatest Books Collection and covers 150 titles, which include more than 600 individual pieces of literature. The lion's share of the disc contains all the works of Shakespeare and the works of Sir Arthur Conan Doyle. In addition, there are a few religious documents (the Bible, Egyptian Book of the Dead, etc.); historical documents (*U.S. Constitution, Articles of Confederation*, the *Gettysburg Address*, etc.), poems, and others. The other editions are expanded versions of the same. The Library of the Future contains 450 titles. The second edition of The Library of the Future (950 titles) adds material by Tolstoy, Twain, Hawthorne, Emerson, and many more. The third edition contains 1,750 titles from a full 100 authors, including Steinbeck, Shaw, and Freud. This edition is also markedly different from the others in that it contains multimedia elements; video clips and illustrations complement the text. Font style and size may be changed as desired. Even though this series has a DOS interface (at least in the first edition that I examined), it does make use of a mouse for menu selection. A search may be made by title, authors, words, or by using a strategy, that is, by choosing fields: countries, categories (subjects), eras, ages, regions (continents), or even specific years or centuries. Within the strategy section AND and OR may be selected for use. Wild cards for groups of letters or words (*) or individual letters (?) may be used. Other search features include screen proximity search, exact-phrase search, and word proximity search. For example, a search for the word "conquered" will return twenty works. When viewing each work, the searched-for word is highlighted. The interface makes it an easy database to use. This is an outstanding value for its low cost.

Name: **Junior DISCovering Authors**
Vendor: Gale Research
Cost: $325
Hardware requirements: IBM PC and compatibles; Macintosh
Comments: Junior Discovering authors provides access to 300 most-often-read literary figures for children and young adults, including Joan Aiken, Lloyd Alexander, Judy Blume, Scott Corbett, Douglas Hill, C. S. Lewis, Anne McCaffrey, Stephen Roos, Gary Soto, and Jane Yolen. Each author entry contains a 1,200- to 1,300-word biographical essay; a portrait; and plot summaries of major and recent works, including information on subjects, themes, characters, time periods and locales; and descriptions and lists of similar books. Lists of movies, plays, and AV adaptations of the author's works are included. It also provides a bibliography of further readings and a list of each author's writings. A menu search can be performed by author name, title, subject term/character, or personal data on authors. An advanced-search mode will search the full text of entries.

Name: **Monarch Notes for Windows**
Vendor: Bureau of Electronic Publishing
Cost: $79.95
Hardware requirements: IBM PC and compatibles; Macintosh (both versions on same disc)
Comments: For the busy person Monarch Notes provides a convenient and fast way to glean the most-important information from a classic work. This CD-ROM edition contains all 200+ guides. In addition, it contains 650 color and black-and-white pictures and illustrations and 226 spoken excerpts. Included are works by Edward Albee, Aristotle, Emily Brontë, Joseph Conrad, William Faulkner, Sigmund Freud, Robert Frost, William Golding, Ernest Hemingway, Henry James, Herman Melville, George Orwell, Edgar Allan Poe, Alexander Pope, Sir Walter Scott, John Steinbeck, Mark Twain, Walt Whitman, Oscar Wilde, William Wordsworth, and many others. A search may be conducted by title, word, phrase, or author. Historical perspective, literary styles, critical commentary, and suggested essay questions accompany each unit.

Further information: Alfred Poor, "Searching for the Right Words," *Computer Shopper*, Jan. 1995, 808.

Name:	**Project Gutenberg**
Vendor:	Walnut Creek CDROM
Cost:	$24.95, semiannual basis per disc; $39.95, individually per disc
Hardware requirements:	IBM PC and compatibles
Comments:	Project Gutenberg is a fascinating effort to reduce the most-significant works in the English language to CD-ROM format. The publisher hopes to have 10,000 volumes on CD-ROM by the year 2001, at a cost of 1 cent per book. It is a semiannual subscription service; all files cumulate with each new issue. There are also selected papers from the International Philadelphia Preprint Exchange and historical texts distributed by Cleveland Free-Net. The April 1994 issue contained the files for 1991, 1992, and 1993. While many truly classic literary works are on disc, there are also many interesting and popular works from different categories. For example, it contains the first million digits of pi, the square root of 2, and the first 100,000 prime numbers (not of too much use to me, but interesting nonetheless). In a more-useful category users will find the Hacker's Dictionary of Computer Jargon, NAFTA Documents, The Hitchhiker's Guide to the Internet, and Data from the 1990 Census. There is also lots of good fiction to read, including books by Edgar Rice Burroughs (e.g., *Thuvia, Maid of Mars*, and even some volumes of the *Tarzan* series), Mark Twain, Jules Verne, *Frankenstein* by Mary Shelley, and many other authors. Some individual works that are also present include *Moby Dick, The Time Machine, Aesop's Fables*, the Bible, *Song of the Lark, O Pioneers!*, The Book of Mormon, *Alice in Wonderland, Paradise Lost*, and many more. Historical and political texts include many early U.S. government documents, selected inaugural addresses, and the *CIA World Factbook*.

The interface is a standard Walnut Creek DOS interface. While it is easy to use, the disc could be improved significantly if the producers would upgrade it to a Windows interface. The disc is "BBS-ready." It contains files that are ready for use with RBBS, PCBoard, Opus, Maximus, SpitFire, Wildcat, and generic files.bbs.

Name:	**Scribner's Writers Series on CD-ROM**
Vendor:	Macmillan New Media
Cost:	$595
Hardware requirements:	IBM PC 386 or later, 2MB free hard-disk space, Windows
Comments:	This exceptional product is both functional and pleasant to

use. It contains 510 essays drawn from several Scribner sets of published works: *African American Writers, American Writers, Ancient Writers, British Writers, European Writers, Latin American Writers, Modern American Women Writers, Science Fiction Writers,* and *Supernatural Fiction Writers.* The system takes only five minutes or less to install. The Windows interface is extremely easy to use. The documents include pleasing fonts, multicolors, and even illuminated initial characters. Boolean logic can be used even by absolute beginners. The main menu divides the database into name, genre (autobiographical/memoirs, children's/juvenile, criticism, essay, journalism, nonfiction, novels, philosophy, plays, poetry, religion, and short stories), time period (twentieth century, nineteenth century, eighteenth century, seventeenth century, sixteenth century, fifteenth century, medieval, and ancient), and nationality (country of origin). Further searching is available by language, race, sex, birth date and death date, or keyword. Any or all of these categories may be invoked at any time, and users may search in more than one file. There is also an excellent search help (hint) file. The actual documents contain what we have all come to expect in Scribner works: high-quality, authoritative analysis and criticism. A selected bibliography follows each entry.

Name:	**Stories of Murder, Mystery, Magic, Terror & More . . .**
Vendor:	World Library
Cost:	$49.95
Hardware requirements:	IBM PC and compatibles, 386 or later, 640K RAM
Comments:	The program works equally well in a DOS or Windows environment, making available the full text of 171 classic stories of mystery and suspense. Included are works from Hans Christian Andersen, Wilkie Collins, Joseph Conrad, Dante, Dostoevsky, Arthur Conan Doyle, Alexandre Dumas, Wolfgang von Goethe, H. Rider Haggard, Nathaniel Hawthorne, Washington Irving, Henry James, Christopher Marlowe, Herman Melville (including the full text of *Moby Dick*), Baroness Orczy, Edgar Allan Poe, Mary Shelley, Robert Louis Stevenson, Bram Stoker, Jules Verne, H. G. Wells, and Oscar Wilde. While not everything may fall neatly into everyone's definition of mystery and terror, the combined works make a formidable recreational and reading tool.

The Windows interface allows for search by title, author, words, or strategy. The strategy choice permits selection by predetermined categories of region, era, country, etc. The search facility makes it so simple to find anything in the 171 titles that it will work the first time and every time for all users. A search for "blood" returned 54 titles with that word and showed each hit in context. The software also permits placement of bookmarks, and it even has an AutoScroll feature that permits readers to set the pace of text scrolling across the screen from 1 (too slow) to 50 (too fast).

Name:	**Twain's World for Windows**
Vendor:	Bureau of Electronic Publishing
Cost:	$39.95
Hardware requirements:	IBM PC and compatibles; Macintosh
Comments:	This disc contains a fascinating multimedia collection of the complete works of Mark Twain, including full-length and short works, essays, speeches, and letters. More than a dozen full-text works about Mark Twain are also included. To add flavor to these materials, a variety of audio and visual information can be accessed by hypertext links throughout. Some of these are outstanding sketches, photos, and video clips and a number of animations. The animations make an ideal feature for young people using the CD. A time line gives details about the history of Mark Twain and the world during his life from 1835 to 1891. The Windows interface makes the product extremely easy to use. All material may be searched. It will provide a marvelous activity for any student of Mark Twain.

Additional similar products available from Bureau of Electronic Publishing include Like the Dickens for Windows and Much Ado About Shakespeare for Windows.

Name:	**Wilson Author Biographies**
Vendor:	H. W. Wilson
Cost:	$299
Hardware requirements:	IBM PC and compatibles, 640K RAM, 3MB free hard-disk space, DOS 3.1 or later, Hayes compatible modem optional
Comments:	The disc covers authors most likely of interest to high school and undergraduate college students. Included are 4,300 authors from 800 B.C. to the present. It includes Wilson Author Series titles: *British Authors before 1800*, *British Authors of the Nineteenth Century*, *American Authors 1600–1900*, *European Authors 1000–1900*, *Greek and Latin Authors: 800 B.C.–A.D. 1000*. The material takes the form of articles about each author's life. Also accompanying

the articles are lists of the author's works and dates of original publication, recent editions published since 1982, and recently published criticism of each author's works. Material is taken from other Wilson publications such as *Humanities Index* and *Biography Index*.

Three search levels make it easy for beginners and advanced researchers to search effectively. A single-subject search mode (browse) will locate authors by searching on author's name or title of a work. Multiple-subject search using Wilsearch mode can be used to search for authors by field: genre, nationality, language, gender, century/period, birthday, and keyword. A command-language search can also be implemented. This system, the same one used by Wilsonline, supports nested Boolean logic, proximity searching, free-text and controlled-vocabulary searching, truncation, ranging, multifile searching, saving of data from a search, and more. In addition, subscribers to Wilson's CD-ROM services also have unlimited online access time to the latest information when required.

Magazines on Disc

Multimedia has also given rise to a new phenomenon, the magazine on a disc. Medio Magazine and NautilusCD are good examples. Both contain text, photos, video, and sound. Kids and adults in the not-too-distant future may well look to CDs such as these for their informational and educational content. Medio Magazine provides an excellent database of hundreds of well-organized research articles of interest to high school or grade school students. NautilusCD is an exciting multimedia look at computer games, current events, photos, and much more. Both of these can be obtained on a subscription basis, providing a monthly, low-cost addition to the collection.

Name:	**Medio Magazine**
Vendor:	Medio Multimedia
Cost:	$59.95 annual subscription of 12 monthly issues
Hardware requirements:	IBM PC and compatibles, 4MB RAM, 4MB hard-disk space, 256-color adapter, sound card, Windows 3.1 or later
Comments:	Medio is a multimedia magazine on a disc that has many features of general interest including travel, sports, and news and is an entertaining and interesting magazine for all age groups. Adults will enjoy the many informative articles on health (drugs, therapies, research, etc.), sports, news, finance, and business. Kids will enjoy the video department with news on sports, news, movie previews, music videos, and short travel films, and an included game. In the issue labeled volume 1, number 2, the entire *Wizard of Oz*, with pictures, is reproduced. The Windows interface uses voice clips to explain everything in significant detail. Another feature is an interactive database of facts and photos to help people in the market for a new car find the right one in the right price range. Some 500 photos accompany the text.

Name:	**NautilusCD**
Vendor:	Metatec
Cost:	$137.40 'for twelve monthly issues
Hardware requirements:	Multimedia IBM PC or compatible 386SX or later, 4MB RAM minimum (8MB recommended), Windows 3.1 or later
Comments:	This is an outstanding product to use to introduce multimedia to a child or adult. It is a magazine on a disc in full stereo with animation, slides, video, and more. As with a print magazine subscription, a new issue arrives each month containing a number of special articles and a central feature or theme. Articles are informative, not just fluff, carefully woven into the multimedia fabric that makes up NautilusCD. Just as with a printed magazine or journal, there is a table of contents. From here it is easy to get to any section or department, including Desktop Media, Entertainment, Education, Industry, and Computer-Ware.

Throughout the disc there are buttons for activating animation, sound, and movies and for running software programs. The Entertainment section offers many games and mental distractions each month. The Desktop Media section offers selected cuts from new Windham Hill music releases and several tracks from upcoming albums from Celestial Navigations. Photography in Desktop Media is fun to browse. Readers will encounter collections of photographs from professionals.

There are several extremely useful features for computer users. One is a database of CD-ROM information, containing many popular-interest titles. Another is an update of news about the computer industry, including product and patent news. ComputerWare usually contains demos of new products such as Microsoft Excel and FaxWorks Pro. Free drivers and computer utilities are also found there. The Education section has a special Kid's Corner for younger users, much like popular magazines have for young people. The Education section also contains some materials for adults. For example, recent issues contained a demo of TriplePlay Plus! Spanish by Syracuse Language Systems.

What I like most about this CD product is that it is for the whole family. Anyone can find much that is exciting and useful in it. "Backpacs" of past issues are available beginning with the January through June 1992 issues. Each Backpac contains six discs.

The Windows interface is quite excellent. It can be user-customized by changing the menu bar and making other changes that can speed use by people already familiar with the product. The Macintosh interface can be similarly customized. The Windows interface makes it easy to access the CD, including the Disk Index and Article Listing. These features make it possible to search for topics, copy shareware to a disk, or print out articles. Link, a communications feature, lets users contact Metatec directly with electronic comments.

Maps

Maps on CD are special because of the ease with which something may be pinpointed and the manner in which the user may "zoom" in or out like a bird to get a better view. Many excellent atlases are on CD-ROM; these cover the world, the United States, and specific cities. Some atlases contain street names and ZIP codes.

However, far more exciting are the maps such as Map'n'Go that assist the user in creating an entire vacation plan complete with route, sights to see, and accommodations.

The most thrilling atlas in the following collection is clearly the Small Blue Planet series. It depicts the earth and its major cities by actual satellite photos for a stunning view. Kids and adults will thrill to this experience.

Name:	**Global Explorer**
Vendor:	DeLorme Mapping
Cost:	$169
Hardware requirements:	IBM PC and compatibles; 4MB RAM required; 3MB hard-disk storage, VGA
Comments:	This easy-to-use world atlas and street map program for the entire world is very well done in bright colors. Users start by selecting a location. The area may be magnified or demagnified 15 levels to take in more detail or greater area. Major features can be accessed by a button side bar that includes a key to the many topographic and political features: railroads, primary roads, secondary roads, major highways, rivers, political boundaries, small towns, oceans and lakes, altitude, national capitals, etc. Locations or streets can be found by using any of several tools on the side bar, including the Street Find search tool. A search may be narrowed by specifying a desired country or geographic or other feature. A distance calculator will determine the shortest distance between any two points. Details about each country include a

picture of the flag plus facts about the country's government, economy, politics, communications network, wildlife, and geography. More than 20,000 of the features on the map come with a short description, including zoos, museums, and many more (a total of 142,100 features). Much of the movement around the map can be done very conveniently without resorting to the menus or buttons. By clicking over an area on any map, the program redraws that section one magnification greater. Other short cuts include pointing and clicking to towns or features on a map, which will provide a short description of the area. Also included is the worldwide network of airline routes. Help files contain troubleshooting tips and many ways to make the most of the program.

Further information: "World-Wise Travelers," *Electronic Learning*, Sept. 1993, 52.

Name: **Map'n'Go**

Vendor: DeLorme Mapping

Cost: $49

Hardware requirements: IBM PC and compatibles, 4MB RAM, 3MB hard-disk space, Windows 3.x

Comments: A computer atlas of the United States, Map'n'Go comes with a variety of exceptional features for mapping and planning trips. Users may instantly select any point in the United States with a variety of magnitudes, zooming in or out. A location also can be found by searching for ZIP code, area code, or place name. Where Map'n'Go excels is in its trip-planning features. For instance, the user selects a starting and ending destination. The program will provide a map with a highlighted route. However, the user may ask the program to provide an alternative, including the shortest route, a preferred route, or the quickest route. In each case, the distance in miles or kilometers will be given as well as a highlighted route map. A preferred speed of travel may also be included in the plan. Another fascinating feature of the program is the database of 4,000 points of interest along the way. Types of highways, tollways, ferries, etc. may be avoided or favored. These may be selected and appended to the user's trip plan. The whole trip plan may be printed out to take along on the trip. The program will provide a guided tour of the route with photos and audio description of features. For route hotels, campgrounds, restaurants, and amenities checklist, users may click on the codes displayed near key points or cities on the maps. Users can, for example, quickly tell if a hotel or motel accommodates pets. Map'n'Go comes with a 128-page oversize travel atlas of the United States.

Name:	**Small Blue Planet: The Real Picture World Atlas 2.0; Small Blue Planet: The Cities Below, The Aerial Atlas of America**
Vendor:	Now What Software
Cost:	$59, Real Picture Atlas; $49.95, Cities Below
Hardware requirements:	Multimedia IBM PC and compatibles, 4MB RAM (8MB recommended); multimedia Macintosh, 4MB RAM (8MB recommended)
Comments:	The Real Picture Atlas is both unique and impressive. The collection of maps includes relief, topographic, photographic, political, and light-sensored maps. World photos are from NASA space flights, spy satellites, and surveillance planes. The zoom feature can zero in on a continent or country. By using the Looking Glass Tool, users may magnify a small portion of a larger map. The tool can be moved around the screen just as a real magnifier might be used. The magnifier can also be set to a different type of map from the one on screen. For instance, when viewing the topographic map of the United States, the magnifier can be set to a political map for exciting and convenient cross reference. Many other features also make this a fascinating way to explore the globe. This new edition has added sound in 70 different languages. When moving around the political globe, a window of phrases opens. The phrases may be spoken in the language of the country the atlas currently highlights.

The Country Almanac section contains political, historical, environmental, and statistical information on each country. The Satellite Gallery section contains eight collections of images obtained from remotely sensed images, the space shuttle, and NASA missions. A convenient control panel to zoom in or out, navigate short distances in any direction, measure distance, cut and paste images, make notes, and much more is always present.

The Cities Below has the same spectacular atlas capabilities of The Real Picture Atlas, but it centers on cities in the United States. It provides a complete historical look at America's towns, villages, and cities from the earliest Native American settlements to the present.

Also available from Now What Software is Earthscapes in Time.

Name:	**StreetInfo**
Vendor:	MapInfo
Cost:	Prices per state range from $225 to $2,995; $25,000 for the entire United States
Hardware requirements:	IBM PC and compatibles; Macintosh
Comments:	StreetInfo covers most areas of physical importance, including rivers, bridges, railroad tracks, etc. Maps are drawn from data supplied from the U.S. Census Bureau's Tiger Information and are accurate to the block and side of street. MapInfo also publishes Canadian StreetInfo.

Military

Jane's Information Group makes many CDs available that cover military information worldwide. These provide an outstanding way to view the content available in print volumes, as well as affording an excellent way to search for specific information about the armed services.

Name:	**Jane's Information Group Series**
Vendor:	Jane's Information Group
Cost:	See below; free demo on CD available
Hardware requirements:	IBM PC and compatibles, Windows
Comments:	Each title in this series contains the information presented in the print edition. The search software is Windows-based to provide multiple access points to information. The index provides a list of fields from which users may select. These include a global search, product title, picture, model, equipment type, manufacturer, etc. Once a satisfactory selection has been found, either the text or any images linked to it may be pulled up. Individual titles include the following:

Jane's Aircraft Identification ($1,350)

Jane's Air-Launched Weapons ($795)

Jane's All the World Aircraft 1989-1990 ($795)

Jane's Ammunition Handbook ($795)

Jane's Armour and Artillery ($795)

Jane's Armoured Fighting Vehicle Retrofit Systems ($795)

Jane's Avionics ($795)

Jane's Battlefield Surveillance ($795)

Jane's Civil & Military Aircraft Upgrades ($795)

Jane's C3I Systems ($795)

Jane's Fighting Ships ($795)

Jane's High Speed Marine Craft ($795)

Jane's Infantry Weapons ($795)

Jane's Land-based Air Defense ($795)

Jane's Military Communications ($795)

Jane's Military Training Systems ($795)

Jane's Military Vehicles and Logistics ($795)

Jane's Naval Identification ($1,350)

Jane's Naval Weapon Systems ($795)

Jane's NBC Protection and Equipment ($795)

Jane's Radar & Electronic Warfare Systems ($795)

Jane's Security and Counter-Insurgency Equipment ($795)

Jane's Strategic Weapons Systems ($795)

Jane's Underwater Warfare Systems ($795)

Nature and Science

Most of the CDs in this section are traditional indexing and abstracting databases useful for research. Each covers several hundred periodicals. Magill's Survey of Science CD-ROM is different in that it contains hundreds of in-depth essays on scientific subjects of interest to students and researchers. The World WeatherDisc can be used to look up and plot the weather for any place on Earth since records have been kept. Some products provide educational tours suitable for younger users. Animals simulates a trip to the San Diego Zoo. The Amazon Rainforest simulates a trip to Brazil and the wilderness. Both discs are highly educational and inexpensive.

Additional products available:

> CRISP Biomedical Research Information on CD-ROM (U.S. Government Printing Office, Superintendent of Documents)
>
> Environmental Periodicals Bibliography on CD-ROM (National Information Services)
>
> GeoArchive on CD-ROM (National Information Services)
>
> Multi-Media Audubon's Mammals (CMC ReSearch)
>
> Oceanographic & Marine Resources—Vols. I & II (National Information Services)
>
> 7 Natural Wonders: A Sierra Club Electronic Guide (InterOptica Publishing)
>
> Species Information Library (National Information Services)
>
> Water Resources Abstracts—Vols. I & II (National Information Services)
>
> Wildlife Worldwide (National Information Services)

Name:	**The Amazon Rainforest (A Sierra Club Electronic Guide)**
Vendor:	InterOptica Publishing
Cost:	$39.95
Hardware requirements:	IBM PC and compatibles; Macintosh (both versions on same disc)

Comments: The Sierra Club has produced a brilliantly conceived CD-ROM. Children and adults will find it educational in a fun and interesting way with exploration of the earth's treasures a rewarding experience. Users can learn where the rainforests of the world are located by using the interactive world and regional maps. Photos of animals and vegetation with accompanying text provide a rich learning environment. Vivid photographs can also be watched in narrated shows of 15 to 20 slides each.

Using video clips, users will see a variety of rainforest subjects. These cover the canopy of the forest, the animals, gold mining, cattle ranching, native inhabitants, and logging. Animations are also used to explain important ecological concepts of the rainforest, including Rainforest Energy during the Day, Recycling Rainforest Nutrients, Rainforest Energy at Night, and The Hydrological Cycle. Facts and Figures provides a fun way to learn the essentials of rainforests such as their sizes, ages, and distribution around the earth. Flora and Fauna is an online essay with hypertext that provides links to other text and images on the disc. Other online hypertext essays are Man and the Rainforest and Geography. An interactive glossary provides another useful learning tool.

The Sierra Club has produced a series of CDs similar to this one, including The Blue Whale, The Grand Canyon, The Great Barrier Reef, and The Indian Monsoon.

Name: **The Animals**
Vendor: Software Toolworks (MindScape)
Cost: $119.95
Hardware requirements: Multimedia; IBM PC and compatibles; Macintosh
Comments: This magnificent multimedia program disc is an adventure at the San Diego Public Zoo. It is highly educational and will be an interesting experience for children as well as adults. The main menu is a map of the complete park. By scanning the map with the cursor and then clicking, an area is selected. These areas include the research center, temperate forest tropical rain forest, kids area, stories area, information, inside the zoo, island, grassland, savanna, zoo gardens, tours, tropical dry forest, nursery, library, tundra, montane, and desert. Tours are provided. Animals in various groups, such as the great apes, can be visited. The program contains video clips, sounds, descriptions, and pictures. The stories area gives audio presentations of how the zoo started, how it cares for baby animals, feeding time, animal quizzes, and more.

The kids area also has numerous features for young people such as storytime, guessing animal sounds game, facts about the animals, baby animals, and more. An alternative way of accessing information is by the alphabetical list of animals or through the Library. The Library is not filled with books but with pictures and other media. Pressing a button plays a clip of actual animal sounds. Pictures, video clips, and animal sounds are accessible alphabetically here. Directions for each section of the program are clearly expressed and neatly arranged in an information kiosk. Children will spend hours learning about the zoo playing this CD.

Name:	**Biological & Agricultural Index**
Vendor:	H. W. Wilson
Cost:	$1,495
Hardware requirements:	IBM PC and compatibles, 640K RAM, 3MB free hard-disk space, DOS 3.1 or later, Hayes compatible modem optional
Comments:	The database contains indexing of 225 important life sciences and agricultural periodicals from July 1983. It is updated and cumulated monthly. Included are animal husbandry, biochemistry, biotechnology, botany, ecology, environmental science, food science, forestry, genetics, horticulture, microbiology, nutrition, soil science, veterinary medicine, zoology, and others. It also includes a separate index of current book reviews. Three search levels make it easy for beginners and advanced researchers to search effectively. A single-subject search mode (browse) will locate authors by searching on author's name or title of a work. Multiple-subject search using Wilsearch mode can be used to search for authors by field. A command-language search can also be implemented. This system, the same one used by Wilsonline, supports nested Boolean logic, proximity searching, free-text and controlled-vocabulary searching, truncation, ranging, multifile searching, saving of data from a search, and more. In addition, subscribers to any of Wilson's CD-ROM services also have unlimited online access time to the latest information when needed.

Name:	**Fish & Fisheries Worldwide**
Vendor:	National Information Services Corporation
Cost:	$695
Hardware requirements:	IBM PC and compatibles, 512K RAM available
Comments:	The Fish & Fisheries Worldwide database contains a variety of information sources. Fisheries Review (1971 to present),

from the U.S. National Biological Survey, has more than 90,000 citations. Fish Database (1960 to present), from the Fish and Wildlife Reference Service, contains more than 7,000 citations. Fishlit (1985 to present) provides more than 40,000 records from more than 1,000 journals worldwide. Aquaculture (1970 to 1984), from the National Oceanic & Atmospheric Administration, lists more than 10,000 citations. Fish Health News (1978 to 1985) is the same as the print publication of the U.S. National Biological Survey, Technical Information Services Division. Each database on this disc may be searched separately or as a group. A standard NISC disc interface provides search modes for novice, advanced, and expert levels with full Boolean, proximity, and field-specific retrieval capabilities.

Name:	**Magill's Survey of Science CD-ROM**
Vendor:	EBSCO Publishing
Cost:	$1,150, one-time purchase
Hardware requirements:	IBM PC and compatibles, 640K RAM, 5MB hard-disk space
Comments:	Magill's Survey of Science contains four separate sets of essays: Earth Science Series, published in 1990; Physical Science Series, published in 1992; Applied Science Series, published in 1993; and Life Science Series, published in 1991. There are more than 1,500 full-text essays with a total of more than 11,000 pages. These essays give an outstanding overview of most aspects of science. Some examples of the essays are "The Abyssal Sea Floor," "Acoustics," "Absolute Zero Temperature," "Food Additives," "AIDS," "Electrical Activity of the Brain," "Solar Cells," "Cement," "Mars' Craters," "Cyclotrons," "Diesel Engines," "Wildlife Management," "Wind," "Sound Waves," "Welding," and hundreds of other topics. A complete index of essay titles is available from which to choose, or a search will produce a list of titles and abstracts. Each essay contains an overview of the subject, a glossary of relevant terms, and a bibliography. Drawings and other images are linked to the text and may be retrieved to further illustrate concepts and ideas.

The software will allow local collection holdings to be tagged in the database and marked with up to ten lines of text for quicker location and identification of library materials. Menu-driven DOS-based search software makes it easy for first-time or inexperienced users to find what they need. Though there are no Windows features, the program is well organized. Advanced users may conduct a more-sophisticated search using truncation, wild cards, and proximity/phrase searches.

Name:	**Oceans Below**
Vendor:	Software Toolworks (MindScape)
Cost:	$49.95
Hardware requirements:	Multimedia IBM PC and compatibles, 33 MHz or faster recommended, 1MB RAM, 580K free hard-disk space, 256 color graphics with 512K video memory, SoundBlaster or Audio Spectrum sound card, DOS 5.0 or later, mouse; Macintosh
Comments:	This well-crafted multimedia program contains many pleasing visual elements that make it especially pleasing for children but also fun for adults. The overall effect is a pleasant way to learn about the sport of skin diving and the oceans, fish, and ecology. The program uses video clips, slides, and sound in its presentation of underwater life and diving skills. On board the boat, users may click on dive info to learn about skin diving and scuba gear. From a world map a variety of locations are available.

Name:	**Wilson Applied Science & Technology Abstracts; Applied Science & Technology Index**
Vendor:	H. W. Wilson
Cost:	$2,495, Wilson Applied Science & Technology Abstracts; $1,495, Applied Science & Technology Index
Hardware requirements:	IBM PC and compatibles, 640K RAM, 3MB free hard-disk space, DOS 3.1 or later, Hayes compatible modem optional
Comments:	Wilson Applied Science & Technology Abstracts contains abstracts (since March 1993) of 50 to 150 words and indexing (since October 1983) for 400 important periodicals in the areas of science and technology. Each month 5,000 new records are added. Applied Science & Technology Index contains indexing only. Three search levels make it easy for beginners and advanced researchers to search effectively. A single-subject search mode (browse) will locate authors by searching on author's name or title of a work. Multiple-subject search using Wilsearch mode can be used to search for authors by field. A command-language search can also be implemented. This system, the same one used by Wilsonline, supports nested Boolean logic, proximity searching, free-text and controlled-vocabulary searching, truncation, ranging, multifile searching, saving of data from a search, and more.

Name:	**World WeatherDisc**
Vendor:	WeatherDisc Associates
Cost:	$295
Hardware requirements:	IBM PC and compatibles; Macintosh
Comments:	The PC version of this software is DOS-based. The World WeatherDisc is an ideal tool for anyone who wants to track world weather trends and patterns. There is an immense amount of information. The data sets are divided into global and United States. The global data sets contain world monthly surface station climatology, worldwide airfield summaries, Comprehensive Ocean-Atmosphere Data (COAD) ship observation data, worldwide consolidated tropical cyclones data set, world monthly weather records—upper air, and Sadler tropical climatology. The U.S. data sets include local climatological data from 286 primary stations in the United States and overseas territories, U.S. station climatological summaries at 1,826 stations across the continental United States, climatic division data, U.S. monthly normals of temperature and precipitation, U.S. freeze data, daily weather observations for major U.S. stations, historical sunshine data, station historical data file, tornado data, thunderstorm beginning and ending times, and lightning statistics derived from storm data. All of the data sets vary as to the time periods covered. Some stretch from 1929 to 1992.

The software is very easy to use. Raw weather data may be viewed, graphed, or exported to disk. World weather units may be selected as English or metric units. There are no fancy features such as push buttons or pull-down menus, but the program makes available an enormous amount of data in a highly organized and easy-to-use format.

Newspaper and Periodical Indexes and Full Text

While it is possible to get full text, cumulative editions of many different journals and magazines on a disc, the cost of doing so makes it out of reach for many libraries. Most small libraries are limited to one or two major papers on CD. This saves storing hundreds of old newspapers or cabinets of microfilm. Since most newspapers on CD are not issued until several months after the paper edition, a CD does not eliminate the need to maintain a paper inventory for at least a few months.

The most expensive time to purchase a newspaper on disc is when it is current; the least expensive way is to buy backfiles during an original subscription period. The manufacturer is usually willing to offer them at a substantial discount to obtain a new customer.

Some libraries have opted to offer some databases, including newspaper and periodical indexes, through an online service such as the Internet or DIALOG. There are advantages to going online or using a CD-ROM. A specific library should analyze its options and judge accordingly. A potential advantage of online services is that they can be updated more frequently than a CD-ROM. Many online services, however, are not updated any more frequently than the monthly CD-ROM that arrives with a subscription service. Some CD-ROM vendors provide an online connection as an additional service.

Additional products available:

Academic Search (EBSCO Publishing)

Anthropological Literature on Disc (G. K. Hall)

Avery Index on Disc (G. K. Hall)

Black Studies on Disc (G. K. Hall)

Computerworld (CW Communications)

Middle Search (EBSCO Publishing)

New England Journal of Medicine (New England Journal of Medicine)

Primary Search (EBSCO Publishing)

San Francisco Chronicle (KR Information OnDisc)

San Jose Mercury News (KR Information OnDisc)

USA Today (Context Systems)

Washington Times (Newsbank)

Name:	**Academic Abstracts; Academic Abstracts Full Text Elite**
Vendor:	EBSCO Publishing
Cost:	$3,399, monthly; $2,999, academic year—August through May; $999, quarterly
Hardware requirements:	IBM PC and compatibles, 640K RAM (2MB recommended), DOS 5.0 or later, 5MB hard-disk space required; Macintosh, 1.5MB RAM, System 6.0.5 or later, 1MB hard-disk space; printer optional; 2-disc CD capacity is recommended for Academic Abstracts Full Text Elite
Comments:	Academic Abstracts and Academic Abstracts Full Text Elite were designed for small college or preparatory school libraries. They are published quarterly, monthly, or for an academic year (August through May). Academic Abstracts contains abstracts of more than 800 journals, studies, digests, reviews, and quarterlies. Academic Abstracts Full Text Elite also contains the full text for 125 titles. Journals include *Consumers Reports*, *Contemporary Drug Problems*, *Contemporary Sociology*, *Criminology*, *Datamation*, *Diabetes in the News*, *Earthquakes & Volcanoes*, *The Economist*, *Esquire*, *Facts On File*, *Issues in Science & Technology*, *Journal of Teacher Education*, *The Journal of Wildlife Management*, *Oceans*, *Personal Computing*, *Publishers Weekly*, *Reason*, *Sail*, *The Saturday Evening Post*, and many others. They cover the subject areas of sociology, sports, music, business, economics, engineering, philosophy, law, and art.

These databases come with a variety of options, many excellent features, and an outstanding online tutorial for beginners. They are DOS-based with no mouse or other Windows options. However, they are easy to use. Both basic and advanced searching are supported by a menu-driven system that allows for Boolean operators OR, AND, and proximity searching. The wild cards for character (?) and truncation (*) are also available. Advanced or enhanced searching makes available more options, including limiting material to cover stories from magazines, finding only items that are owned by the library, selecting by a date range or number of pages (including <, >, or exact number), and combining previous search results by number into a new search. This advanced mode also searches the entire citation of an article. Results are available in three ways. The title list contains subject, title, and source of the article. The detailed display contains more-complete bibliographic information and an abstract of the article, ISSN, and source. Full text is available for some items, including all book reviews. Results may be printed out to paper as a bibliography or downloaded (copied) to disk. Special codes for local custom enhancements of the database are also available, including program colors, accumulation of statistics, local notes, limitation on the number of hits per search, and various printing options and page formatting.

Name: **Biography and Genealogy Master Index on CD-ROM 1995 Cumulation**

Vendor: Gale Research

Cost: $1,250, first year; $350, subsequent annual updates

Hardware requirements: IBM PC and compatibles

Comments: This two-CD set contains the complete 21 volumes of Gale's *Biography & Genealogy Master Index* compiled into a single source. Data have been collected from 2,100 volumes of current and retrospective biographical dictionaries and *Who's Who*s since 1975. People included date from classical to modern times. Information includes biographee's name, birth and death years, and full-source publication (title, author/editor, publisher, year of publication, volume/edition number, and whether a portrait is provided with the biography). Disc A is used to conduct name searches; Disc B is used for extended searches. An extended search will provide a full-text name search or a search by birth or death year, portraits, source name, or publication year. The database may be marked to indicate which of the sources for citations are owned by the local library or are available at nearby libraries.

Name: **Biological Abstracts**

Vendor: SilverPlatter

Cost: Contact vendor

Hardware requirements: IBM PC and compatibles; Macintosh

Comments: Biological Abstracts database is updated quarterly. It contains bibliographic citations and abstracts in the biological and biomedical fields, including current research reports. More than 250,000 records are indexed each year.

Name:	**Books in Print with Book Reviews Plus; Books in Print Plus; Books out of Print with Book Reviews Plus; Ingram Books in Print with Book Reviews Plus; Ingram Books in Print Plus**
Vendor:	Bowker-Reed Reference Electronic Publishing
Cost:	Books in Print with Book Reviews Plus: $1,595 one year, $4,546 three years; Books in Print Plus: $1,095 one year, $3,121 three years; Books out of Print with Book Reviews Plus: $395 one year, $1,126 three years; Ingram Books in Print with Book Reviews Plus: $1,833 one year; Ingram Books in Print Plus: $1,330
Hardware requirements:	IBM PC and compatibles; Macintosh (Books in Print packages only)
Comments:	Books in Print with Book Reviews Plus offers more than 230,000 reviews from 12 reviewing media: *Publishers Weekly, Library Journal, School Library Journal, Choice, Booklist, University Press Book News, BIOSIS, Bookstore Journal, Voice of Youth Advocates, Kirkus Reviews, Reference and Research Book News,* and *Sci-Tech Book News.*

Books in Print Plus provides access to more than 42,000 U.S. publishers. The system can be used to interface with 22 distributors for electronic ordering, including Baker & Taylor, Blackwell, Midwest, PUBNET, Academic Book Center, Research Books, Brodart, American Overseas Book Company, Random House, and others. A search for a book may be made by author, publisher, title, ISBN, subject, keyword, LCCN, series title, or children's subject. A search may be further narrowed by defining it as juvenile or youth or by specifying grade level. Two or more searches may be combined. The resulting hits may be displayed in the form of a catalog card, if desired. Other display formats include *Books in Print* standard, MARC tagged, order form, custom, detailed, Ingram. The order format contains provisions for electronic orders, purchase orders, or special orders. Search results may be printed or saved to disk. A batch search may also be made. Boolean search terms AND, OR, and ANDNOT may be used, along with truncation and replacement wild card for any letter.

Books out of Print provides access to more than 600,000 books that are out of print or out of stock since 1979.

Further information:	Anita Amirrezvani, "Great CD ROMs for Fun and Profit," *PC World*, Dec. 1993, 239.

Name:	**Book Review Index on CD-ROM**
Vendor:	Gale Research
Cost:	$1,295; $495, annual updates
Hardware requirements:	IBM PC and compatibles
Comments:	Contains 2.5 million book review citations since 1965 in more than 500 publications to more than 1 million titles, including classical novels, new reference books and magazines, children's books, cookbooks, and textbooks. Journals indexed include *Choice*, *The New Yorker*, *New York Times Book Review*, *Atlantic Monthly*, *Time*, and *National Genealogical Society Quarterly*. Each citation contains the author, editor and/or illustrator's name, title being reviewed, source of the review, date and volume number of the source, page number on which it appears, type of book being reviewed, and in some cases the approximate word count. The database may be searched by title, author, reviewing journal, document type, and publication year of review.

Name:	**Business Index Select; Business ASAP Select**
Vendor:	Information Access Company
Cost:	Business Index Select: $2,000 with 12 monthly updates, $1,700 with 9 monthly updates from September to May; Business Index Select with Business ASAP Select: $4,000 with 12 monthly updates, $3,700 with 9 monthly updates
Hardware requirements:	IBM PC and compatibles
Comments:	The Information Access databases differ in coverage of business, tax, accounting, job hunting, investments, management, mergers and acquisitions, and key industry and market trends. Business Index Select contains indexing and abstracts of articles from some 240 business journals, including six-month coverage of the *Wall Street Journal*. If purchased with Business ASAP Select, some 100 of the journals are included full text. Coverage of each journal is for the most recent 24-month period. Some of the journals are *ABA Banking Journal*, *Academy of Management Journal*, *Illinois Business Review*, *Journal of Consumer Affairs*, *Real Estate Today*, *U.S. Industrial Outlook*, and *Working Woman*. The interface is standard InfoTrac. It provides for two levels of searching, depending on the sophistication of the user. Full Boolean and keyword searching permits an efficient subject search. Results can be printed out to paper.

Name:	**Business Source**
Vendor:	EBSCO
Cost:	$1,495, monthly subscription
Hardware requirements:	Macintosh, System 6.0.5 or later, 1.5MB RAM, 1MB hard-disk space
Comments:	The Business Source database contains keyword access to the full text of two-year coverage of 48 rotating, selected journals. An additional 500 business-related journals, including the *Wall Street Journal*, are indexed. Topics of interest include economics, management, accounting, banking, labor, public relations, communications, marketing, and finance. The database includes quarterly reviews, trade magazines, and journals. Each has a 50-word indicative abstract and Library of Congress subject headings. The software will allow local collection holdings to be tagged in the database and marked with up to ten lines of text for quicker location and identification of library materials. Menu-driven search software makes it easy for first-time or inexperienced users to find what they need. Advanced users may conduct a more-sophisticated search using truncation, wild cards, and proximity/phrase searches. Some of the full-text journals include *The American Economist, Economic Trends, Federal Reserve Bank of New York, International Trade Forum, Hastings Center Report, Kiplinger's Personal Finance Magazine, Money, Technology Review, Women in Business*, and many others. The following are indexed and abstracted: *Accounting Review, Adweek Western Advertising News, Byte, Computers & Operations Research, Crain's Chicago Business, The Economist, Financial Review, Fund Raising Management, Government Product News, Journal of Occupational & Organizational Psychology, Long Range Planning, Management Japan, Marketing News, Monthly Labor Review, PCWeek, Personnel Review, Technology Review, Training, Trusts & Estates*, and many others.

Name:	**Chicago Tribune**
Vendor:	Newsbank
Cost:	$1,450, current year; $950, each backfile
Hardware requirements:	IBM PC and compatibles
Comments:	This database covers the *Chicago Tribune*, one year per disc, text only. Installation software comes on two floppy disks and must be reinstalled each January when the new year starts. The search process is made as simple as possible since this is intended as a public access database. Users must initially

choose which year they want to search. Two search levels provide some support for both new and advanced users. Level I provides search using the operators AND, OR, NOT, NEAR, TO, or SAME. Headlines or articles may be displayed, depending on user needs or whether the user wants to further narrow the search. The program automatically prompts users for additional search terms to help reduce the number of hits. Level II provides a menu of fields by which a search may be limited: text, headlines, index terms, caption, dateline, and author. Overall, this is an easy database to use and one that is popular with the public.

Name: **CNN Newsroom Global View**

Vendor: Softkey Software Products

Cost: $99 for single users; $149 for schools and libraries

Hardware requirements: IBM PC and compatibles, 640K RAM, 1MB hard-disk space, sound card

Comments: Intended for ages 14 to adult, CNN Newsroom Global View is an interesting news and world almanac. It includes an atlas, a gazetteer, charts, and graphs. It contains a large volume of video segments in addition to text-based stories.

Further information: Alfred Poor, "Spin Doctor," *Computer Shopper*, Dec. 1993, 560.

Name: **Consumer Index to Product Evaluations and Information Sources**

Vendor: National Information Services Corporation (in cooperation with Perian Press)

Cost: $695, annual subscription with semiannual updates

Hardware requirements: IBM PC and compatibles, 512K RAM available

Comments: This database contains two consumer tools: Consumers Index and Consumer Health & Nutrition Index. Consumer Index contains information on more than 25,000 product evaluations, recalls, and warnings. Articles are from more than 100 journals. Its 8,000 abstracts add coverage of travel and transportation, finances, food, computers, etc. Consumer Health & Nutrition Index indexes more than 8,500 articles about health, transportation, the home, etc., using more than 4,000 subject headings. The source of this information is a core of 80 consumer magazines (*Harvard Medical School Letter, Nutrition Today, Men's Health, American Baby*, and many others), medical-center publications, and health-related newsletters. A full-text search may be conducted on the entire database or only on specific sections. The operators AND, OR, NOT, and NEAR may be used. A wild card (*) is also supported.

Name:	**Essay and General Literature Index**
Vendor:	H. W. Wilson
Cost:	$695
Hardware requirements:	IBM PC and compatibles, 640K RAM, 3MB free hard-disk space, DOS 3.1 or later, Hayes compatible modem optional
Comments:	With its main thrust in the humanities and social sciences, Essay and General Literature Index is an author-and-title index to essays published in collections. The database contains essays and articles from January 1985. It includes a single-alphabet, subject-author index to collections of essays by single authors. Citations include page references and references for variant forms of authors' names. Three search levels make it easy for beginners and advanced researchers to search effectively. A single-subject search mode (browse) will locate authors by searching on author's name or title of a work. Multiple-subject search using the Wilsearch mode can be used to search for authors by field: genre, nationality, language, gender, century/period, birthday, and keyword. A command-language search can also be implemented. This system, the same one used by Wilsonline, supports nested Boolean logic, proximity searching, free-text and controlled-vocabulary searching, truncation, ranging, multifile searching, saving of data from a search, and more. In addition, subscribers to any of Wilson's CD-ROM services also have unlimited online access time to the latest information when needed.

Name:	**Ethnic NewsWatch CD-ROM**
Vendor:	SoftLine Information
Cost:	Contact vendor
Hardware requirements:	Contact vendor
Comments:	The database consists of general-reference, multicultural information. It includes the full text from 85 newspapers and magazines from ethnic and minority presses, including African-American, Arab-American, Asian-American, Hispanic/Latino, Jewish, and Native American. The total CD consists of 85,000 full-text articles with 3,000 new articles each month. Spanish and English publications may be searched in either language using keyword search.

Name: **Facts On File News Digest**

Vendor: Facts On File

Cost: $795, quarterly; $695, annual without updates (without subscription to print version); $595, annual (with subscription to print version); $295, annual update

Hardware requirements: IBM PC and compatibles, 2MB RAM, 5MB hard-disk space, DOS 5.0 or later; Macintosh, System 6.0.5 or later, 1.5MB RAM, 1MB hard-disk space

Comments: The Facts On File database begins at 1980 and contains an index of more than 600,000 entries; a full-text digest from more than 75 world newspapers; and more than 50,000 abstracts of major events, companies, organizations, and news subjects. It also includes an atlas composed of 300 U.S., European, and world satellite survey maps. The EBSCO search software performs menu-driven searches on a basic level or more-sophisticated searches with wild cards; truncation; Boolean AND, OR, and NOT; and proximity search. Hypertext links provide quick access from text to maps or from abstracts to articles. A cross reference is provided for *Facts On File News Digest* print version as well.

Further information: Philip Bishop, *Home-Office Computing*, July 1992, 64.

Name: **Front Page News Plus Business on CD-ROM for the Macintosh**

Vendor: Buckmaster Publishing

Cost: $149 for 4 discs, issued quarterly

Hardware requirements: IBM PC and compatibles; Macintosh

Comments: Front Page News is an annual publication that contains approximately 245,000 full-text articles from 15 different news sources and wire services: Newsgrid News, United Press International, TASS, PR Newswire, DPA, Kyodo, IDG PR Service, Chinese News Agency, Latin American News Agency, Agence France-Presse, Comtex, Business Wire, and others. The low cost of this database makes it outstanding for small libraries or school libraries that wish to provide access to a wide selection of current information in an easy-to-use, highly accessible, and well-organized format. Students will find it extremely useful for gathering information for term papers and other research. Adults will find it useful to have so much diverse information at their fingertips.

Each article contains news service reference, newspaper reference, etc. The material is organized with a runtime version of Folio Corporation's Folio View Search Engine, a Windows-like interface that uses windows and a mouse cursor. Articles can be browsed one by one by heading or text. Each article is numbered, and if the number for an article is known, it can be entered for direct access. Search terms may be truncated or guessed at if uncertain using the word wheel. A search can use AND, OR, NOT or EXCLUSIVE OR. There are online help functions, but the online manual that is provided explains how Folio View Search Engine works, not Front Page News specifically. Search results may be saved to disk as a generic word processing file or as a DOS text file, or they can be printed. Subscription includes quarterly updates.

Name: **InfoTrac Magazine Index Select; Magazine Index Plus; Magazine ASAP; Magazine ASAP Select II; Magazine ASAP Select I; General Periodicals Index—Public Library Version**

Vendor: Information Access

Cost: InfoTrac Magazine Index Select: $1,800, regular; $1,400, school year. Magazine Index Plus: $2,880, regular; $2,100, school year; $950 add-on backfile. Magazine ASAP: $1,000. Magazine ASAP Select: $1,800, regular; $1,400, school year. Magazine ASAP Select I: $1,000. General Periodicals Index—Public Library Version: $8,500, regular; $1,950, backfile

Hardware requirements: IBM PC and compatibles

Comments: These databases offer a wide range of choices for the public and academic libraries for popular periodicals indexing, abstracting, and full text. InfoTrac Magazine Index Select provides abstracting of more than 200 periodicals. It indexes and abstracts popular magazines as well as the *New York Times*.

Magazine Index Plus provides coverage of more than 400 magazines plus the current two months of the *New York Times* and the *Wall Street Journal*. Most entries contain long abstracts. Citations are coded to InfoTrac's Magazine Collection microfilm system.

Magazine ASAP provides full text (ASCII computer code) of 250 magazines as indexed in Magazine Index Plus.

Magazine ASAP Select I provides the full (ASCII computer code) text of approximately 50 magazines (indexed in Magazine Index Plus). Magazine ASAP Select II provides text of 100 titles.

General Periodicals Index—Public Library Version contains the greatest number of indexed journals with 1,100. It also includes the *New York Times*, the *Wall Street Journal*, and the *Christian Science Monitor*. This database provides excellent business as well as popular magazine coverage. Titles have location codes to full text in Magazine and Business Cbllection microfilm systems.

All of these databases are easy to use. Data is organized by the *Library of Congress Subject Headings* as the main authority with additional up-to-the-minute headings supplied by Information Access Corporation. A subject guide search finds the topic plus the subjects before and after the topic since they are organized alphabetically. Headings include topics; personal, corporate, or product names; and titles of books, movies, plays, etc. Hits are presented in reverse chronological order with the most recent first. A special feature allows the library to include "library subscribes to journal" when applicable. Citations may be printed out per a maximum number as specified by the library.

Name:	**KR Information OnDisc**
Vendor:	KR Information OnDisc
Cost:	Contact vendor for prices of individual products
Hardware requirements:	IBM PC and compatibles
Comments:	KR Information OnDisc is a family of products taken from the DIALOG online databases. These include dozens of databases in the fields of business information (e.g., American Banker, Canadian Business & Current Affairs, Commerce Business Daily, Corporate America, and Directory of U.S. Importers & Exporters), education and humanities (e.g., Grants Database; The Philosopher's Index; Women in the U.S.: Collections of the Schlesinger Library, Radcliffe College; and International ERIC), health and biomedicine (e.g., Health Devices Alert, International Pharmaceutical Abstracts, Healthcare Product Comparison System, MEDLINE, and MEDLINE Clinical Collection), law and government (e.g., Federal Register, TRADEMARKSCAN—Federal, and TRADEMARKSCAN—State), newspapers and journals (e.g., Boston Globe, Consumer Reports, Detroit Free Press, Journal of Commerce & Traffic World, Los Angeles Times, Miami Herald, Newsday and New York Newsday, NewsWave, Philadelphia Enquirer, San Francisco Chronicle, and San Jose Mercury News), and science and technology (e.g., Advanced Materials; Aerospace Database; Chemical Business NewsBase; DOE Energy Science and Technology; Ei ChemDisc; Ei CivilDisc; Ei Compendex Plus; Ei EEDisc;

Ei Manufacturing; Ei Energy & Environment Disc; Ei MechDisc; Ei Page One; Environmental Chemistry, Health & Safety; Kirk-Othmer Encyclopedia of Chemical Technology; METADEX/Materials Collection: Metals, Polymers, Ceramics; NTIS; Nuclear Science Abstracts; Paper, Printing & Packaging Database; Petroleum Abstracts; and Polymer Encyclopedia).

One other collection of databases is the Economist Intelligence Unit Regional Business Intelligence Series. This collection contains Asia-Pacific Business Intelligence, Volume I: North Asia and Australasia; Asia-Pacific Business Intelligence, Volume II: Southeast Asia and Indian Subcontinent; East European Business Intelligence; Latin American Business Intelligence; and West European Business Intelligence.

Name:	**LegalTrac on InfoTrac**
Vendor:	Information Access
Cost:	$3,500
Hardware requirements:	IBM PC and compatibles
Comments:	LegalTrac is an index to more than 800 publications, beginning in 1980, including all major law reviews, seven legal newspapers, bar association journals, and law specialty publications. Data are organized by the *Library of Congress Subject Headings* as main authority, with additional timely headings supplied by Information Access Corporation. A subject-guide search finds the topic on an alphabetical word wheel. Headings include personal, corporate, or product names and titles of books, movies, plays, etc. Bibliographic citations for the search are presented in reverse chronological order to allow the most recent to appear first. A special feature allows the library to include "library subscribes to journal" when applicable. Citations may be printed out per a maximum number as specified by the library.

Name:	**Library Literature V. 2.5.1**
Vendor:	H. W. Wilson
Cost:	$1,095
Hardware requirements:	IBM PC and compatibles, 640K RAM, 3MB free hard-disk space, DOS 3.1 or later, Hayes compatible modem optional
Comments:	The database contains library literature from December 1984 to the present. A search may be made by a single-subject search using the browse wheel. A multiple-subject search (Wilsearch) may also be used for 1, 2, or 3 subjects including a personal name, title words, journal name, organization,

Dewey number, or year. A command-language disc search is also useful.

Name:	**Magazine Article Summaries; MAS FullTEXT Select; MAS FullTEXT Elite**
Vendor:	EBSCO Publishing
Cost:	$399 to $3,199, depending on frequency, FullTEXT Select, or FullTEXT Elite subscription
Hardware requirements:	IBM PC and compatibles, 640K RAM, 2MB recommended, DOS 5.0 or later, 5MB hard-disk space required; Macintosh, System 6.0.5 or later, 1.5MB RAM, 1MB hard-disk space; printer optional; 2-disc capacity is recommended for MAS FullTEXT Select and MAS FullTEXT Elite
Comments:	Magazine Article Summaries, updated monthly, contains abstracts for more than 450 different magazines of a general-interest nature, the *New York Times*, and thousands of *Magill Book Reviews*. MAS FullTEXT Select adds the full text of approximately 60 of the magazines. MAS FullTEXT Elite adds the full text of approximately 125 of the magazines. Some of the magazines covered include *Canadian Business*, *Car & Driver*, *Center Magazine*, *Chinatown News*, *Chicago*, *The Christian Century*, *Commonweal*, *Compute!*, *Cricket*, *Creative Classroom*, *Current History*, *Esquire*, *Field & Stream*, *Football Digest*, *Forbes*, *Foreign Affairs*, *Fortune*, *The Futurist*, *Gourmet*, *The New Republic*, *Omni*, *Opera News*, *Publishers Weekly*, *Time*, *Washingtonian*, *Wilson Library Bulletin*, and many others. Topics covered by these magazines are centered around medicine, sports, the arts, health, science, nutrition, business, education, and politics.

The database comes with a variety of options, many excellent features, and an outstanding online tutorial for beginners. It is DOS based with no mouse or other Windows options; however, it is easy to use. Basic and advanced searching are supported. Both are menu driven and allow for Boolean operators OR and AND, proximity searching, and wild cards for character (?) and truncation (*). Advanced or enhanced searching makes available more options, including limiting material to magazine cover stories, finding only items that are owned by the library, selecting by a date range, number of pages (including <, >, or exact number), or combining previous search results by number into a new search. This advanced mode also searches the entire citation of each article. Results are available in three ways. The title list contains the subject, title, and source of the article.

The detailed display contains more-complete bibliographic information and an abstract of the article, ISSN, and source. Full text is available for some items, including all book reviews. Results may be printed out to paper as a bibliography or downloaded (copied) to disk. Special codes for local custom enhancement of the database are also available, including program colors, accumulation of statistics, local notes, limitation on the number of hits per search, and various printing options and page formats.

Name: **Newspaper Abstracts; Newspaper Abstracts National**
Vendor: UMI
Cost: Newspaper Abstracts: $3,185, all nine papers, 1989+, $345 each for two backfiles; Newspaper Abstracts National: $2,600
Hardware requirements: IBM PC and compatibles, 1MB RAM, 490K free RAM, 2MB hard-disk space per ProQuest database installed plus 10MB disk space to run after installation, DOS 3.3, 1.44MB floppy
Comments: Newspaper Abstracts contains indexes and abstracts of a selected group of popular U.S. daily newspapers. Backfiles are available for 1985 through 1988. The database covers the *Christian Science Monitor*, *New York Times*, *Wall Street Journal*, *Washington Post*, *Atlanta Constitution/Journal*, *Boston Globe*, *Chicago Tribune*, *Los Angeles Times*, and *USA Today*. An abridged version, Newspaper Abstracts National, covers only the *Christian Science Monitor*, *Los Angeles Times*, *Wall Street Journal*, *New York Times*, and *Washington Post*. Backfiles are available for 1985 to 1987.

Searchware for these two products makes it convenient for public use by people with little or no search experience. A search may be made using the fields that are readily available. A search may also be made using Boolean AND, OR, and NOT for search terms. Truncation and field-limiting and proximity searching are also permitted. Any search set may be saved for reuse or for combining with other sets. The results screen for titles shows source, publication date, location of the article in the publication, and availability of the source material.

Name: **Newsweek Interactive**
Vendor: Newsweek
Cost: $24.95
Hardware requirements: Multimedia IBM PC and compatibles, 4MB RAM, DOS 5.0, hard-disk drive with 3MB free, mouse, SoundBlaster
Comments: This multimedia version of *Newsweek* is published quarterly and contains the full text of the news magazine for each three-

month period. To add to the multimedia tone of the disc, there are four hours of radio interviews from the weekly program *Newsweek on the Air*. Other material on the disc includes 200 *Washington Post* articles that are related to the *Newsweek* feature articles and are arranged in folders. Both the *Newsweek* and *Washington Post* texts are searchable. Special feature articles created for this disc edition cover major topics such as global earth environment and the future of baseball. These include videos, animations, photo essays, and interviews in the presentations.

Name:	**PCI (Periodicals Contents Index)**
Vendor:	Chadwyck-Healey
Cost:	$7,500 per segment
Hardware requirements:	IBM PC and compatibles, 640K RAM, 2MB hard-disk space, DOS 3.1 or later
Comments:	This database provides bibliographic access to academic journal articles from 1800 to 1980, available in two volumes per year. Each volume contains indexing for approximately 750,000 journal articles and consists of either North American or non-North American periodicals. The total of the volumes contains in excess of 2,200 titles and more than 6 million citations from journals judged to be of scholarly value. The complete table of contents for each journal is given.

   A search may be conducted by title, author, and journal title. A search may be restricted by language of the journal, journal's subject (the index puts each title into one of 37 different subject headings), the year of publication, or a range of dates. Boolean operators can also be used. Browsing by title and issue or table of contents is also easy, as well as by the indexes of keywords, authors, headings, journal titles, and subjects. Local library holdings may be appended to the database.

Name:	**ProQuest Dissertation Abstracts**
Vendor:	UMI
Cost:	$2,395, 1993+ for two-disk set; prices vary for archival sets
Hardware requirements:	IBM PC and compatibles, DOS 3.3, 1MB RAM, 490K free RAM, 2MB hard-disk space per ProQuest database installed plus 10MB hard-disk space to run after installation, 1.44MB floppy
Comments:	The database contains 1.2 million doctoral dissertations and masters theses from 1988 to the present plus some material

to 1861. Two sets are available: Dissertation Abstracts A: Humanities and Social Sciences and Dissertation Abstracts B: Sciences and Engineering. Publications contained in the database come from more than 1,000 universities worldwide, including nearly all major North American graduate schools. Complete bibliographic data and abstracts are included for all items since July 1980.

ProQuest Searchware makes it convenient for public use by people with little or no search experience. A search may be made using the fields provided or by using Boolean AND, OR, and NOT for search terms. Truncation and field-limiting and proximity searching are also permitted. Any search set may be saved for reuse or combined with other sets. The results screen for titles shows source, publication date, location of the article in the publication, and availability of the source material.

Name:	**ProQuest General Periodicals**
Vendor:	UMI
Cost:	Contact vendor
Hardware requirements:	IBM PC and compatibles, DOS 3.3, 1MB RAM, 490K free RAM, 2MB hard-disk space per ProQuest database installed plus 10MB hard-disk space to run after installation,1.44MB floppy
Comments:	This periodical index contains abstracts and articles of general-reference periodicals from January 1986 to the present. Four different versions of this database are available: General Periodicals Research I, General Periodicals Research II, General Periodicals Select, and General Periodicals Library. Research I contains abstracting and indexing of 1,000 titles from 1986, including full-image views (articles as they appear in the source publication with photos, graphs, illustrations, etc.) of 300. Research II contains abstracting and indexing of approximately 1,600 titles from 1986 plus full-image views of 350. General Periodicals Select contains abstracting and indexing of more than 500 titles from 1986 that are specifically relevant to research in undergraduate programs, with full-image views of 200. General Periodicals Library contains abstracting and indexing of approximately 500 titles since 1986, chosen to be of interest to public libraries. Some 300 are full-image views.

ProQuest Searchware makes it convenient for public use by people with little or no search experience. A search may be made using the fields abstract, authors, compilers, date, illustrations, ISSN, issue, journal, journal code, length, names, number, product, reviews, subjects, title, type, and volume. A search may also be made using Boolean AND, OR, and NOT for search terms. Truncation and proximity searching are also permitted.

Name:	**ProQuest News Service (Full-text) Databases**
Vendor:	UMI
Cost:	Contact vendor
Hardware requirements:	IBM PC and compatibles, DOS 3.3, 1MB RAM, 490K free RAM, 2MB hard-disk space per ProQuest database installed plus 10MB hard-disk space to run after installation, 1.44MB floppy
Comments:	Updated monthly, this database contains the full text from *CBS News Transcripts*, *NBC News Transcripts*, *Federal News Service*, and major U.S. newspapers for the current year plus two backfile years. Each newspaper is offered as a separate subscription: *New York Times*, *Wall Street Journal*, *Wall Street Journal Europe*, *Asian Wall Street Journal*, *USA Today*, and *Washington Post*.

ProQuest Searchware makes it convenient for public use by people with little or no search experience. A search may be made using the fields that are readily available. A search may also be made using Boolean AND, OR, and NOT for search terms. Truncation and field-limiting and proximity searching are also permitted. Any search set may be saved for reuse or combined with other sets. The results screen for titles shows source, publication date, location of the article in the publication, and availability of the source material.

Name:	**Readers' Guide Abstracts; Readers' Guide Abstracts Select Edition**
Vendor:	H. W. Wilson
Cost:	$1,995
Hardware requirements:	IBM PC and compatibles, 640K RAM, 3MB free hard-disk space, DOS 3.1 or later, Hayes compatible modem optional
Comments:	Readers' Guide Abstracts contains indexing from January 1983 and abstracting from September 1984 for all articles contained in all 240 periodicals already indexed in *Readers' Guide to Periodical Literature* plus coverage of the *New York Times*. More than 85,000 abstracts are included each year, averaging 125 words each. Readers' Guide Abstracts Select Edition only provides coverage of selected articles in the same periodicals and the *New York Times*.

Three search levels make it easy for beginners and more-advanced researchers to search effectively. A single-subject search mode (browse) will locate authors by searching on author's name or title of a work. Multiple-subject search using Wilsearch mode can be used to search for authors by field. A command-language search can also be implemented. This system, the same one used by Wilsonline, supports nested Boolean logic, proximity searching, free-text and controlled-vocabulary searching, truncation, ranging, multifile searching, saving of data from a search, and more. In addition, subscribers to any of Wilson's CD-ROM services also have unlimited online access time to the latest information when needed.

Name:	**Readers' Guide to Periodical Literature**
Vendor:	H. W. Wilson
Cost:	$1,095
Hardware requirements:	IBM PC and compatibles, 640K RAM, 3MB free hard-disk space, DOS 3.1 or later, Hayes compatible modem optional
Comments:	Updated monthly, this database indexes 240 popular magazines of interest to school, college, and public libraries. Three search levels make it easy for beginners and more-advanced researchers to search effectively. A single-subject search mode (browse) will locate authors by searching on author's name or title of a work. Multiple-subject search using Wilsearch mode can be used to search for authors by field. A command-language search can also be implemented. This system, the same one used by Wilsonline, supports nested Boolean logic, proximity searching, free-text and controlled-vocabulary searching, truncation, ranging, multifile searching, saving of data from a search, and more. In addition, subscribers to any of Wilson's CD-ROM services also have unlimited online access time to the latest information when needed.

Name:	**Science Citation Index**
Vendor:	Institute for Scientific Information
Cost:	Contact vendor; one year's data per disc, updated quarterly with annual cumulation, annual cumulations for previous years may be purchased separately
Hardware requirements:	IBM PC and compatibles; Macintosh
Comments:	This index contains more than 600,000 references to the citations at the end of scientific articles contained in approximately 3,300 science and technology journals. It is an aid

to researchers in locating research and updates to previous research, following the work of a particular researcher or institution, or verifying bibliographic information. A search may be carried out by citation, title word, author's name, author's address or institutional affiliation, or journal; it may be limited to the latest quarterly update or to a specific language or document type. The database supports both Boolean search and truncation. Citations may also be drawn from a citation dictionary and a dictionary of search terms. Search strategies may be saved for later use. Results may be viewed as titles or as complete records with author(s), title, source, language, document type, references, and a document order number or document delivery through ISI. The database will also indicate how many records exist that are related to the search results. Search results may be collected into sets for printing, saving, or combining with other search results. Saved results may be used with a word processor or database management software.

Name:	**The Serials Directory**
Vendor:	EBSCO Publishing
Cost:	$525 quarterly
Hardware requirements:	IBM PC and compatibles, 640K RAM (2MB recommended), DOS 5.0 or later, 5MB hard-disk space required; printer optional
Comments:	The Serials Directory CD contains all of the information in the print version, including 200,000 U.S. and international titles. Library of Congress classification numbers, Dewey decimal, universal decimal, National Library of Medicine, CODEN designations, and MARC control numbers are attached to each record. Other information includes former title/new title name(s), price, publisher's name, address, telephone and fax numbers, editor's name, languages, frequency, circulation, ISSN Register, and other information. Local holdings may be highlighted with notes (up to ten lines) to speed up retrieval of materials. The search software is menu-driven and easy to use. Truncation, wild cards, and proximity searches are supported for advanced search. A search may also be limited to a specific field to retrieve titles that are within specified parameters using greater than ($>$) or less than ($<$), etc. Titles within a given price range or above or below a certain price threshold may be found using this technique. Also included on the disc is Copyright Clearance Center information: a separate index of titles accepting advertising, a

separate index of titles accepting book reviews, and a separate peer-reviewed index.

Name:	**Social Sciences Citation Index**
Vendor:	Institute for Scientific Information
Cost:	Contact vendor; one year's data per disc, updated quarterly with annual cumulation, annual cumulations for previous years may be purchased separately
Hardware requirements:	IBM PC and compatibles, 640K RAM, 3MB hard-disk space; Macintosh
Comments:	The CD contains bibliographic data, including descriptions and abstracts, on more than 130,000 source items in more than 3,300 science and technical journals plus 1,400 social science journals, for a total of more than 1,650,000 cited references. It is an aid to researchers in locating research and updates to previous research, in following the research of a particular researcher or institution, or in verifying bibliographic information. A search may be carried out by citation, title word, author's name, author's address or institutional affiliation, or journal; it may be limited to the latest quarterly update or to a specific language or document type. The database supports both Boolean search and truncation. Citations may also be drawn from a citation dictionary and a dictionary of search terms. Search strategies may be saved for later use. Search results may be viewed as titles only or as complete records with author(s), title, source, language, document type, references, and a document order number or document delivery through ISI. The database will also indicate how many records exist that are related to the search results. Search results may be collected into sets for printing, saving, or combining with other search results. Saved results may be used with a word processor or database management software.

Name:	**Time Almanac on CD-ROM**
Vendor:	Compact Publishing
Cost:	$79.95
Hardware requirements:	486 IBM PC or later and compatibles, multimedia, Windows 3.1 or later, 4MB RAM
Comments:	News junkies and students will love this exciting reference tool. It is packed with useful features for understanding and learning about current events. This multimedia CD contains *Time* magazine covers and more than 25,000 news articles

from 1989 to the first week of 1995. Additional materials cover decade highlights since 1923. Election highlights of all presidential campaigns since 1924 are offered through multimedia coverage providing videos and speeches of candidates. To test a user's knowledge of current events the disc contains "Newsquest," a set of 1,500 questions. The 1993 version has been loaded with statistics to give readers access to the *U.S. Statistical Abstract*, area codes, ZIP codes, and postal rates. The complete contents of the *1994 CIA World Factbook* and State Department notes on 200 countries are also on the disc. This information makes excellent source material for term papers. Students can research murder, rape, and other crimes; the judiciary (including the Supreme Court and its decisions); the history of capital punishment; science and technology outlays by the government; and many other areas of interest. The detailed U.S. map that is also online can be used to learn where events in the almanac occurred. The calendar of events provides dates for holidays for the year, hurricane names, celestial events (phases of the moon, equinoxes, etc.), and much more.

Searching for text is easy and can be done by a word list. Specific phrases can be searched if typed in. The browse feature will list all articles by date and title for quick recall. The CD contains 78 video clips of important historical news. It is issued annually.

Further information:	"'Time Almanac' Offers Wealth of Data at Rich Price," *San Jose Mercury News*, Aug. 22, 1993.
Name:	**Ulrich's PLUS**
Vendor:	Bowker-Reed Reference Electronic Publishing
Cost:	$495, 1-year subscription, issued every 13 weeks; $1,411, 3-year subscription
Hardware requirements:	IBM PC and compatibles
Comments:	Ulrich's PLUS contains purchasing information for more than 83,000 publishers in 215 countries. It includes more than 149,000 regularly and irregularly issued serials and more than 47,000 that have stopped publication. There are 75 data elements in each record. A search may include title; subject; publisher; editor; abstracted index; ISSN; area code; U.S. state and ZIP code; country code; circulation; CODEN; Dewey decimal number; class number; document delivery availability; online/CD-ROM vendor; price (U.S.); keyword; year first published; media code; special features; special index; publication code; and status code. The database also

includes editorial descriptions of many titles and contains some 87,000 fax numbers and 21,000 telex numbers of publishers. Eight display and output formats include standard Ulrich's listing, catalog card, MARC-tagged, order form, custom detailed, electronic order, and custom. The program supports electronic ordering from any vendor accepting the standard SISAC format. Its downloading feature saves records in ASCII format. Document supplier notations are included for ADONIS, British Library Document Supply Centre, Chemical Abstract Service, Congressional Information Service, Engineering Information, Faxon, Swets, UnCover, and UMI.

Name:	**U.S. Business Reporter**
Vendor:	KR Information OnDisc
Cost:	$2,495; $995, current-year; $995, archival year; updated bimonthly
Hardware requirements:	IBM PC and compatibles; Macintosh
Comments:	This database includes selected company news from BusinessWire and full text from business sections of 16 metropolitan newspaper databases. Researchers may seek information on industry trends, market opportunities, business executive profiles, and stock offerings for state or city.

Name:	**Washington Times & Insight**
Vendor:	Wayzata Technology
Cost:	$26.10
Hardware requirements:	IBM PC and compatibles, DOS 4.0 or later, Windows 3.1 or later; Macintosh 6.0.7 or later, 2MB of free RAM
Comments:	The system uses the search software TextWare 4.0 Lite for Windows. The information in this database contains the *Washington Times* and *Insight on the News* (a weekly news magazine) from January 1991 through June 1994. The *Washington Times* is available in two separate files that let users browse chronologically from beginning to end, if desired. A full-text search supports Boolean logic, phrase, or proximity searches using AND, OR, NOT, ANDNOT, XOR, and ORNOT. Two ways to search are with a word wheel or a command line. Search histories are maintained by the system so that they may be quickly repeated. The software is flexible and contains a myriad of features for local configuration. Other features include sticky notes, bookmarks, connections to outside programs, and word-and-image links. The system includes a viewer for PCX (graphic) images.

Recreation and Travel

Recreational activities such as sports, hobbies, and travel may now be enhanced with the aid of CD-ROM databases. Sports CDs comprise many more categories than are included in this section. Baseball fans will love Total Baseball and Microsoft Complete Baseball. Both provide a mass of statistics that can be searched and sifted. Travel CDs offer trip planning, mapping, and sightseeing opportunities.

Additional products available:

Key Action Traveler; Key Action Traveler for Windows (Softkey Software Products)

The Story of the World Cup 1930–1994 (Attica Cybernetics)

Name:	**Everywhere USA Travel Guide**
Vendor:	Deep River Publishing
Cost:	$59.95
Hardware requirements:	IBM PC and compatibles, 4MB RAM, 3MB hard-disk space, Windows 3.1 or later, DOS 3.3 or later, sound card
Comments:	Everywhere USA Travel Guide is an exciting two-disc, multimedia travel guide to the United States. One disc covers areas east of the Mississippi River, and one covers the land west of the Mississippi. The database includes 6,000 pictures of historic and scenic locations that are suggested as travel destinations. Dozens of short videos with sound offer some insight into attractions such as ballooning, comedy clubs, the arts, and nature that are grouped by state or by type of attraction. The photos are quite outstanding and can be viewed continuously as a slide show presentation. There are from one to three photos grouped together with any attraction.
	While it is easy to find travel books with lots of pictures, this package has some features that make it unique and

worthwhile. Attractions of interest to the user can be located in several ways. They may be narrowed by state, each with a listing of individual attractions. The New York State listing, for example, contains approximately 200 different locations. They may also be selected by viewing thumbnail images of the photographs, eight at a time. When one image is selected, a map may be called up to locate it. Other important information immediately available on the screen is the cost of the attraction, the time of year it is available, and the days and hours during which it is open. Several paragraphs describe the nature of the location in a nutshell. An address and phone number for each are also given.

Beyond the basics, however, the Travel Guide comes equipped with a variety of advanced search features. Push buttons will specify attractions according to whether they are free, children's activities (such as camping, beaches, hiking, tours, dining), or handicapped accessible. Attractions can also be limited by month or even day of the week when they are open. Two or more criteria can be linked with the operators of AND or OR. Though it is not possible to search for random text, nor is it possible to include both search operators at one time (e.g., while "camping AND hiking AND handicapped accessible" is valid, "camping AND hiking OR handicapped accessible" is not valid). Such searches can be done for a specific state or for the entire United States. Results may be printed out or a bookmark placed to mark a particular attraction for later recall.

Name:	**HAM Radio**
Vendor:	Chestnut Software
Cost:	$19.95
Hardware requirements:	IBM PC and compatibles
Comments:	Enthusiasts of ham radio operation will find this a highly useful and feature-packed CD with its many program listings and utilities. The program listings contain bulletin board system software, FCC regulations, DX, FAX, frequency lists, maps, radio clusters, satellite tracking, TTY, contest information, club information, exam assistance and study aids, Morse code, antenna programs, and much more. All of the programs are compressed. The interface will load them directly to a hard drive.

Name:	**Microsoft Complete Baseball**
Vendor:	Microsoft
Cost:	$79.95
Hardware requirements:	IBM PC and compatibles, 4MB RAM, 2 MB hard-disk space, Windows 3.x, sound card, 256-color graphics adapter
Comments:	Microsoft Complete Baseball is a multimedia adventure into the history of the major leagues. It contains information on the teams, players, history, records, and even a trivia quiz. The interface is flawless. Each menu is filled with baseball cards, photos, or other baseball nostalgia. Most selection is by push button, but there is also a search facility in each section.

Fans who like statistics will especially enjoy the records section. This lists the top 50 players for 12 different statistics, including at bats, home runs, RBIs, strikeouts, etc. The list can be filtered by including or not including batters, pitchers, or relief pitchers. Records are available separately for player season or player year. Statistics also are given for teams, including for team season and team year. Individual player information gives a biography and photo of most players (a few are labeled unavailable). The chronicle section contains a history of baseball, baseball stories, awards, previous leagues, and the *New York Times* 100 Players. The almanac is a year-by-year retrospective of baseball. A narrative describes the season, with push-button options for the World Series, final standings, league leaders, all-star games, and awards and honors. There are photos interspersed throughout, along with occasional introductory video clips of famous home runs, etc.

The trivia quiz is, in a word, *hard*. If you don't know anything about baseball, pass this up. Two levels (both hard) ask random multiple-choice questions about teams and players. In level one players get three chances, in level two players get only one.

Another exciting feature is the "Microsoft Baseball Daily," an online modem service for the hardcore baseball fan that connects users with a downloaded baseball infosheet each day of the regular season. It contains league-leader updates, the day's highlights, player and team statistics, etc. A sample is already loaded on the disc. Any additional copies require registration and are $1.25 per issue.

Microsoft has produced the best computer baseball product to date with this easy-to-use, colorful, statistically and historically useful program.

Name:	**National Parks of America**
Vendor:	Multicom Publishing
Cost:	$59.95
Hardware requirements:	IBM PC and compatibles
Comments:	This database of the national park system provides an excellent way in a colorful multimedia environment to find the right park for specific interests. The national parks are divided into regions: Pacific Northwest, Great Lakes Region, Northeast, Southeast, Outer Region (Alaska and Hawaii), and Golden West. Each region is further subdivided into states. It is also possible to access information by the index, which will take users directly from the main menu to any state. The "Travel Plan" section includes a search that can be limited by categories of interest (backpacking, boating, camping, first aid, fishing, food/supplies, handicap accessibility, hiking, lodging, pets, skiing) and by region and state to provide a useful listing of parks. Information may be printed out. Music (though not always the most enjoyable) will play during parts of the presentation. For each park, a slide presentation and text narrative show and explain points of interest, activities (guided and self tours, museums, visitor centers, trails, etc.), mailing addresses, telephone numbers, travel directions, best times to visit (including notes on seasonal temperatures, peak tourist month, snow, etc.), and general information about exhibits, campgrounds, fisheries, etc.

Name:	**Total Baseball**
Vendor:	CMC Research
Cost:	$69.95
Hardware requirements:	IBM PC and compatibles, 640K RAM, SVGA with 512K of video memory capable of 640×480 and 256 colors; Macintosh, System 6.0.5 or later, 2MB RAM
Comments:	Baseball fans will love the more than 500 images of players, teams, and ballparks, along with many nostalgic audio moments in baseball history. The main database is a statistical number cruncher. There are stats on more than 13,000 players. This includes batting, pitching, and fielding registers for all major league players; the top 100 all-time, life-time, and single-season leaders; and the Most Valuable Player, Cy Young, Rookie of the Year, and Hall of Fame awards. Appendixes include "Rules and Scoring and Rules Changes to 1919," "Rules and Scoring with Rule Changes from 1920 to the Present," "Forfeit and No Decision Games" (with some brief explanation as to why each was ended

the way it was), "Pitcher Lifetime Fielding," "Glossary of Statistical Terms," "City Series," "Ultimate Baseball Library" (a massive bibliography divided by topics such as statistics, guidebooks, Negro leagues, and umpiring), and team and league abbreviations. While a few of the other baseball CD-ROM products may offer a snappier appearance with a Windows interface, none offers any more-complete or -detailed accounting for the enthusiast.

Religion

Laypersons, scholars, and religious officials alike have always desired greater access to religious documents to look up specific words, events, or passages. Several of the CDs listed in this section are an entire biblical reference library. The Bible Library contains 9 different versions of the Bible as well as 20 other reference books. Use of CD-ROM reduces search time to a fraction of the time it takes to find something in paper volumes.

Additional products available:

The Bible Library (Sony Electronic Publishing)

Creation Stories (Time Warner Interactive Group)

The New Oxford Annotated Bible (Oxford University Press)

Name:	**The Bible Library**
Vendor:	Ellis Enterprises
Cost:	$69
Hardware requirements:	IBM PC and compatibles, 640K RAM
Comments:	Bible Library contains 9 versions of the Bible and 20 additional Bible reference books. This makes it the most extensive Bible reference CD looked at in this section. It is a CD intended for research, not for browsing or casual reading. The Bible versions available are The Living Bible, American Standard, King James, New King James, New International, Revised Standard, Simple English, Romanized, and Romanized Unaccented. The reference works, which will assist clergy in study or preparation for sermons or other Bible-related activities, are *Easton Illustrated Dictionary*, *Elwell's Evangelical Dictionary*, *Gary Home Bible Commentary*, *Life and Times of Jesus the Messiah*, *Literal Translation*, *Micro Bible*, *Henry Concise Commentary*, *Osbeck's 101 Hymn Stories*, *Sermon Outlines*, *Strong's Greek Dictionary*, *Strong's Hebrew Dictionary*, *Theological Wordbook of the*

Old Testament, Vine's New Testament Dictionary, and *Vine's Old Testament Dictionary*. Any number of the Bible versions may be searched concurrently and displayed. The Bible verse citation (e.g., John 3:16) is displayed as well, if the field of "citation" is chosen. The Boolean operators of AND and OR are allowed.

The DOS interface is less than inviting. It would work better if it were a Windows environment. Still, it is not complicated, and the average user will find it easy to make a search from one or more of the Bible or reference volumes. There is online help (F1) that is needed, especially since there are too many annoying function keys without a quick screen reference. These can be either written down or memorized. Search results may be printed out or written to a disk file. An extensive manual is available on disc that can be printed out or viewed. It contains installation instructions, operating and search tips, potential problems, and error messages.

Name:	**CD-ROM Judaic Classics Library, 3d edition**
Vendor:	Davka
Cost:	$549
Hardware requirements:	IBM and compatibles, 640K RAM required, 2MB hard-disk storage
Comments:	The database contains a collection of original Judaic texts, including Tanach, Babylonian Talmud, Aggadic Midrashim, Zorah, Talmud Yerushlmi, Mishneh Torah, Rashi on Chumash and Talmud, and four commentaries on the Torah. Texts may be searched using up to eight search terms at the same time and Boolean operators and proximity search terms.

Name:	**The Holy Bible CD-ROM**
Vendor:	Advantage Plus Distributors
Cost:	$14.95
Hardware requirements:	IBM PC and compatibles, Windows or DOS, hard-disk drive optional
Comments:	Both Windows and DOS versions are contained on the CD. The Windows version is delightful to read and use. Full control of font type and size make it useful for anyone who needs a larger, clearer image. This CD contains the Online Bible Version 6.1 and the King James Version, *Thayer's Greek Lexicon* and Brown, Driver & Briggs *Hebrew Lexicon, Original Thompson Chain Topics*, the *New Topical Textbook*, the entire *Treasure of Scripture Knowledge* of more than 580,000 cross references, Strong's numbers,

1769 Authorized Version, 1890 Darby Bible, 1898 Young's Literal Translation, *1917 Scofield Verse Notes*, and the French/German/Spanish translations of the Bible. The Seedmaster Bible is also included. It contains an "Exhaustive Word List" for all of the translations and Strong's numbers. The Seedmaster Bible also allows users to run more than one version of the Bible simultaneously.

Finding one's way around such a mass of information is relatively simple using the program's search capabilities. For instance, a search can be performed in an entire version of the Bible or in any range of books and verses, and it allows for Boolean search terms. A special edit feature permits another version of the Bible to be opened and copied or altered as necessary and placed in the notepad. The program contains extensive context-sensitive help files, though some areas are left without much documentation (e.g., the program contains few hints about the use of the excellent power button bar). All in all, the program is filled with many sophisticated features.

Name:	**Soncino Talmud on CD**
Vendor:	Davka
Cost:	$299
Hardware requirements:	IBM PC and compatibles, Windows 3.1 or later, 4MB RAM; Macintosh, 4MB RAM
Comments:	This library of original texts includes the complete Soncino English text of the Talmud. Also included are original Hebrew and Aramaic texts of the Talmud and Hebrew text of Rashi's commentary of the Talmud. A search may be made and text is scrolled in both English and Hebrew. The Windows interface is convenient for search and display. A simple search may be conducted, or one can involve Boolean operators AND, OR, and NOT. Complex logic can be used to include phrases, also with Boolean operators and proximity search, parentheses, and combinations of Boolean operators. A wild card (*) may be used for prefixes or suffixes or for embedded letters (in Hebrew only). Search results may be copied, pasted, saved to disk, or printed.

Sociology

Many CD databases present a wide variety of information about the human condition, including marriage, death, crime, race relations, and the stages of human development. Perhaps the best, or at least the most-comprehensive, index to such literature is the Cross-Cultural CD; however, it is expensive, making it beyond the reach of many smaller libraries. Social Science Source is less expensive and more practical for the small library seeking to improve its access to general social literature.

Name:	**Cross-Cultural CD (Human Sexuality and Marriage)**
Vendor:	SilverPlatter Information
Cost:	$5,980, full set; $1,495, per volume
Hardware requirements:	IBM PC and compatibles, 512K RAM available, 2.5MB hard-disk space
Comments:	Individual volumes in this set include: Human Sexuality, Marriage, Family Life (volume 1); Crime and Social Problems (volume 2); Old Age, Death and Dying (volume 3); Childhood and Adolescence, Socialization and Education (volume 4); and Religious Beliefs and Religious Practices (volume 5). It includes information from 1,000 books on psychology, sociology, and anthropology and focuses on 60 different societies around the world from the nineteenth and twentieth centuries. The Human Sexuality and Marriage volume contains information on dating behavior, eroticism, frequency of sex, ideals of beauty, incest taboos, orgasm, pornography, prostitution, rape, symbolism, homosexual marriage, honeymoon, love, marriage by exchange, wife capture, wife purchase, and much more.
	Retrieval software is SilverPlatter's WinSPIRS for Windows users or PC-SPIRS for DOS users. WinSPIRS provides an excellent data interface. If available online, multiple databases may be searched simultaneously. Both truncation

(*) and wild cards (?) are supported. The operators AND, NEAR, NOT, OR, WITH, and IN can be used. A thesaurus provides ample subject access; an index provides additional easy access to information. Each citation in these databases includes the following fields: author, record control number, publication date, descriptors, geographic focus, outline of cultural materials subject codes, page number(s) in source, publisher information, cultural summary citations, society, cultural summaries note, full text of the excerpt, title, and period of time researched.

Name: **Popline on CD-ROM**

Vendor: National Information Services Corporation

Cost: $695 annual subscription with semiannual updates

Hardware requirements: IBM PC and compatibles, 512K RAM available

Comments: This disc contains a database of population studies. Some 200,000 citations and abstracts are included for published and unpublished population literature, including family planning and related health issues. Some specific topics include maternal and child health, practices to ensure child survival, breastfeeding, child immunization, population dynamics, primary health care, overpopulation, health care instruction, family planning programs, policies on migration, sexually transmitted diseases, AIDS, law/policy on reproduction, and much more. Information coverage is from 1827 to the present, gathered from government reports and publications, international agencies, family planning organizations, clinical medicine and health databases, monographs, laws, bills, court decisions, conference papers, theses, dissertations, newspaper articles, and others. The standard NISC disc interface provides search modes for novice, advanced, and expert levels with full Boolean, proximity, and field-specific retrieval capabilities.

Name: **Social Issues Resources Series**

Vendor: Social Issues Resources Series

Cost: Researcher: $1,450 for software only, $1,250 for renewals of software only; Government Reporter: $950 for software only, $700 annual updates; Discover: $650 for software only, $475 for annual updates; Index-Only: $190 for annual updates; inquire for work stations hardware/software packages or multimedia

Hardware requirements: IBM PC and compatibles, 512 K RAM, 7MB hard-disk space; Macintosh, System 7, 3MB RAM, 10MB hard-disk space

Comments: SIRS Researcher CD-ROM contains full-text articles from more than 800 domestic and international sources: newspapers, magazines, and government publications from 1988 to the present and graphics such as maps, diagrams, and other illustrations. It can be searched by subject headings that are indexed according to the Library of Congress subject headings. "Title browse" lets users search groups of articles under a topic. "Keyword search" uses a combination of words within separate search fields. Improvements in the 1995 edition include management features to track patron usage, an on-screen dictionary, and article summaries for new full-text articles.

SIRS Government Reporter on CD-ROM contains documents published by federal departments, agencies, and commissions. Information includes analyses, statistical data, charts, tables, graphs, and maps. A search may be made by category (subject tree), department or agency browse, keyword search (with Boolean operators, proximity searching, and truncation), or background notes on countries (U.S. State Department).

SIRS Discover CD-ROM is a separate product designed for younger patrons to promote reading, research, language, and writing skills. It contains full-text articles drawn from more than 300 magazines and newspapers. The database also contains a subset of articles written by children ages 18 and younger. Users have access to an on-screen dictionary, notepad, article summaries, and four reading level categories: primary, upper primary, middle, and upper middle. Articles may be printed or downloaded to disk. A search may be made by category (subject tree) or by keyword search (with Boolean operators, proximity searching, and truncation). The program comes with a complement of teaching materials and an *Educator's Guide*.

The SIRS Index-Only CD-ROM is an index to the SIRS Print Information Systems. Bibliographic citations found during a search in this tool correspond to articles in the SIRS print series.

Name: **Social Science Source**
Vendor: EBSCO Publishing
Cost: $995, annual subscription with bimonthly updates; $495, annual subscription with three updates
Hardware requirements: IBM PC and compatibles, 640K RAM, 5MB hard-disk space, CD player with two-disc capacity recommended

Comments: Social Science Source is an index and abstract service with coverage of 353 journals in political science, economics, international relations, sociology, psychology, and public policy. Some begin in 1984. Of these, 23 journals are full-text searchable with tables, charts, and graphic images. Articles may be printed out for patron use. Some of the full-text articles are "Aging," "Congressional Quarterly Weekly Report," "Foreign Policy," "Journal of Social Psychology," "Journal of General Psychology," "Monthly Labor Review," "National Review," "Public Health Reports" and "World Press Review." Abstracted journals include *Journal of International Affairs*, *Journal of Comparative Family Studies*, *Labor History*, *Mankind Quarterly*, *Mother Jones*, *NATO Review*, *NEA Today*, *The Nation*, *Philosophical Quarterly*, *The Population Bulletin*, *Public Administration Review*, *Studies in Philology*, *Working Mother*, *Technology and Culture*, *Vital Speeches*, and *Youth and Society*.

Searching may be conducted by keyword, subject, full Boolean logic, phrase, and proximity. Local library holdings may be marked in the index to accelerate retrieval. Up to ten lines of notes may be included for each title detailing interlibrary loan availability, etc. Collection development statistics will track usage by title.

Name: **Welcome to Africa**
Vendor: Walnut Creek CDROM
Cost: $39.95
Hardware requirements: IBM PC 386 or later and compatibles, 256-color VGA, Windows 3.1 or later
Comments: The major attraction of this CD is the 450 pictures contained on it. The Windows interface makes it possible to choose numerous viewing categories, including theme, topic, or place, or to choose from among 200 keywords. The pictures are quite spectacular and give users a great sense of the African continent. They include wildlife, scenery, people, and culture. Additionally, the disc contains a role-playing game. The user takes the role of a villager who must make decisions about what to plant, what to buy, etc. Another activity enables users to "write their own book" using words and pictures.

Name: **Wilson Social Sciences Abstracts; Social Sciences Index**
Vendor: H. W. Wilson
Cost: $2,295, Wilson Social Sciences Abstracts; $1,295, Social Sciences Index

Hardware requirements: IBM PC and compatibles, 640K RAM, 3MB free hard-disk space, DOS 3.1 or later, Hayes compatible modem optional

Comments: Updated with 3,000 new records each month, Wilson Social Sciences Abstracts contains abstracts and indexes of 415 important English-language social science periodicals. Included is a separate index to reviews of current books in social science. Subjects covered include community health, economics, law and criminology, minority studies, policy studies, psychology and psychiatry, sociology, urban studies, and more. Abstracts range from 50 to 150 words. Indexing is from February 1983 and abstracting from January 1994.

Social Science Index contains indexing only, without abstracts. Three search levels make it easy for beginners to use and for more-advanced researchers to search effectively. A single-subject search mode (browse) will locate authors by searching on author's name or title of a work. Multiple-subject search using Wilsearch mode can be used to search for authors by field. A command-language search can also be implemented. This system, the same one used by Wilsonline, supports nested Boolean logic, proximity searching, free-text and controlled-vocabulary searching, truncation, ranging, multifile searching, saving of data from a search, and more. In addition, subscribers to any of Wilson's CD-ROM services also have unlimited online access time to the latest information when needed.

Telephone Directories

CD-ROMs make it much easier to search for one telephone number among 80 million residential telephone numbers and 12 million business numbers. A good national directory can now be purchased for less than forty dollars. Occasionally, there is a complaint about the accuracy of these national telephone directories, and they do have errors in them. However, one, PhoneDisc, claims to be 97 percent accurate. In any case, most libraries have little access to any but the local telephone directory in paper because of cost and storage problems. Disc-based phone directories make a welcome and worthwhile addition, but no library should fail to stock the local print phone directory.

Additional product available:

MetroSearch Library (Metromail)

Name:	**American Business Phone Book**
Vendor:	American Business Information
Cost:	$149
Hardware requirements:	IBM PC and compatibles
Comments:	The more than 10 million business addresses and telephone numbers compiled on this disc are from 5,000 Yellow Pages directories in the United States and Canada. Easy to install and simple to use, this product can be searched by key word, company name (within a city, state, or entire country), geographic area (ZIP code, area code, city, or state), type of business (using SIC codes or Yellow Pages headings). A search can also include the Boolean operators AND or OR.

Name:	**Canada Phone**
Vendor:	Pro CD
Hardware requirements:	IBM PC and compatibles, 4MB RAM
Cost:	$149
Comments:	The CD contains white pages directories for all major Canadian cities.

Further information:	John McCormick, "Guard Your Time and Shelf Space with These CD-ROM Phone Books," *Government Computer News*, Mar. 21, 1994, 45.

Name:	**Direct Phone**
Vendor:	Pro CD
Cost:	$79
Hardware requirements:	IBM PC and compatibles, 4MB RAM
Comments:	This CD phone directory is advertised as a directory for home use. It contains the same number of entries (80 million) as Select Phone. This two-CD set is also less expensive than its business counterpart, which has four CDs. However, it has fewer features and search capabilities. Also, the SIC code is not included. Searches may be made by name, street, city, state, and ZIP or area code; wild card searches are also permitted. Information contained within includes name, address, city, state, ZIP code, and telephone number. Information gleaned from the directory may be printed or saved to disk for unlimited and unrestricted use into any database, word processor, spreadsheet, or contact management software. Printed output can be in delimited or fixed-length ASCII, business card format, or mailing label format. The CD provides autodial capability for a Hayes-compatible modem. The disc's name search feature makes it easy to scan potential correct entries when only a partial name is known.
Further information:	Deborah Cole, "Pro CD Offers 3 National-Directory Discs," *MacWeek*, Dec. 13, 1993, v. 7, no. 48, 15.

Name:	**Euro Pages**
Vendor:	Pro CD
Cost:	$49
Hardware requirements:	IBM PC and compatibles, 4MB RAM required
Comments:	The Euro Pages telephone directory CD contains numbers for 150,000 companies, manufacturers, and distributors from the following countries: Austria, Belgium, Switzerland, Germany, Denmark, Spain, Great Britain, Hungary, Italy, Ireland, Luxemburg, Norway, The Netherlands, Sweden, Finland, Greece, Poland, Croatia, Slovenia, The Czech Republic, and The Slovak Republic. Products, services, and activities of each company are indexed and divided into 19 key sectors and 600 subheadings. Access is also available through 6,000 keywords.

Name:	**North American Facsimile Book**
Vendor:	Quanta Press
Cost:	$304.95
Hardware requirements:	IBM PC and compatibles
Comments:	This database contains more than 150,000 business fax numbers in the United States, Canada, and Mexico.

Name:	**PhoneDisc USA (Residential East and West)**
Vendor:	Digital Directory Assistance
Cost:	$79
Hardware requirements:	IBM PC and compatibles; Macintosh
Comments:	This extremely easy-to-use CD makes available many millions of residential telephone numbers in the United States. Numbers are divided into two discs (East and West), and are available separately. The database takes the form of a wheel, so it is easy to browse among the entries. As letters are typed, the wheel spins to the closest entry. The current entry is highlighted in a box in the lower right corner of the screen.

Search criteria may be specified in several ways, including by city and state. The database lists names, addresses, cities, states, ZIP codes, and phone numbers. The software is set up to access more than one CD drive if more than one is available. Databases can be changed from the menu with no loss of time or additional software. The autodial feature automatically dials a number from the directory if the computer is connected to the phone lines. Printing entries to paper is flexible. Entries from the database may be printed out singly by current entry or as a batch by selecting a group by first and last entry. Complete help is available as an online file.

Name:	**ProPhone Business+One**
Vendor:	Pro CD
Cost:	Contact vendor
Hardware requirements:	IBM PC and compatibles, DOS 3.1 and later, 512K RAM
Comments:	ProPhone contains 7 million business listings organized in an easy-to-use format. It is very useful for finding businesses by subject categories, not just by name. While there are no Windows features, they are largely unnecessary. There are no limitations on use.

Listings may be searched by name or SIC code and then subdivided by heading, address, city, state, ZIP code, or area code. The easiest and most straightforward way to find something is to simply enter the name. A word wheel allows guessing the names one letter at a time. If a specific name is not known, a subject search can be performed by entering one of the more than 2,000 SIC codes. This is extremely useful in pinpointing a certain category of industry. If the number is not known, the heading field, a listing of subject headings that pinpoint specific SIC codes, may be used. Apparently, the only Boolean operator allowed is OR. No searching for words or phrases within a name is allowed.

Once a listing has been found, the name, full address, telephone number, and the number of employees (if available) is given. A special count feature will tell how many listings there are for any specific search criteria or for the entire directory. (The count I did for the entire directory I used returned 6,661,439 listings.) Once a search has been completed, the browse function (F4) permits scanning through the listings. A dial feature will automatically dial a selected listing using an available modem. Setup can be used to specify modem parity, pulse or tone dial, com port, etc. Search results can be printed in galley form, as business cards or mailing labels, as a disk file, or in ASCII delimited format.

Name:	**Select Phone**
Vendor:	Pro CD
Cost:	$299, single copy; $399, 4 quarterly issues; $999, LAN version
Hardware requirements:	IBM PC and compatibles, 386 or later; Macintosh
Comments:	The five-disc set contains 80 million phone numbers in the United States, both residential and business. The database may be searched by any field: name, street address, city, state, ZIP code, area code, telephone number, business heading, and SIC. Reverse searching and sort are also supported for name, address, business, or telephone number. This is an unrestricted database and may be used with any word processor, spreadsheet, or database that supports delimited ASCII or .dbf format. Search results may be output as labels, business cards, or galleys. Features include Boolean logic and wild-card searching. Any number in the database may be autodialed with a Hayes-compatible modem.

United States Information and Statistics

A world of statisics and facts are available about the United States on CD-ROMs. Some products are familiar as print directories. These include the 9-Digit ZIP Code Directory, Compact Disc Federal Register, Staff Directories on CD-ROM Plus, and the U.S. Code on CD-ROM. All are easier to use than their paper counterparts and can be searched quickly and efficiently. Other databases include directories for locating federal grants and funding, military personnel and bases, historic places, and even U.S. voters.

Name:	**9-Digit ZIP Code Directory**
Vendor:	American Business Information
Cost:	$49
Hardware requirements:	IBM PC and compatibles, 4MB RAM, 3MB available hard-disk space, DOS 5.0 or later, Windows 3.1 or later
Comments:	With this CD any ZIP code in the United States may be obtained by searching for the complete address for a 9-digit ZIP code or the city and state for a 3- or 5-digit ZIP code. Any ZIP code may be entered to find the city and state. Alternately, an address may be entered to find the correct ZIP code.

Name:	**Compact Disc Federal Register**
Vendor:	Counterpoint Publishing
Cost:	$367.50
Hardware requirements:	IBM PC and compatibles
Comments:	The database contains the full text of the daily *Federal Register* for the preceding six-month period. Charts, tables, and diagrams are all included.

Name: **County and City Data Book; Statistical Abstract of the United States**

Vendor: U.S. Bureau of the Census

Cost: $125, County and City Data Book; $50, Statistical Abstract of the United States

Hardware requirements: IBM PC and compatibles, 640K RAM, DOS 3.3 or later

Comments: County and City Data Book contains a wealth of current statistics on counties, cities of more than 25,000 population, and 11,000 places that have a population of more than 2,500. Information is from the 1990 census and features race, age, education, income, housing, and labor force statistics with comparisons with 1980. Statistics also involve spending patterns and tax burdens for city and local governments, unemployment figures, personal income growth, and health resources. Statistical Abstract of the United States 1994 contains about 1,400 data tables from federal government agencies, including information on crime, health, education, elections, recreation, housing, agriculture, and employment. Tables also give state rankings for many topics, including infant mortality rates, number of physicians per population, educational attainment, etc. Search software, compatible with dBASE format, supports a search for term, phrase, or tables.

The Bureau of the Census makes a number of other CD-ROM census-related products available as well: American Housing Survey, Census of Agriculture, Census of Population and Housing, County Business Patterns, Current Population Survey, Economic Censuses, Import and Export Data, TIGER/Line, and USA Counties.

Name: **Federal Grants and Funding Locator**

Vendor: Staff Directories

Cost: $295, annual subscription

Hardware requirements: IBM PC and compatibles, 512K RAM, 20MB hard-disk space

Comments: Information on 1,300 federal grant programs is included in this database. Searches may be conducted by program name, federal agency, grant requirements, dollar amount, deadlines, funding guidelines, and past funding data. The database is updated summer and winter.

Name: **Information U.S.A.**

Vendor: InfoBusiness

Cost: $69.95

Hardware requirements: IBM PC and compatibles

Comments: A treasury of government-giveaway information comprises this database. Some 30,000 economical or free sources of information are provided, along with ways to seek out free advice from 70,000 experts. All federal domestic-assistance programs are included.

Further information: David M. Stone, "Knowledge Is Everything," *Windows Sources*, Sept. 1994, 38.

Name: **Microsoft Stat Pack**
Vendor: Microsoft
Cost: $134.95
Hardware requirements: IBM PC and compatibles, 512K RAM
Comments: U.S. government statistics on this CD give economic, political, demographic, business, trade, agricultural, and industrial trends. Some of the documents include *Agricultural Statistics*, *Statistical Abstract of the United States*, *Public Land Statistics*, *Area Wage Survey*, and *Business Statistics*.

Name: **Military Contracts/Procurement Locator**
Vendor: Staff Directories
Cost: $695, annual subscription, updated quarterly
Hardware requirements: IBM PC and compatibles, 512K RAM, 20MB hard-disk space
Comments: The database contains information on military contracts, contractors, and subcontracting leads. The five parts of this database are

> Military Contractors Locator, which includes 225,000 Department of Defense contracts awarded during the previous twelve months; searchable by 88 fields
>
> Military Dictionary of Terms/Acronyms, with more than 80,000 entries explaining military terms, ranks, titles, buildings, codes, weapons systems, and military jargon
>
> Small Business and Subcontracting Locator
>
> S.I.C. Code Database, containing Standard Industrial Classification code information
>
> Contractors Currently Barred from Department of Defense Contracts, including reason, terms, and length of disbarment

Searchable data fields include agency or contractor name, reporting period of fiscal year, SIC/Weapons/Product service code, location of contractor or performance, foreign contracts, subject index, dictionary/acronyms, SIC code data, small business opportunities, and disbarred contractors.

Name: **Military Personnel/Base Locator**
Vendor: Staff Directories
Cost: $495, annual subscription, updated spring, summer, and fall
Hardware requirements: IBM PC, 512K RAM, 20MB hard-disk space
Comments: The database contains current U.S. military personnel information. The three parts of this database are

> Military Personnel Locator, containing information taken from the Department of Defense phone book and information from the *Federal Staff Directory* on more than 128,000 military and civilian personnel

> Military Base Locator, including data on more than 1,000 military bases worldwide, each with 130 fields of information including host commands, tenant commands, base function, commanding generals, base closures, locations, community and family information, history, names, addresses, and telephone and fax numbers

> Military Dictionary of Terms/Acronyms, including more than 80,000 entries that explain military terms, ranks, titles, buildings, codes, weapons systems, and military jargon

The database is searchable by dictionary/acronyms, person name, title, rank, base location or name, agency or organization, activities or command on base, and specialties or tasks.

Name: **National Register of Historic Places Index**
Vendor: Buckmaster Publishing
Cost: $295
Hardware requirements: IBM PC and compatibles; Macintosh
Comments: Information on more than 57,000 historic places in the United States and its territories is the basis of this CD. Records were drawn from the Department of the Interior and the National Park Service. Details on each site include its name, state, county, street address, city, ZIP code, category of place, reference number, criteria indicators, and certification date. Buckmaster also publishes the Place-Name Index.

Name:	**Staff Directories on CD-ROM Plus**
Vendor:	Staff Directories
Cost:	$495, annual subscription, updated twice each year
Hardware requirements:	IBM PC and compatibles, 512K RAM, 20MB hard-disk space
Comments:	Staff Directories contains basic information on more than 100,000 federal government staffers, including the Executive branch, the Judiciary, and Congress. Staff from the *Congressional Staff Directory*, *Federal Staff Directory*, and *Judicial Staff Directory* and the *World Factbook* are all included. A search may be conducted for congressional staff members by congress member's name and district, city/county/ZIP code, staffer's name or title, committees and subcommittees, and biographical data, as well as a full-text subject search. Executive staff members may be searched by federal executive's name/title/office, biographical data, location/address, or full-text subject search. A judicial search may be conducted by judge's name, biographical data, individual's name/title, court name/city/county, or by a full-text subject search.

Name:	**U.S. Code on CD-ROM**
Vendor:	U.S. Government Printing Office
Cost:	$34
Hardware requirements:	IBM PC and compatibles, 640 K RAM, 1/2MB hard-disk space
Comments:	The full text of all 50 titles of the *U.S. Code* and its supplements to January 2, 1992, are on this CD-ROM. Also included is the Table of Popular Names. Retrieval software for DOS (I-Search) and Windows (Personal Librarian) is included.

Name:	**Voters on CD**
Vendor:	Aristotle Industries
Cost:	$3,500
Hardware requirements:	IBM PC and compatibles, 640K RAM, 1MB hard-disk storage
Comments:	All registered voters in the United States as of 1985 are listed on this CD-ROM. Data may be sorted and exported by names, addresses, and telephone numbers.

Utilities

There has been a tremendous explosion in the number of useful utilities available for PCs. Most of the products listed in this section are intended for use by the library staff on their office PCs. Copyright restrictions make it prohibitive to circulate most, though not all, of the items listed (shareware excepted). Cyberdelic Screen Savers for Windows is a good example of an outstanding product that can be circulated to patrons. In this category are included screen savers (products that take over the screen of an inactive computer to prevent burn-in). Screen savers also offer a variety of distracting and amusing colors, animations, and even audio. There are screen savers based on popular TV and movie culture, including *Star Trek* and the *Simpsons*. ROMaterial is a collection of icons, sounds, and other visuals for use with Windows. Kudo CD Manager is a product for organizing and maintaining a collection of CDs. Kudo CD Publisher is a product for mastering a CD. Some libraries will wish to master a CD to house their local-history newspaper index and photo collection.

Name:	**Cyberdelic Screen Savers for Windows**
Vendor:	Quantum Axcess
Cost:	$19.95 (shareware)
Hardware requirements:	IBM PC and compatibles, 2MB free hard-disk space, Windows 3.1 or later, DOS 5.0 or later
Comments:	Cyberdelic Screen Savers contains more than 100 low-cost screen saver programs. The disc is shareware. Patrons and staff may use or share the programs as they wish, but they bear the responsibility of sending in the registration and any required fee if they continue to use the program. The disc interface is excellent, giving the basic information about each screen saver when highlighted from the list (author's name, basic note describing the screen saver, and the amount of the shareware fee). Any saver on the list may be immediately installed to hard drive by pushing an install button. Savers fall into several functional categories. Some can be run (tested)

directly from the CD; many must be installed to hard drive first, however. Some are merely modules to other programs such as AfterDark. The screen savers range from some that are either ordinary or average in excitement to those that are quite good. Some even include sounds such as popping corn. Many are silly, such as MediaScreen Top Gun (which blasts holes in the computer screen from which blood then flows) or the cow or chicken mooing or clucking across the screen. Several versions of a roller coaster ride are quite good, though they would have been better with sound effects. Nearly all savers have variable options that allow them to be customized for greater enjoyment. The interface also allows users to see a list of currently installed screen savers on a system as well as those that have been removed and archived.

Name:	**Kudo CD Manager**
Vendor:	Imspace Systems
Cost:	$130
Hardware requirements:	IBM PC and compatibles, 4MB RAM, 3MB free hard-disk space, Windows 3.1; Macintosh II and later, System 6.x (System 7 for Drop and Drag), 4MB RAM, 2MB free hard-disk space
Comments:	This system is useful for organizing, managing, and accessing CD-ROMs. An image catalog of a CD-ROM collection can be created that allows menu choices. A menu can be created for the contents of one CD or more than one. Content may be accessed in several ways, including visual browsing, viewing hundreds of images simultaneously on the screen, or finding and sorting with logic (AND, OR, IS, IS NOT, CONTAINS, $=$, $>$, $<$, $\geq$, and $\leq$). The program supports 35 file formats (BMP, EPSF, GIF, JPEG, etc.).

Name:	**Kudo CD Publisher**
Vendor:	Imspace Systems
Cost:	$500
Hardware requirements:	IBM PC and compatibles, 4MB RAM, 3MB free hard-disk space, Windows 3.1; Macintosh II and later, System 6.x (System 7 for Drop and Drag), 4MB RAM, 2MB free hard-disk space
Comments:	Libraries may master their own CD-ROMs for special collections, such as local history, using this product. Text, digital graphic images, photographs, movies, and sound formats are supported.

Name: **Lightning CD**
Vendor: Lucid
Cost: $29.95
Hardware requirements: IBM PC and compatibles
Comments: One of the problems with CD-ROM drives is speed. This add-on product is designed to enhance the performance of a CD-ROM drive by making it faster. The basic tool is a cache, a place in RAM where information is stored in case it is needed again. Quite often a computer will need to access the same information it last accessed. When this is the case, then finding it in RAM is much faster than loading it from the CD, which is very slow in comparison. For this to work correctly, the work station should have lots of RAM available to use; otherwise, the RAM available for other operations may shrink. This system will work well for some operations and not at all for others. Lightning CD will autoconfigure for the best amount of RAM, or it will allow the user to predetermine the amount of RAM (from 32K to 99K). In addition to faster CD-ROM drive operation, this software also includes several other utilities, including a screen accelerator, keyboard accelerator, a screen blanker, a tree delete, and a disk-watch function.

Name: **ROMaterial**
Vendor: Moon Valley Software
Cost: $29.95
Hardware requirements: IBM PC and compatibles, sound card
Comments: This CD includes quite a variety of add-on products all in one place: screen savers, icons, cursors, wallpapers, sounds, and other options. When ROMaterial is activated, all features are available from an always available button pad. The pad may be set to be always "on top" of all other windows (so it is easy to find).

The program's 500 icons will add color and sparkling variety to any desktop. They represent all manner of applications and symbols and can be selected from a convenient notebook for instant use. It is easy, for example, to select from among 200 cursors. This is lots of fun since they range from every imaginable form of black or white or outline arrow, hand, happy face, hypodermic needle, lightning, magnifying glass, atomic symbol, and skateboard (my favorite) to animals, food, and esoterica of all sorts. Both icons and cursors can be animated. A variety of moving icons will perform perpetually on the screen, if desired (e.g., a hand pulling a file out of the file cabinet). By carefully manipulating the icons on your desktop, it is easy to have a three-ring circus performing even when nothing is going on. The mouse cursor can be set to a moving object such as a mouse or an angel after so many seconds idle.

Several types of screen savers come with ROMaterial, including slide show and video savers. A number of video clips come with it. Some of these are animal tricks, space footage, animation, etc.

A wallpaper changer is also included with 100 wallpapers. ROMaterial also installs ICONHEARIT, which has some 500 sound effects. Six foreign languages and five English and American accents will liven up the work day. When activated, ICONHEARIT will pronounce all Windows events using any of the programmed voices. Other installed sounds include animal noises, machinery, and musical instruments. While the basic system and all icons are transferred to the hard drive on installation, other components, such as the video and slide screen savers, are transferred only as requested by the user, saving disk space.

Another product, ROMaterial Again, contains many business-related materials. It offers much more of the same, including new voices (male, robot, chipmunk, etc.), lots of wallpaper in many areas (comedy, history, people, etc.), work-related sounds (typing, printing, etc.), and screen breaks. While inexpensive and amusing, the only real problem with either of these two products is their need for disk space if too many of their features are used at one time.

Name:	**Windows Heaven**
Vendor:	Most Significant Bits
Cost:	$10, volume 1 for Windows; $19, volume 2 for multimedia
Hardware requirements:	IBM PC and compatibles, Windows 3.x
Comments:	Windows Heaven contains a wide variety of freeware and shareware at a low price for use with the Windows operating system. It has an excellent interface for viewing and installing the programs. Categories include communications, drivers, education, fonts, games, genealogy, general, graphics, home business, icons, printing, programming, religion, screen savers, sound, music, utilities, wallpapers, and word processing. The communications category contains terminal software, e-mail utilities, and even a complete BBS (powerBBS), and others. There are many Windows drivers for graphics, printing, and the mouse. There are many educational

programs for all age groups, including the Constitution, astronomy, chemistry, genetics, and even learning the ABCs and 1-2-3s. Fonts contains a variety of fonts for use with Windows ATM and a copy of FontMonster, a font editing and management program for Truetype and Type1 fonts. Fonter, another font management program, is also included, as are others. There must be well over 100 games, mostly minor board games, but interesting nonetheless. Two programs assist in the maintenance of a family tree. Graphics includes screen utilities and hundreds of bitmap images for use as wallpaper or slides. Some of these graphics utilities are quite sophisticated, including PhotoLab, a photo-imaging package. Home Business includes many useful programs: checkbook, to-do list, almanac, address book, calendar, calculator, etc. One program, The Library, keeps track of thousands of book references. The icon directory contains several libraries of icons plus utilities for their management. Word processing utilities include some programs for organizing and retrieving documents. One of these, Fileware, works directly with Microsoft Word. One curious program, Finish Line, "learns your vocabulary and style as you type, then shows likely words and phrases in a window." Pressing a single key will then finish the sentence.

This is an outstanding CD for librarians and for the general public. Since it is shareware, patrons will be responsible for sending in the fee for registering any specific software package.

Name:	**Wired for Sound Pro CD**
Vendor:	Aristosoft
Cost:	$39.95
Hardware requirements:	IBM PC and compatibles, 4MB RAM, 10MB hard-disk space, Windows 3.x, SoundBlaster sound card
Comments:	This disc is an economical way to make a desktop much more expressive. It comes with 400 talking icons, 50 animated icons, 400 wallpapers, 2,800 sound effects, and 100 designer cursors. In addition, it allows the computer to quickly take on human elements with 7 celebrity impressions such as Clint Eastwood, Arnold Schwartzenegger, Homer Simpson, and George Bush. Once installed and activated, the program will use the selected voice whenever a Windows command is performed. A variety of other features also talk, including Talking Solitaire and Minesweeper (the versions of these two programs also allow you to cheat at these games!). The

clock will tell time in any voice, including foreign languages such as French and Russian. Any of the 2,300 sounds may be attached to activities within Windows. Also included are 75 video clips of people, animals, and things. A Personal Information Manager (PIM) is fun and attractive and can be used as an appointment book that talks. Four screen savers of dynamic outdoor images will also liven up a work area. A person who is all work and no play, however, should probably pass on this one.

Discount and Mail Order CD-ROM Vendors

Crimson Software Distribution
207 S. Villa, Ste. 215
Villa Park, IL 60181
(708) 833–3611

MacMall
2645 Maricopa St.
Torrance, CA 90503
(800) 222–2808

MacWarehouse
1720 Oak St.
P.O. Box 3013
Lakewood, NJ 08701
(800) 255–6227

Most Significant Bits, Inc.
37207 Colorado Ave.
Avon, OH 44011
(800) 755–4619
Fax: (216) 934–1386

Multimedia Specialists
P.O. Box 55164
Madison, WI 53705
(800) 233–0010

PC Connection
6 Mill St.
Marlow, NH 03456
(800) 800–1111

Software Support International
2700 N.E. Andresen Rd., Ste. A-10
Vancouver, WA 98661
(800) 356–1179

Surplus Software Inc.
489 N. Eighth St.
Hood River, OR 97031
(800) 753–7877

Tiger Software
CD-ROM Buyer's Guide
One Datran Center, Ste. 1500
9100 S. Dadeland Blvd.
Miami, FL 33156
(800) 238–4437

Vendor Name and Address List

Area codes in some metropolitan areas are changing because the phone companies are running out of numbers. Therefore, some of the numbers listed herein may have different area codes as soon as next year. If you experience difficulty, please consult the operator.

A. M. Best Co.
Ambest Rd.
Oldwick, NJ 08858
(908) 439–2200
Fax: (908) 439–3296

Abacus Software, Inc.
5370 52nd St. SE
Grand Rapids, MI 49513
(800) 451–4319, (616) 698–0330
Fax: (616) 698–0325

Advantage Plus Distributors, Inc.
14202 Carlson Cir.
Tampa, FL 33626
(813) 885–1478
Fax: (919) 362–8294

Allegro New Media
387 Passaic Ave.
Fairfield, NJ 07004
(800) 424–1992, (201) 808–1992
Fax: (201) 808–2645

American Business Information
5711 S. 86th Cir.
P.O. Box 27347
Omaha, NE 68127
(402) 593–4523
Fax: (402) 331–6681

Apogee Software Productions
P.O. Box 496389
Garland, TX 75049
(214) 278–5655

Applied Optical Media Corp.
1450 Boot Rd., Bldg. 400
West Chester, PA 19380
(800) 321–7259, (215) 429–3701
Fax: (215) 429–3810

Aristosoft, Inc.
7041 Koll Center Pkwy.,
Ste. 160
Pleasanton, CA 94566
(800) 278–6768, (510) 426–5355
Fax: (510) 426–6703

Aristotle Industries
205 Pennsylvania Ave. SE
Washington, DC 20003
(800) 243–4401, (202) 543–8345
Fax: (202) 543–6407

Astronomical Research Network
206 Bellwood Ave.
Saint Paul, MN 55117–1909
(612) 488–5178

Attica Cybernetics Ltd.
9234 Deering Ave.
Chatswort, CA 91311
(800) 721–2475
Fax: (818) 701–8714

Books That Work, Inc.
2300 Geng Rd., Bldg. 3, Ste. 100
Palo Alto, CA 94303
Direct sales: (408) 644–2024
Fax: (415) 812–9700

BookWorm
(Products available through Educational Resources)
1550 Executive Dr.
Elgin, IL 60123
(800) 624–2926, (708) 888–8300

Bowker–Reed Reference Electronic Publishing
121 Chanlon Rd.
New Providence, NJ 07974
(800) 323–3288
Fax: (908) 665–3528

Brodart Automation
500 Arch St.
Williamsport, PA 17705
(800) 233–8467, (800) 666–9162
Fax: (717) 327–9237

Broderbund Software
500 Redwood Blvd.
Novato, CA 94948
(415) 382–4400
Fax: (415) 382–4587

Buckmaster Publishing
Rt. 3
P.O. Box 56
Mineral, VA 23117
(800) 282–5628, (703) 894–5777

Bureau of Electronic Publishing
141 New Road
Parsippany, NJ 07054
(800) 828–4766
Fax: (201) 808–2676

Career Guidance Foundation
8090 Engineer Rd.
San Diego, CA 92111
(800) 854–2670

Chadwyck–Healey, Inc.
1101 King St.
Alexandria, VA 22314
(800) 752–0515, (703) 683–4890
Fax: (703) 683–7589

Chestnut Software, Inc.
2 Park Plaza, Ste. 205
Boston, MA 02116–1049
(617) 542–9222
Fax: (617) 542–9220

Chilton Professional Automotive
One Chilton Way
Radnor, PA 19089–0230
(800) 995–1554, (215) 964–4000
Fax: (215) 864–4745

ChipSoft
6330 Nancy Ridge Rd., Ste. 3
San Diego, CA 92121-3290
(602) 295–3110

CMC ReSearch, Inc.
7150 S.W. Hampton St.
Ste. C–120
Portland, OR 97223
(800) 854–9126, (503) 242–2567
Fax: (503) 242–0519

Columbia University Press
562 W. 113th St.
New York, NY 10025
(212) 316–7126

Compact Publishing, Inc.
201 Broadway
Cambridge, MA 02139
(617) 494–1200

Compton's NewMedia, Inc.
2320 Camino Vida Roble
Carlsbad, CA 92009–1504
(800) 862–2206, (619) 929–2500
Fax: (619) 929–2577

Context Systems, Inc.
2935 Bayberry Rd.
Hatboro, PA 19040
(215) 675–5000

Corel Corp.
The Corel Bldg.
1600 Carling Ave.
Ottawa, ON, CD K1Z 8R7
(800) 772–6735, (613) 728–8200
Fax: (613) 728–9790

Counterpoint Publishing
20 William St.
P.O. Box 928
Cambridge, MA 02140
(617) 547–4515

Creative Multimedia Corp.
514 N.W. 11th Ave., Ste. 203
Portland, OR 97209
(503) 241–4351
Fax: (503) 241–4370

CW Communications, Inc.
375 Cochituate Rd.
P.O. Box 9171
Framingham, MA 01701–9171

Davka Corp.
7074 N. Western Ave.
Chicago, IL 60645
(800) 621–8227, (312) 465–4070

Deep River Publishing, Inc.
P.O. Box 9715–975
Portland, ME 04104
(800) 643–5630, (207) 871–1684

DeLorme Mapping
Lower Main St.
P.O. Box 298
Freeport, ME 04032
(800) 452–5931, (207) 865–1234

Design Publishers
800 Siesta Way
Sonoma, CA 95476
(707) 939–9306
Fax: (707) 939–9235

Digital Directory Assistance, Inc.
70 Atlantic Ave.
P.O. Box 648
Marblehead, MA 19453
(800) 284–8353, (617) 639–2900

Dimensional International
Zephyr One, Calleva Park
Aldermaston, England RG7 4QZ
+44 (0) 734 810077
Fax: +44 (0) 734 8166940

Disclosure, Inc.
5161 River Rd.
Bethesda, MD 20816
(800) 754–9690

Discus Knowledge Research, Inc.
Toronto, ON, Canada
(800) 587–4321

DRI/McGraw–Hill
Lexington, MA
(617) 863–5100
Fax: (617) 860–6861

Dun's Marketing Services
Three Sylvan Way
Parsippany, NJ 07054-3896
(800) 526–0651, (201) 605–6000

Dynamic Graphics, Inc.
6000 N. Forest Park Dr.
P.O. Box 1901
Peoria, IL 61656
(800) 255–8800
Fax: (309) 688–5873

EBook, Inc.
1009 Pecten Ct.
Milpitas, CA 95035
(408) 262–0502

EBSCO Publishing
P.O. Box 2250
Peabody, MA 01960
(508) 535–8500
Fax: (508) 535–8545

EduCorp
7434 Trade St.
San Diego, CA 92121
(800) 843–9497, (619) 536–9999
Fax: (619) 536–2345

Ellis Enterprises, Inc.
3445 W. Memorial Dr., Ste. C
Oklahoma City, OK 73134
(800) 729–9500, (405) 749–0273
Fax: (405) 751–5168

Encyclopaedia Britannica
Britannica Centre
310 S. Michigan Ave.
Chicago, IL 60604
(800) 432–0756
Fax: (312) 294–2138

Epic Megagames
10406 Holbrook Dr.
Potoma, MD 20854
(301) 983–9771

Expert Software, Inc.
P.O. Box 144506
Coral Gables, FL 33114–4506
(800) 759–2562
Fax: (305) 448–2074

Facts On File, Inc.
460 Park Ave. S
New York, NY 10016
(212) 683–2244

Fairfield Language Technologies
122 S. Main St., Ste. 400
Harrisonburg, VA 22801
(800) 788–0822, (703) 432–6166
Fax: (703) 432–0953

Firstlight Productions
15353 N.E. 90th St.
Redmond, WA 98052–9818
(800) 368–1488, (206) 869–6600
Fax: (206) 869–6605

Follett Software Co.
809 N. Front St.
McHenry, IL 60050
(800) 323–3397, (815) 344–8700
Fax: (815) 344–8774

G. K. Hall & Co.
Macmillan Distribution Ctr.
100 Front St.
P.O. Box 500
Riverside, NJ 08075–7500
(800) 257–5755
Fax:(800) 562–1272

Gale Research, Inc.
(800) 877–4253
Fax: (313) 961–6083

GeneSys
400 Dynix Dr.
P.O. Box 19010
Provo, UT 84605
(801) 223–5262

Grolier Electronic Publishing, Inc.
Sherman Tpke.
Danbury, CT 06816
(800) 285–4534, (203) 797–3530
(203) 797–3197

H. W. Wilson Company
950 University Ave.
Bronx, NY 10452
(212) 588–8400

HarperCollins Interactive
10 E. 53rd St.
New York, NY 10022
(800) 424–6234, (212) 207–7000
Fax: (212) 207–7433

Hopkins Technology
421 Hazel Ln., Ste. 200
Hopkins, MN 55343
(800) 397–9211, (612) 931–9376
Fax: (612) 931–9377

The HyperGlot Software Co., Inc.
(subsidiary of The Learning Co.)
6204 Baum Dr.
P.O. Box 10746
Knoxville, TN 37939–0746
(800) 726–5087
Fax: (615) 588–6569

IDG Books Worldwide Inc.
919 E. Hillsdale Blvd.
Foster City, CA 94404-9691
(800) 434–3422, (415) 655–3000

Imspace Systems Corp.
2665 Ariane Dr., Ste. 207
San Diego, CA 92117–3422
(800) 488–5836, (619) 272–2600
Fax: (619) 272–4292

InfoBusiness, Inc.
887 S. Orem Blvd.
Orem, UT 84058
(800) 657–5300, (801) 221–1100
Fax: (801) 225–0817

Information Access Co.
362 Lakeside Dr.
Foster City, CA 94404
(800) 227–8431, (415) 378–5200

Institute for Scientific Information
3501 Market St.
Philadelphia, PA 19104
(800) 336–4474, (215) 386–0100
Fax: (216) 386–2911

Interactive Multimedia Pursuits
P.O. Box 14620
Fremont, CA 94539
(510) 797–9087
Fax: (510) 797–9088

InterActive Publishing Corp.
300 Airport Executive Park
Spring Valley, NY 10977
(914) 426–0400
Fax: (914) 426–2606

Interactive Ventures, Inc.
1380 Corporate Center
Center Curve #305
Eagan, MN 55121
(800) 692–4000, (612) 686–0779
Fax:(612) 686–0721

InterMedia Interactive Software, Inc.
3624 Market St., Ste. 302
Philadelphia, PA 19104
(215) 387–3059
Fax: (215) 387–3049

InterOptica Publishing
300 Montgomery St., Ste. 201
San Francisco, CA 94104
(800) 708–7827, (415) 788–8788
Fax: (415) 788–8886

Interplay Productions, Inc.
17922 Fitch Ave.
Irvine, CA 92714
(800) 969–4263, (714) 553–6655
Fax: (714) 252–2820

J & D Distributing
P.O. Box 1375
Orem, UT 84059–1375

Jane's Information Group
1340 Braddock Pl., Ste. 300
Alexandria, VA 10452
(703) 683–3700

Johnston & Company
P.O. Box 446
American Fork, UT 84003
(801) 756–1111
Fax: (801) 756–0242

Knox Computer Systems, Inc.
10055 Barnes Canyon Rd., Ste. K
San Diego, CA 92121
(619) 535–0771
Fax: (619) 535–0773

KR Information OnDisc, Inc.
Marketing Dept.
Attn. B. Ramirez
3460 Hillview Ave.
Palo Alto, CA 94303
(800) 334–2564
Fax: (415) 254–8350

Laser Resources, Inc.
20620 South Leapwood Ave.
Carson, CA 90746
(800) 535–2737, (310) 324–4444
Fax: (310) 324–9999

Lawyers Cooperation Publishing
(800) 828–6373

Library Corp.
Research Park
Inwood, WV 25428
(800) 325–7759, (404) 591–0089

Library of Congress
Cataloging Distribution Service
Customer Services Section-CD
P.O. Box 75640
Washington, DC 20541–5017
(202) 707–6100
Fax: (202) 707–1334

Lintronics Publishing Group
1991 Mountainside Dr.
Blacksburg, VA 24060
(703) 552–7204
Fax: (703) 552–9261

Lotus Development Corp.
55 Cambridge Pkwy.
Cambridge, MA 02142–1295
(800) 426–7682
Fax: (617) 693–3512

Lucid Corp.
101 W. Renner Rd., Ste. 450
Richardson, TX 75082
(214) 994–8100
Fax: (214) 994–8103

Macmillan New Media
Scribner Reference
124 Mount Auburn St.
Cambridge, MA 02138
(800) 328–8830, (617) 661–2955
Fax: (617) 868–7738

MapInfo Corp.
1 Global View
Troy, NY 12180
(800) 327–8627, (518) 285–6000
Fax: (518) 285–6060

MECC
N. Brookdale Corp. Center
6160 Summit Dr.
Minneapolis, MN 55430
(800) 685–MECC, (800) 228–3504
Fax: (612) 569–1551

MecklerMedia
20 Ketchum St.
Westport, CT 06880
(203) 226–6967
Fax: (203) 454–5840

Media Vision, Inc.
47300 Bayside Pkwy.
Fremont, CA 94538
(510) 770–8600
Fax: (510) 770–9592

Medical Economics Data Co.
680 Kinderkamack Rd.
Oradell, NJ 07649
(201) 262–3030

Medio Multimedia, Inc.
P.O. Box 10844
Salinas, CA 93912
(800) 788–3866
Fax: (408) 655–6071

Merriam-Webster
(800) 201–5029, (413) 734–3134

Metatec Corp.
7001 Discovery Blvd.
Dublin, OH 43017

Metromail
(800) 234–1489

Microsoft Corp.
One Microsoft Way
Redmond, WA 98052
(800) MSPRESS, (800) 426–9400
Fax: (206) 883–8101

Moody's Investors Service
99 Church St.
New York, NY 10007
(800) 995–8080, (212) 553–0442
Fax: (212) 553–4700

Moon Valley Software, Inc.
21608 N. 20th Ave.
Phoenix, AZ 85027
(800) 473–5509, (602) 375–9502
Fax: (602) 993–4950

Morningstar
225 W. Wacker Dr.
Chicago, IL 60606
(800) 866–3472, (312) 696–6000
Fax: (312) 696–6001

Most Significant Bits, Inc.
15508 Madison Ave.
Lakewood, OH 44107
(216) 529–1888, (216) 221–4411

Multicom Publishing, Inc.
1100 Olive Way, Ste. 1250
Seattle, WA 98101
(800) 850–7272, (206) 622–5530
Fax: (206) 622–4380

National Archives
(800) 234–8861

**National Information Services
    Corp.**
Wyman Towers
3100 St. Paul St., Ste. 6
Baltimore, MD 21218
(410) 243–0797
Fax: (410) 243–0982

New England Journal of Medicine
P.O. Box 803
Waltham, MA 02254–0803

New Riders' Publishing
201 W. 103rd St.
Indianapolis, IN 46290

Newsbank, Inc.
58 Pine St.
New Canaan, CT 06840
(800) 243–7694

Newsweek, Inc.
The Newsweek Bldg.
P.O. Box 408
Livingston, NJ 07039
(800) 634–6850
Fax: (212) 350–4929

North Coast Software
265 Scruton Pond Rd.
Barrington, NH 03825
P.O. Box 459
(603) 664–6999
Fax: (603) 664–7872

Now What Software
2303 Sacramento St.
San Francisco, CA 94115
(800) 322–1954, (415) 885–1689
Fax: (415) 922–1265

NTC Publishing Group
4255 W. Touhy Ave.
Lincolnwood, IL 60645
(708) 679–5500

OCLC Forest Press
6565 Frantz Rd.
Dublin, OH 43017
(800) 848–5878

On-Line Computer Systems, Inc.
20251 Century Blvd.
Germantown, MD 20874
(800) 922–9204, (301) 428–3700

Orange Hill/New Media Schoolhouse
Market Plaza
P.O. Box 390
Pound Ridge, NY 10576
(914) 764–4104
Fax: (914) 764–0104

Oxford University Press
Electronic Publishing
(212) 679–7300 ext. 7370
Fax: (212) 725–2972

P-80 Systems
(304) 744–7322

P T R Prentice Hall
113 Sylvan Ave.
Englewood, NJ 07632
(201) 592–2863
Fax: (201) 592–2249

Panatech Corporation
600 Boulevard South, Ste. 104
Huntsville, AL 35802
(205) 883–3528
Fax: (205) 883–3526

Parsons Technology, Inc.
One Parsons Dr.
P.O. Box 100
Hiawatha, IA 52233-0100
(800) 223–6925, (319) 395–9626
Fax: (319) 395–0102

Pergamon Press, Ltd.
Irwin House
118 Southwark St.
London, SE10SW 10452
44–928–1404

Perian Press
P.O. Box 1808
Ann Arbor, MI 48106
(313) 434–5530

Pixel Perfect, Inc.
P.O. Box 410129
Melbourne, FL 32941-0129
(800) 788–2099, (407) 777–5353
Fax: (407) 777–0323

Power Up!
P.O. Box 7600
San Mateo, CA 94403
(800) 851–2917

Prentice Hall Professional Software
2400 Lake Park Dr.
P.O. Box 723597
Atlanta, GA 31139
(404) 432–1996
Fax: (404) 435–5036

Pro CD, Inc.
8 Doaks Ln.
Little Harbor
Marblehead, MA 01945
(617) 631–9200
Fax: (617) 631–9299

Quanta Press, Inc.
1313 Fifth St. SE, Ste. 208C
Minneapolis, MN 55414
(612) 379–3956
Fax: (612) 623–4570

Quantum Axcess
240 N. Fifth St., Ste. 330
Columbus, OH 43215
(614) 228–3903
Fax: (614) 228–5284

Random House Reference and Electronic Publishing
201 E. 50th St.
New York, NY 10022
(800) 733–3000, (212) 751–2600
Fax: (212) 572–4997

Redgate Communications Corp.
Beachland Financial Center
660 Beachland Blvd.
Vero Beach, FL 32963
(800) 333–8760, (407) 231–6904

Reed Technology and Information
20251 Century Blvd.
Germantown, MD 20874-1196
(800) 922–9204, (301) 428–3700
Fax: (301) 428–2903

Resource International Publishing Co.
Route 1, P.O. Box 168
Milford, TX 76670
(817) 582–7373

Roth Publishing, Inc.
185 Great Neck Rd.
Great Neck, NY 11021
(800) 899–ROTH
Fax: (516) 829–7746

SAMS Publishing
11711 N. College Ave.
Carmel, IN 46032
(317) 573–2500

ScanRom Publications, Inc.
401 Church Ave.
Cedarhurst, NY 11516
(516) 295–2237
Fax: (516) 295–2240

SelectWare Technologies, Inc.
29200 Vassar, Ste. 200
Livonia, MI 48152

SilverPlatter Information, Inc.
100 River Ridge Dr.
Norwood, MA 02062
(800) 874–1130, (617) 769–2599

Social Issues Resources Series (SIRS), Inc.
P.O. Box 2348
Boca Raton, FL 33427-2348
(800) 232–7477, (407) 994–0079
Fax: (407) 994–4704

Softbit, Inc.
One Whitewater
Irvine, CA 92715
(714) 251–8600
Fax: (714) 261–7977

Softkey Software Products, Inc.
201 Broadway, 3rd Fl.
Cambridge, MA 02139
(800) 377–6567, (617) 374–1450
Fax: (617) 577–7903

SoftLine Information, Inc.
65 Broad St.
P.O. Box 16845
Stamford, CT 06905
(203) 968–8878
Fax: (203) 968–2370

Software Toolworks (MindScape)
60 Leveroni Ct.
Novato, CA 94949
(800) 234–3088, (415) 883–3000
Fax: (415) 883–3303

Sony Electronic Publishing
One Lower Ragsdale Dr.
Monterey, CA 93940
(800) 654–8802
Fax: (408) 375–7130

Staff Directories, Ltd.
P.O. Box 62
Mount Vernon, VA 22121
(703) 739–0900
Fax: (703) 739–2964

John Dee Stanley
6959 California Ave. SW
Seattle, WA 98136

Sumeria, Inc.
329 Bryant St., Ste. 3d
San Francisco, CA 94107
(915) 904–0889

SWL, Inc.
5383 Hollister Ave.
Santa Barbara, CA 93111
(800) 933–5383, (805) 964–7724
Fax: (805) 967–7094

Syracuse Language Systems
719 E. Genesee St.
Syracuse, NY 13210
(315) 478–6729

Taft Group
835 Penobscot Bldg.
645 Griswold St.
Detroit, MI 48226
(800) 877–TAFT

Time Warner Interactive Group
2210 W. Olive Ave.
Burbank, CA 91506
(800) 482–3766, (818) 955–9999
Fax: (818) 973–4552

Tri-Star Publishing
275 Gibraltar Rd.
Horsham, PA 19034
(215) 441–6490

UMI
300 N. Zeeb Rd.
Ann Arbor, MI 48106
(313) 761–4700
Fax: (502) 589–5572

Updata
1736 Westwood Blvd.
Los Angeles, CA 90024
(310) 474–5900

U.S. Bureau of the Census
Customer Services
Washington, DC 20233–8300
(301) 763–4100

U.S. Government Printing Office
Superintendent of Documents
P.O. Box 371954
Pittsburgh, PA 15250
(202) 783–3238
Fax: (202) 512–2250

Viacom New Media
648 S. Wheeling Rd.
Wheeling, IL 60090
(800) 877–4266, (708) 520–4440
Fax: (708) 459–7456

Virtual Reality Laboratories
(800) 829–8754, (805) 545–8515
Fax: (805) 781–2259

Visible Ink Software
835 Penobscot Bldg.
Detroit, MI 48226
(800) 735–4686

VRontier Worlds
809 E. South St.
Stoughton, WI 53589

Walnut Creek CDROM
4041 Pike Lane, Ste. D–891
Concord, CA 94520
(800) 786–9907, (510) 674–0783
Fax: (510) 674–0821

**Walt Disney Computer Soft-
ware, Inc.**
500 S. Buena Vista St.
Burbank Centre, 20th Fl.
Burbank, CA 91521–6380
(800) 688–1520, (800) 228–0988
(818) 973–4015
Fax: (818) 846–0454

Wayzata Technology, Inc.
16221 Main Ave. SE
P.O. Box 807
Prior Lake, MN 55372
(800) 735–7321, (612) 735–7321

West Publishing Corp.
615 Merrick Ave.
Westbury, NY 11590
(800) 255–2549
Fax: (800) 245–4522

Wheeler Arts
66 Lake Park
Champaign, IL 61821–7101
(217) 359–6816
Fax: (217) 359–8716

World Book Educational Products
101 N.W. Point Blvd.
Elk Grove Village, IL 60007
(800) 433–6580, (708) 290–5300

World Library, Inc.
2809 Main St.
Irvine, CA 92714
(800) 387–2687

ZCI Publishing
1950 Stemmons, Ste. 4044
Dallas, TX 75207–3109
(800) POWERCD
(214) 746–5555
Fax: (214) 746–5560

Zedcor
4500 E. Speedway Blvd., Ste. 22
Tucson, AZ 85712
(800) 482–4567, (602) 881–8101
Fax: (602) 881–1841

Ziff Communications Co.
One Park Ave.
New York, NY 10016
(800) 827–7889, (212) 503–4400

Computer Periodicals of Interest

CD-ROM Professional
Pemberton Press, Inc.
11 Tannery Ln.
Weston, CT 06883
(203) 227–8466

CD-ROM Today
P.O. Box 51478
Boulder, CO 80323

CD-ROM World
P.O. Box 3000
Denville, NJ 07834
(800) 783–4903

Compute
P.O. Box 3244
Harlan, IA 51593
(800) 727–6937

ComputerLife
P.O. Box 55880
Boulder, CO 80322
(800) 926–1578

Computer Shopper
Ziff-Davis Publishing Co.
One Park Ave.
New York, NY 10016
(212) 503–3500

MacWeek
Ziff-Davis Publishing Co.
One Park Ave.
New York, NY 10016
(212) 503–3500

MacWorld
MacWorld Communications, Inc.
501 Second St., 5th Fl.
San Francisco, CA 94107
(415) 243–3235

PC Computing
Ziff-Davis Publishing Co.
One Park Ave.
New York, NY 10016
(212) 503–3500

PC Magazine
Ziff-Davis Publishing Co.
One Park Ave.
New York, NY 10016
(212) 503–3500

Shareware Magazine
1030–D E. Duane Ave.
Sunnyvale, CA 94086
(408) 730–9291

Glossary

Analog   The continuous wave signal used by the telephone line. A pattern is determined based on changes in the signal. Opposite of "digital," which generates a series of separate (discrete) signals in the form of *1*s and *0*s.

ASCII   For American Standard Code for Information Interchange; an agreed-upon standard of 128 letters, numbers, and other symbols, each represented by a set of seven digits (*1*s and *0*s).

Backup   A second or additional copy on a disk of a program or data.

BASIC   For *B*eginner's *A*ll-Purpose *S*ymbolic *I*nstruction *C*ode; originally created as a teaching language but eventually gained a following as an important high-level computer language.

Batch   Multiple instructions or data executed as a group, often as if typed from the keyboard (especially when used as a macro).

Baud   Bits per second transmitted. Typically, data speed is 300 (300 bits per second), 1,200, 2,400; 9,600; 14,400; 28,800; 57,600 baud; etc. Since each computer character requires about 10 bits (including stop, start, etc., bits), this amounts to 30, 120, 240, etc., characters per second.

Bit   The smallest unit of information that a computer can process, either a *1* or a *0*. Bits are combined into groups of eight or more to form a byte.

Bit–mapped graphics   Graphics are shown as an actual representation of the object (by *1*s and *0*s) rather than by a formula. The opposite of "object-oriented graphics."

Bulletin board system (BBS)   An interactive online database that may have a number of features, including multiple lines in; upload/download for public domain and shareware programs, and electronic mail; conference areas; etc. Usually, though not always, operated on a local microcomputer. Some operate on national networks such as the Source or CompuServe.

Bundled   Software that comes with the hardware, often including a word processor and a database management system, to make the system more marketable.

Byte   Generally, 8 bits used during transmission, though stop and start bits may make it 10 bits. A byte is basically a computer word (character) such as *W* or *1*.

Cache   A CPU cache is composed of special high-speed chips for the temporary storage of instructions for the CPU to speed the overall operation of the computer. It holds data and instructions going between the CPU and regular memory. Since the cache chips are closer to the speed of the CPU than is regular memory, subsequent use of these instructions is faster. A disk cache is an area in memory to which disk information is copied. Subsequent use of this information is faster because memory access is always much faster than disk access. A CPU contains an internal cache as well.

CAD   For *C*omputer *A*ided *D*esign; special design software, high-speed work stations, and special hardware (e.g., scanners) used to design products.

Caddy   A small, protective plastic container for each CD that is inserted into the drive door if required by the CD-ROM drive.

CD-R   For *CD-R*ecordable; a disc that can be written to, but only once. Such a disc has advantages over WORM drives (write once, read many) in that it can be read by any CD-ROM drive, not just by the CD-R drive. It can be used as a master from which multiple CDs may be made.

CD-ROM   For *C*ompact *D*isk–*R*ead *O*nly *M*emory; a storage device that differs in several important ways from conventional disk drives in that a CD-ROM will hold several hundred megabytes of data and is more difficult to damage.

Central Processing Unit   (CPU) The central brain or processor of the computer where timing, routing of data, and other decisions are made.

CGM   For *C*omputer *G*raphics *M*etafile; a graphics file format.

Chip   The basic hardware unit of microcomputer technology, made of silicon.

Circuit board   A board that contains a number of chips and controls a device such as a printer or modem, or houses the RAM and ROM (memory) of the computer.

Click art   Another name for clip art that is in electronic format.

Clip art   Artwork available from many sources that can be loaded into a desktop publishing or graphics package and used to complete a document.

Clipboard   An area to which data (text or graphics) is clipped and stored for later recall.

Clone   A computer that emulates a more-popular brand to capitalize on the market.

Command language   An English-like computer language used with programs such as dBASE to produce more-sophisticated programs.

Compiler   A program that takes a BASIC or other high-level language program and converts it into the machine code of the computer.

Crash A total, and usually sudden, system failure.

Cursor Usually a flashing square that points to where the next character on the computer screen will appear.

Desktop publishing Creating camera-ready copy with the computer and printer, often entailing a laser printer for high-quality production. Also refers to simpler products produced on a dot matrix printer and programs such as The Print Shop.

Digital *1*s and *0*s (digits) that are added into bytes to form computer words or characters, as opposed to the analog or continuous signal of the telephone lines.

Disk drive The mass-storage device that reads and writes on a disk. These data-storage devices come in many sizes and types and may be built in or external to the computer.

Diskette The media on which data are stored and retrieved in a disk drive.

Documentation The printed or online manuals that give the instructions for use of a program.

DOS For *D*isk *O*perating *S*ystem; the master control program that manages the filing system and interfaces with the disk drives.

Dots per inch (dpi) A measurement of resolution usually applied to printers and monitors. The greater the dpi, the better the resolution. For most desktop publishing application printing 300 dpi is acceptable.

Download To receive a program into a computer from a (usually) remote or distant computer. Opposite of "upload." The program can then be copied to disk for future use.

Driver A program that gives the computer control over a device such as a printer, a scanner, etc. Wrong driver selection or the lack of a driver is a frequent reason for computer problems. Microsoft CD-ROM Extensions (MSCDEX) is a driver necessary for operating most CD-ROM disk drives.

Electronic mail (e-mail) Sending messages electronically. May be done locally through a bulletin board system or nationally through a nationwide network.

EMS For *E*xpanded *M*emory *S*pecification; the way in which PCs access additional RAM memory. A special EMS driver is required to make use of this feature.

EPS For *E*ncapsulated *P*ost*S*cript; a file format of the printer page-description language PostScript. The file will contain an image description.

Error message A computer message that something is wrong, for example, "Disk Full."

Font A complete set of letters, numerals, and symbols in a particular typeface or style.

GIF   For *G*raphics *I*nterchange *F*ormat; a bit-mapped graphics file format created by CompuServe.

Graphics tablet   An input device that allows the user to draw or trace objects that are then digitized for computer use.

Hacker   Though originally a term used to describe a computer enthusiast, it now means someone who uses a computer for destructive purposes, such as crashing bulletin boards, invading mainframes illegally, and other mischievous acts.

Hardcopy   Printed computer data.

Hardware   The nuts-and-bolts parts of the computer that can be seen and felt, such as the monitor, chips, keyboard, and disk drives.

HyperCard   An Apple Computer tool for developing complex applications of graphics, text, sound, video, and data.

Hypertext   Analogous to hyperspace in science fiction novels; it will get you to another spot in the document or even to other documents by just clicking on a highlighted word or choice. For example, if a user is reading about dinosaurs in an online text, by pressing the name in a list of dinosaurs a picture of a dinosaur will appear. Often hypertext is used to provide additional information or definitions to users who are less familiar with the subject. The relationships between parts of text so linked are known as "hyperlinks."

Icon   A graphic representation of an object, such as a file folder, trash can, or bomb, or a graphic representation of a command.

Integrated software   Software that does more than one thing, usually word processing, database management, spreadsheet, telecommunications, and graphics.

Interactive   Computer programs that require a human response. Noninteractive software (demo programs, for instance) will run without human intervention.

Jewel box   The most common form of CD storage container. A small plastic storage device not much larger than a CD that offers substantial protection from abuse. Some jewel boxes may house as many as 4 CDs.

Jukebox   A device that stores multiple CDs, also called a CD changer. It changes CDs as requested by the user in much the same way that a music jukebox changes CDs. Inexpensive changers will house 6 CDs at one time, with only one accessible at any given moment. Larger, more expensive changers will house as many as 100 CDs.

Local area network (LAN)   A system that connects computers for sharing data, files, electronic mail, and expensive peripherals.

Macro   Provides for the use of a single control character to take the place of inputting something longer. For instance, a single control character may take the place of a long sentence. In word processing, a macro may be used to insert the time, date, or even boilerplate for parts of form letters and documents. Macros may be custom made for any purpose.

Mainframe computer   A large computer usually requiring air conditioning and a special room and support.

MegaHertz (MHz)   A measure of computer speed; the internal clock speed (central processing unit) of a microcomputer. Speeds range from 4 to well over 120 MHz. Most computers may be set at two different speeds, slow and fast (turbo). Many microcomputers may be also be upgraded by replacing the CPU or by adding another one to get a faster computer.

Memory   A computer's ability to store and hold data. Data are usually stored temporarily in the computer's chips and more permanently on hard or floppy disk drives.

Microcomputer   A small desktop or home computer. The distinctions between the different sizes of computers blur more each year as the large ones decrease in size and the small ones increase in power.

MIDI   For *M*usical *I*nstrument *D*igital *I*nterface; a widely used protocol for the interchange of various types of musical information between a computer, synthesizers, and musical instruments.

Modem   From *mo*dulator/*dem*odulator; a device for translating the digital code of the computer into the analog code of the telephone line and back again. Two modems (one at each end) are required for two computers to communicate over the telephone. Computers can be directly connected without modems if they are close enough to connect with a cable.

Monitor   The screen that displays the computer's answers or data.

Morphing   A special effect often seen on television, especially in commercials and rock videos, when animals, people, or machines, for example, are transformed from one to another in a rather natural and interesting way, as if melting from one to the other.

Mouse   A small, hand-operated object that moves the cursor on the screen as the mouse is moved on the desktop.

Multimedia PC   A personal computer specially equipped to play sound, animation, video, and slides.

Object-oriented graphics   Graphics that are represented and created by mathematical formulas. Opposite of "bit-mapped graphics."

Parity   A method for checking the accuracy of data transmission by adding up the data bits to a total that must be either odd or even. If the proper addition is not made by the computer, the data are rejected and must be retransmitted.

PCX   A bit-mapped graphics file format. It was developed by Zsoft Corporation.

Peripheral   Any device that is not part of the computer proper, whether internal or external to the computer housing. Peripheral devices include modems, printers, disk drives, and graphics tablets.

Photo CD   A system devised by Kodak for putting up to 100 high-quality photographs on one CD. Such CDs are called multisession CDs when additional pictures are added after the original set. A multisession drive is required to read such a CD.

PICT   (PICTure) PICT is a Macintosh vector graphics file format.

Printer   A device for printing out hardcopy of the computer results. Printers may be dot matrix, daisywheel, inkjet, or laser.

Public domain   Software without copyright restrictions.

Pull-quote   A statement taken from an article and emphasized in larger type to highlight some important point. Sometimes called "callout."

QEMM   A DOS memory manager that works with a 386 computer or later.

RAM   For *R*andom *A*ccess *M*emory; memory in a computer that changes as the computer uses it.

ROM   For *R*ead *O*nly *M*emory; memory that already has a program stored on it. The computer can read this memory or stored information but cannot change or add to it.

Runtime version   Some programs require other programs to function normally. Since not everyone may own the second program, manufacturers of some programs have included a runtime version of the additional program to make it a self-contained program. The runtime version will not run outside this environment for which it was specifically created.

Scanner   A device that can take a photo or other image on paper and digitize it for use with computers.

Screen saver   Any program that works to prevent monitor burn-in or damage to an unattended computer monitor. Usually, after a period of time, specified by the computer user, during which the computer has not been used, the screen saver program activates itself. Then a blank screen or animated cartoons or other spectacles appear on screen. Any visuals change position or scenes so the visual is not static.

Shareware   Copyrighted software that is freely distributed. If the user wishes to continue to use it, a license fee must be remitted to the owner of the software as stipulated in the software itself.

Software   The invisible part of the computer; the set of instructions that tells the hardware what to do with the data it receives.

Spreadsheet   The electronic version of the accountant's pad. Formulas and data may be entered, and the results are calculated immediately. A second set of data or a change in any data element will result in a recalculation of the entire spreadsheet, making it possible to judge the effect of changes in budgets, for example, very quickly.

Style sheet   A template for desktop publishing. All attributes for a document are retained in the style sheet for future use.

Telecommunication   Communication over long distances through telephone lines, satellite, or other means.

Template   A form, electronic or paper, that represents work someone has prepared but that may be used over and over with different sets of data. An example is the spreadsheet in which formulas have been placed for creating a budget. Since any two businesses that use the same kind of budget can use the same formulas, they can use the same template.

Terminal   A place where people may interface with a computer, through a keyboard, monitor, or printer. The computer need not be present; it can be reached through either the telephone lines with a modem or directly through cable (known as hardwiring) in a local area network.

Thumbnail   A miniature representation of a page to see how it will look when actually printed.

TIFF   For *T*agged *I*mage *F*ile *F*ormat; a bit-mapped graphics file format developed by Aldus and Microsoft.

Upload   To accept data into a computer. The opposite of "download," which is to send data to another computer.

Utility program   Any program that has as its function the care and maintenance of the computer or other software is termed a "utility." These programs include virus-protection programs, disk-maintenance programs, data-compression programs, and even screen savers.

Virtual reality (VR)   A computer simulation. The ultimate simulation is virtual reality. The ultimate possibility with this concept is the holodeck on *Star Trek: The Next Generation*, where users cannot differentiate between what is real and what is simulated. Nothing in the real world today is even close to this distant future. The term therefore applies to an approximation. Generally, if on the computer screen it is possible to inspect an object by moving around or over it in the same way that the real object could be inspected, then it is termed "virtual reality." Most manufacturers of games, however, don't bother to distinguish between good and mediocre VR and pathetic VR in their hype.

Virus   A destructive program that replicates itself to cause mischief.

Wallpaper   In a graphical user interface (GUI) the computer monitor represents a desktop. The surface of that desktop may be represented with any graphic or pattern desired by the user. Virtually thousands of wallpaper styles have been created. Any digitized picture can be used as a wallpaper. A GUI can be set to change the wallpaper each time the computer is booted, providing a fresh start each day.

WAV   A Windows sound file.

Wild card   A search may be enhanced or broadened with the use of a wild card, usually an asterisk, question mark, or exclamation point. A wild card tells the computer program to search for all variations of a spelling as indicated by the wild card. For example, the term "computer" will find only the one term, but "comput*" might locate compute, computer, computers, etc. An exclamation point (!) can often be used to substitute for a single letter.

Word Processing   A software program that allows users to rearrange and revise text (sentences, words, etc.), without having to retype everything before hardcopy is produced. Often these programs come with "spellers" that check documents for suspect words (possibly misspelled words).

Work station   An area that contains the necessary equipment (furniture, outlets, table, etc.) for work with a computer. The place at which a person with a computer works. Such places should have good lighting and comfortable seating.

Bibliography

CD-ROM

Adams, Charlotte. "The Top 20 CD-ROM Hits You Should Know." *Federal Computer Week*, June 6, 1994, S4.

Andres, Clay. "Three On-Line Dictionaries." *MacUser*, June 1994, 58.

Benford, Tom. *Welcome to CD-ROM*. New York, NY: MIS Press, 1993.

Berger, Pam, and Susan Kinnell. *CD-ROM for Schools: The Definitive Handbook*. Wilton, Conn.: Online, 1994.

Blankenhorn, Dana. "Review of Dr. Schueler's Home Advisor Medical Pro CD-ROM." *Newsbytes*, July 15, 1994, 7.

Branscum, Deborah. "Software Shopping by CD-ROM: Electronic Catalogs Want Your Business." *MacWorld*, May 1994, 173.

Brownstein, Mark. "Buyer's Guide to External CD-ROM Drives." *PC Laptop Computers Magazine*, Sept. 1994, 32.

Buckler, Grant. "Corel Launching Clip Art CD-ROM at CES." *Newsbytes*, Jan. 4, 1994.

Coffey, Margaret. "How Business Exploits CD-ROM." *Computer Weekly*, Feb. 24, 1994, 38.

Crotty, Cameron. "Soncino Talmud CD-ROM." *MacWorld*, Apr. 1994, 50.

Dunn, Nancy E. "CD-ROM Network Guide." *MacWorld*, Aug. 1994, 151.

Eckhardt, Robert C. "The Oxford English Dictionary." *MacWorld*, Apr. 1994, 77.

Ehrenman, Gayle C. "Medio Magazine." *PC Magazine*, Sept. 13, 1994, 468.

———. "The Legends of Oz." *PC Magazine*, June 14, 1994, 478.

Erlanger, Leon. "Roll Your Own CD." *PC Magazine*, May 17, 1994, 137.

Fay, Natalie. "Berlitz Japanese." *MacWeek*, Aug. 1, 1994, 45.

Fridlund, Alan J. "Clip-Art Kit on CD-ROM Is a Bargain." *InfoWorld*, May 2, 1994, 129.

Gliedman, John. "Random House Dictionary on CD-ROM Is an Unabridged Delight." *Computer Shopper*, Mar. 1994, 784.

Gold, Steve. "32,000 London Streets on CD-ROM." *Newsbytes*, June 20, 1994.

Hicks, Adam A. "Adding onto Print Shop, CD-ROM Style." *PC Magazine*, May 17, 1994, 68.

————. "CD-ROM Guide to Your Own Private Eden." *PC Magazine*, June 28, 1994, 61.

Keizer, Gregg. "Interactive Literature Gets Serious: The Complete Maus." *Computer Shopper*, July 1994, 766.

LaGuardia, Cheryl. *A CD-ROM Primer*. New York: Neal-Schuman, 1994.

Langberg, Mike. "Buy This Comedy Disk and Joke Might Be on You." *San Jose Mercury News*, Feb. 27, 1994, 6E.

Levitan, Arlan. "Twain's World Brings the Life and Times of Samuel Clemens to Disc." *Computer Shopper*, Feb. 1994, 827.

Lohr, Steve. "The Silver Disk May Soon Eclipse the Silver Screen." *New York Times*, Mar. 1, 1994, A1.

Mallory, Jim. "Leonardo da Vinci in 3D on Mac CD-ROM." *Newsbytes*, July 13, 1994, 7.

————. "Multimedia Book to Include Software on CD-ROM." *Newsbytes*, Aug. 11, 1994.

————. "New CD-ROM Journeys to the Planets." *Newsbytes*, May 25, 1994.

————. "72 More Titles Added to InfoNow CD-ROM." *Newsbytes*, May 2, 1994.

————. "29-Volume Encyclopedia on CD-ROM for Macintosh." *Newsbytes*, July 15, 1994.

Marshall, Patrick. "Quad-Speed CD Jukebox Is a Steal." *InfoWorld*, July 4, 1994, 77.

Mossberg, Walter S. "CD-ROM Software That Quietly Goes About Your Business." *Wall Street Journal*, Aug. 18, 1994, B1.

Murphy, Catherine. *CD-ROMs for School Libraries: An Evaluative Guide to Collection Building*. Medford, N.J.: Learned Information, 1994.

Myers, Ben. "CD-ROM Heaven: $2,495 Pioneer Jukebox Handles 18 Disks at Once." *PC Magazine*, July 1994, 42.

Ohlson, Karen J. "Stock Your Digital Bookshelf." *MacUser*, June 1994, 40.

Perry, James. M. "Can't Get Enough of a Book? Buy a CD-ROM." *Wall Street Journal*, May 23, 1994, B1.

Quain, John R. "Multimedia Stravinsky: The Rite of Spring." *PC Magazine*, July 1994, 508.

———. "300 Clemens Titles on CD-ROM." *PC Magazine*, Jan. 11, 1994, 426.

Rabinovitz, Rubin. "$79 Random House Dictionary: Look It up Under Bargain." *PC Magazine*, Jan. 25, 1994, 56.

Rathbone, Andy. *Multimedia and CD-ROMs for Dummies*. San Mateo, Calif.: IDG Books, 1994.

Richards, Trevor. "Growth of CD-ROM Software: 1989–1994." *Computers in Libraries*, Jan. 1995, 76.

Rohan, Rebecca. "Microsoft's Cinemania 94 Brings Screen Gems to CD-ROM." *Computer Shopper*, Mar. 1994, 780.

Said, Carolyn. "Multimedia CD-ROM Titles Find Their Place in Business." *MacWeek*, Mar. 21, 1994, 61.

Senechal, Ann. "Books in Hyperspace: When and How Does CD-ROM Format Make a Book Better?" *Aldus Magazine*, July 1994, 40.

Snell, Jason. "Microsoft Works CD-ROM Adds Multimedia." *MacUser*, Oct. 1994, 30.

Spector, Lincoln. "Shareware CD From the Authors." *PC World*, Feb. 1994, 94.

Stephenson, Peter. "Going Underground for Security." *LAN Times*, May 23, 1994, 56.

Trivette, Donald B., and Julie Cohen. "The Home Reference Library." *PC Magazine*, Dec. 7, 1993, 584.

Valas, George. "Comparison of Some Widespread CD-ROM Information Retrieval Software Packages." *Online & CD-ROM Review*, vol.18, 211.

Vaughan-Nichols, Steve J. "Reliable, Removable, and Rewritable Optical Drives." *Computer Shopper*, Dec. 1993, 182.

Welch, Nathalie. "Macs Connect with Phone CD-ROM." *MacWeek*, June 6, 1994, 6.

Wilkinson, David. "Multiple Database Operation on the Stand-Alone Public CD-ROM System: Considerations for System Management." *CD-ROM Librarian Magazine*, July/Aug. 1992.

Willmott, Don. "PC Magazine on CD-ROM." *PC Magazine*, Sept. 13, 1994, 170.

Wingerson, Katherine M. "Bookshelf 1994." *MacWeek*, Aug. 1, 1994, 44.

CD-ROM in Libraries

Gillespie, Thom. "Best Buys: What to Collect in Multimedia." *Library Journal*, Feb. 1, 1995, 40.

Lubelski, Greg W. "Multimedia to Go: Circulating CD-ROMs at Geauga County Public Library." *Library Journal*, Feb. 1, 1995, 37.

St. Lifer, Evan. "Catching on to the 'Now' Medium: LJ's Multimedia Technology Survey." *Library Journal*, Feb. 1, 1995, 44.

Hardware and Software

Banks, Michael A. *The Modem Reference*. New York: Brady, 1992.

Crawford, Sharon. *Your First Modem*. San Francisco: Sybex, 1994.

Dewey, Patrick R. *202+ Software Packages to Use in Your Library*. 101 Micro Series. Chicago: American Library Association, 1992.

Freedman, Alan. *The Computer Glossary*. New York: Amacom, 1995.

Goodman, John. *Memory Management for All of Us*. Indianapolis: SAMS Publishing, 1993.

Halliday, Caroline M. *Hayes Modem Communications Companion*. San Mateo, Calif.: IDG Books, 1994.

Lowe, Doug. *The Only DOS Book You'll Ever Need*. Fresno, Calif.: Murach, 1994.

McLaughlin, Robert, Susan B. Sasser, and Mary Ralston. *Fix Your Own PC*. 2d ed. New York: MIS:Press, 1992.

Robinson, Phillip. *Welcome to Memory Management*. New York: MIS:Press. 1994.

Rosch, Winn L. *The Hardware Bible*. Indianapolis: Brady, 1994.

Shatz-Atkin, Jim. "The Ultimate Guide to Children's Software." *MacUser*, Dec. 1994, 97.

Stinson, Craig. *Running Windows 3.1*. Redmond, Wash.: Microsoft Press, 1992.

Windows

Jamsa, Kris. *Jamsa's 1001 Windows Tips*. Las Vegas, Nev.: Jamsa Press, 1993.

Mace, Pau, Angus Mace, and Jeffrey Gordon. *Paul Mace's Tools for Windows*. New York: Random House Electronic Publishing, 1994.

Index

Patrick R. Dewey has served as the director of the Maywood (Illinois) Public Library District since 1984. The previous ten years he spent as a reference librarian and branch head in the Chicago Public Library system. Prior to that he was editorial librarian for *Playboy*. He attended Oakland University in Rochester, Michigan, and received his MSLS from Wayne State University in Detroit. Dewey has written eighteen books, including five books in the ALA 101 Micro Series; several guides to interactive fiction and adventure games; and directories for bulletin board systems, comic book dealers, and fan clubs. He also teaches microcomputer applications in libraries at Rosary College in River Forest, Illinois.